AUTOBIOGRAPHY OF
Ald. JOHN WILSON, J.P., M.P.

A RECORD OF A STRENUOUS LIFE

REPRINTED FROM

"THE DURHAM CHRONICLE"

PUBLISHED BY THE
PROPRIETORS OF "THE DURHAM CHRONICLE"
SADLER STREET, DURHAM

1909

CONTENTS.

ALDERMAN JOHN WILSON, J.P., M.P.

AUTOBIOGRAPHY

OF

ALDERMAN JOHN WILSON, M.P.

A RECORD OF A STRENUOUS LIFE.

CHAPTER I.—PRELIMINARY.

To the Editor of the "Durham Chronicle."

Sir,—Of all the friends that we, the miners of this county, have had, none have rendered us greater service than the "Durham Chronicle." We were not so highly favoured when we started as now, but towards us you have not changed. From the earliest moment of our struggle after union until now we have had free access to your columns. Even when our construction of sentences was of the crudest kind, you bore with many of us. My first attempts to use the pen to denounce wrongs and demand rights were made in the "Durham Chronicle." Many a time since then free access has been afforded me, and now I am going to trouble you with a new and somewhat longer insertion. If I had a better subject I should ask your favour with greater boldness, for I would have been more eloquent. But we cannot all have the great ones of the earth to write about—some of us must be content to take more lowly subjects. Further, I am writing somewhat under compulsion, and you know that always acts as a clog to writing. I need not say I have a great regard for the subject, and I feel confident you will extend to me on this occasion the favour I have found in the columns of the "Chronicle" for at least 33 years without hindrance.

I have been many a time urged by different friends to place on record an outline of my life.

These kind people believe that some good influence might accrue from it, and especially to our young men, who might learn how to appreciate the blessings of a good home, and kind parents anxious for their good; to be careful not to waste their early, youthful days in evil, instead of using that period as the Spring and sowing time of their life, having some connection with and relation to the harvest of their maturity, and to inspire them with the thought that there are possibilities of usefulness within them, if they will but use the opportunities which are lying around them, and which are amplifying every day; for I may without charge of conceit say that my life may be summed up in three sentences: Neglect in youth and early manhood; regret (remaining yet) for such neglect; and keen and anxious endeavour to redeem that which is unredeemable, for time once lost is "gone for ever." The efforts of mature life can never make up for the lost opportunities of youth.

In that reasoning lies the whole justification for placing on record this outline of what has been a life of struggle; but there were three serious objections which were and are still present with me. First, I am in entire agreement with John Foster that it is a difficult thing for a man to write his autobiography. There is in us all a desire to show ourselves off as well as we can, and thus magnify our virtues and strong points and lessen the vices and weak places. The appetency or desire for the approval and praise of our fellows (of which McCosh makes such good use in his Method of Divine Government) is strong within us, and we are apt to colour everything which will induce and assure us of it. This militates against an impartial autobiography. We want the power "to see oursels as others see us," and thus be saved from the innate pride which holds sway in the human breast, and leads us to magnify or minimise as the purpose may be suited and the desired praise secured.

I hesitated in the second place because I did not think my life of sufficient importance to the general public to warrant it, except in the one point already mentioned. It is true I have been active, and perhaps not a little obtrusive in the opinion of some, but this has been more local than general. I have striven, but it has been on the principle of the good housewife who believes it is her first duty to keep her own door-step clean before she bothers with those of the whole town. With me Durham has held the chief place, and it does so yet, and will so long as I can do anything in man's affairs. The people amongst whom I was born and (with a short break or two) have lived and struggled after a better life are, as they have been, the objects of my care.

I have a third reason. I am not a diarist; I am not a Pepys. My action in that respect is more in harmony with that described by Mark Twain, who started on a tour with a firm resolve to keep a regular and full diary, but at the end of a week found himself a few days behind with his record. I make resolves every New Year's Day, but when the year is very young (beyond a bare business item) I find myself a serious resolve breaker. I must, therefore, depend upon my memory. I will be candid, and state that there are certain matters which I shall bury, as they are not creditable or in the least useful, but I will guarantee the truth of what is written, and while it is but little of this great world's affairs I can speak of, I will deliver a round, unvarnished tale of a life

which, from beginning until now, has been a struggle, but which has had a full measure of help and blessing. More than the deserts deserved.

If anyone does me the honour to read this outline of a life which you, sir, are kind enough to publish, they must disabuse their minds of anything romantic, and prepare for a dull journey. What they will find is a matter of fact outline of a very ordinary life, for I have no eloquence to move men's minds, neither do I desire any. There are two things I shall strive to avoid. I shall not mention the lower side of my life for the purpose of glorying in it. If mentioned at all, it will be for two reasons. One is to give emphasis to that which people know already, viz., that I cannot lay any claim to the angelic. I do not believe in a man making himself out to have been a great criminal in order that he may stand out as one of the sanctified. The second reason is to sufficiently indicate that there has at some point of my life been a right-about-face, and to give prominence to the means by which the change in route was brought about. I here and now declare my regret that such a change was in the least necessary. It would be an unjustifiable piece of prudery to seek to gloss it over. If I did so, and tried to make out that my life from beginning to end had been a white sheet, there are still men alive who would write me down as one who shrunk from the truth—in the words of Mr Birrell, a great truth crusher.

Two thoughts more as preliminaries are necessary. No man ever had stronger parental feelings than I have up to this late day in life.

Although my mother was to me only a dream impressed upon a childish memory, and my father did not set the best example possible, I feel her warm kiss now, and I am confident that no man ever lived in whose breast there was a honester heart than his. Never had a man a friend upon whom he could rely more securely than upon him. The remembrance of them fills me with a spirit of pure ancestor worship. When I see old men treated with indifference by their sons, allowed to battle with poverty and carry a heavy burden of sorrow and anxiety, while their sons waste in dissipation in a few hours that which would bring the old men comfort, my mind is filled with grief at the base ingratitude such neglect indicates. What baser ingratitude can be found than to see an old man in want and his children indifferent whether he starves or not, when they should seek to help and cheer?

The last thought in these prefatory remarks is of a somewhat different kind. It may be that, for clearness sake, names may be mentioned. This will only be where it is absolutely necessary, and not with intent. I have lived in different periods, and in different economic and social conditions. I have seen the great revolution in the relations between employer and employed, and a great mitigation, if not a complete destruction, of the animus and antagonism which existed. The gulf which separated the two sides of the industrial community has been narrowed beyond the dream of possibility forty years ago, and I have no praise for or thanks to the man who seeks to widen it again. Knowing these things, I am sure that

treatment was meted out to men which, with our better knowledge of each, would not be done now; but it is necessary that some idea of the conflict which took place should be given, and that would not be so clear if only vague and general terms were used.

There was a fear of trade unionism, which was not entirely unfounded if we widen our outlook. There had been extravagances committed, but many of these arose from the restricted and unjust conditions under which working men were compelled to sell their labour. As a consequence, if men could not meet in the open, they worked in secrecy and darkness. They were prevented from working collectively and on equal terms before the law, for a working man single in opposition to a capitalist is in an unequal position, even if the law did not increase the inequality, as in those days it did. The consequence was actions were done which would never have been thought of in a state of freedom, and there was a dread generated which prompted managers to practise acts of cruelty which in these days would never be thought of, for we, in our united actions, have shown we can conduct our business in a manly way.

I am Yours
John Wilson

CHAPTER II.—EARLY LIFE.

It appears to me the most natural point to commence an autobiography is to describe the family whence the person sprang. I can boast of no great names so far as my ancestors are concerned, except two—Adam and Noah: I lay claim to these as relations. I am not like a Highlander, who refused to have kinship with the latter. I have read of two Highlanders who were discussing as to whose line ran farthest back. I am not sure as to their clan names, but we will say Macgregor and Macdonald. The latter got his line safely back into the Ark with Noah, but the other, with becoming pride, scorned the idea, and said: "There never was a time when a Macgregor had not a boat of his own." I am not so proud as that. I can with safety go back to the two points I have named, and say at those times my forefathers were equal to any. Since then I cannot boast of any aristocratic or blue-blooded names. Neither can I say that any of them led armies for the purpose of killing men they had never seen nor could have wronged; but this I can say, my immediate relations were respectable tradesmen, who followed their various trades honestly, and who, like Longfellow's village blacksmith, could look the whole world in the face. They kept the cool, sequestered vale of life, and kept it well, as all who knew them would testify. To some there may be nothing to boast of in that. To me there is great cause for rejoicing, because there was honour in the stock.

My grandfather's name was Avery Robinson Wilson. He was born in 1780. His parents kept the Swan Inn, Wolviston, near Stockton. He was a joiner, and died in Sunderland, in 1872, at the ripe age of 92. He had eight sons. To each of these he gave a trade, as, in his opinion, it was better to be a poor man engaged in useful toil than be a rich cumberer of the ground. A drone is a drone, no matter what status he may be engaged in, and it had been part of the old patriarch's creed not to allow an opportunity for such in his family. My father was the third son, and was a butcher to trade. He was the only one who did not keep to his trade, as will be seen shortly, except the brother named Robert, who, although intended for a miller, became a grocer, and for a number of years kept a grocer's shop in Ryhope Village.

Date of Birth.

The date of my birth may be fixed by relating a little episode, or a conversation, I had with a lady some time ago. She had her share of Mother Eve's curiosity, though not so ruinous in its result. Her desire was to know how old I was. She put the question to me in its most straightforward manner. My reply was not so direct. It was after the following manner:— "Madam, I am rather feminine on that subject, but you will know from your reading that Queen Victoria was crowned on June 26th, 1837, and that there was great rejoicing throughout the nation. It has always been a question with me whether the jubilation was because the Queen was crowned or a great man was born, for that was my birthday; and, without entering into the feelings of other people, it was, in my opinion, one of the most important events of English history. For what would all our national events have mattered to me if the great man referred to had never been born?"

Place of Birth.

The date is fixed as the 26th of June, 1837. The place was Greatham, near Hartlepool, in the county of Durham. The house was that belonging to the Old Mill. The site is now covered by the Wesleyan School. I am precise about this, because some other place may some years after this claim the honour. Who can tell? Did not seven cities dispute the honour of being Homer's birthplace? I am determined there shall be no wrangling in future generations about mine. Whether Greatham feels honoured or not because there I first saw the light, I do, because I was so privileged. As I have indicated, there was no glamour of a great name about my family. It was lowly. What matters it? The essential and true estimate is what we are ourselves. It is the finish that counts, and not the start. Not so much who our parents were as what we are ourselves. It is well for us if we have well-to-do, noble living parents. It is much better if they have in us good and noble sons. My mother came from Hamsterley, near Bishop Auckland. Her maiden name was Hannah Sponton. My father at the time of my birth was a labourer, who, in wild ways, had wasted one fortune at least, and thrown away the chances his father and family circumstances gave him, until as a consequence he had got down to the lowest rung.

Conditions of Family.

It may be anticipation, but it will be fitting to enter more fully into the life and circumstances of my father at this time and until his death, when I was twelve years old. He was a combination of poacher and smuggler, and I have heard him tell of cargoes landed near to and upon Castle Eden sands, and many a time have I sat beside him when making his nets for his nightly expeditions in search of game, his well-trained lurcher dog lying beside him, and I looking with boyish admiration at his skill with the "mesh," and pride in his daring (and he was a bold, daring man), thinking of the time when I would be like him, for the father is universally a hero to his son. He was so to me—and to this day I feel in my heart a rising of filial feeling when I, by memory's light, see him as he was—passionate, self-willed, but kind, ready to help and give of his last to do so. Honest and reliable in his dealings with his fellows. The law of the land could lay no charge to him, except in the matters I have mentioned—poaching and occasional smuggling (which pure ethics cannot condemn)—with one exception, which I will relate, as it has a close relationship to my life afterwards.

When I was six weeks old we were living in the part of Easington Lane known as the Brickgarth. My father and a poaching companion (although he preferred to be alone) went from Easington Lane to Castle Eden Dene, and were interrupted in their operations by a gamekeeper. The result of the fray was that the keeper was left for dead, while they made their way home with the game they had caught.

Those who came to the rescue of the wounded man suspected who the poachers were, and followed to our home. When they arrived my mother, with me in her arms, and the other man's wife were in the kitchen, while the two men were upstairs dividing the results of their expedition. Hearing their pursuers questioning the women, who were doing their best to shield their husbands (so I was informed by my father afterwards), the men removed the tiles from the roof and went along to the end of the row, where they got down and separated, and I was assured that my father never had his boots off until he got on to London Bridge. He was a noted walker, and by perseverance (there being no telegraph system such as we have now) he managed to escape apprehension. As a consequence of that act he lived in constant dread of the law officers, and never, to my knowledge, did we live more than six months in any place until we reached Stanhope in Weardale, when I was eleven, and the last nine months of his life was spent there, our home being at lodgings, and father working as a labourer at the quarries.

I enter thus fully into these matters not to boast because of the distance between now and then, but because they form a key to the first twelve years of my life. Whenever I hear a man boasting that he is a self-made man, I am sorry, because I feel confident there is another element in all our lives—the " Divinity that shapes our ends, rough-hew them how we will." Effort and eager watchful desire are needed on our part. I am not dreamer enough to think that a man can wrap himself in indolence and have supernatural uplifting, but I am thankful that I have full confidence in the Divine guidance in our affairs if we are willing co-workers with it. That which, in Shakespearean statement, is known as " the tide in the affairs of men which, taken at the flood, leads on to fortune," but if missed ends in shallows and misfortune. This recognition has been my experience, for there have been events, as there are in the lives of other men, to which no rule of human explanation can be applied satisfactorily.

CHAPTER III.—NATIONAL CONDITIONS.

These, as I have briefly described them, were the domestic circumstances into which I was born, and by which the tendencies of my life at its start were given. It will not be out of place if I set forth in outline a few national conditions as they related more especially to the families like ours. The period stands out prominently as being one of the most important in our history. It can with truth be described as transitional, a transition which presents a vastly different nation to this generation from that of 1837. The geographical construction of our country has altered very little by the encroachment and receding of the sea upon our coasts, but there have been many and marvellous changes in the conditions of the life of the people. In every aspect is this change seen, and by way of describing the condition into which I was born, and indicating the progress made, I will outline a few of those changes.

I cannot, like Tristram Shandy, describe minutely, except I turn to the pages of the historians, and as these are common property, and if written at all are for the enlightenment of subsequent generations, I will avail myself of the information they supply. We are told by one writer that " 1837 marks almost the lowest depth of degradation of the English rural population, and a very low level indeed in the condition of the miner and mill operative." Walpole in his history says : " There are probably persons who have not had occasion to study records of the time who have any notion of the misery into which the poor had fallen. A long apprenticeship had indeed inured them to suffering; but the misery which they endured in 1816 and 1833 was as nothing compared with the protracted wretchedness which commenced in 1837, and continued to 1842. In 1839, 1,137,000 persons were in receipt of relief in England and Wales alone; in 1840 the pauper roll contained 1,199,000; in 1841, 1,299,000; in 1842, 1,429,000. The population of England and Wales at that time amounted to about 16,000,000, so that one person out of every eleven in the country was a pauper. The poor, moreover, lived under conditions which would have made life with high wages horrible, and which made life with low wages intolerable."

The general description of the conditions prevailing at the period of which I write the historian details in a particular manner which is truly appalling. It finds corroboration in every contemporary, with which I need not burden this outline of my life. I propose to take a few aspects of the national life. At the base of the survey I place politics. The nation had been five years under the extended franchise resulting from the Reform Bill of 1832. As illustrative of the political condition of the country prior to this, let me quote the words of a writer of that period :—

" The people of England had little influence and no authority over the Government. It was said that they lived under a representative system, but the system had become so corrupt, there was scarcely a shred of honest representation left in it. Two-thirds of the House of Commons were appointed by peers, or other influential persons. Every great nobleman had a number of seats at his unquestioned disposal. The Duke of Norfolk OWNED eleven members, Lord Lonsdale OWNED nine, and the Duke of Rutland OWNED six. Seventy members were returned by thirty-five places, where there were scarcely any votes at all. Old Sarum had two members, but not one solitary inhabitant; Gatton enjoyed the services of two members, while the voters were seven in number. The right to appoint these two members had been valued at one hundred thousand pounds. The revenue officers, who cast their votes as the Government directed them, controlled seventy elections. Three hundred members, it was estimated, were returned by one hundred and sixty persons. All this time Leeds, Birmingham, and Manchester were unrepresented. Seats were openly offered for sale down to the very eve of the Reform Bill. Hastings had been so often sold for £6,000 that her market price was perfectly established. Generally the purchaser was expected to belong to the same political party with the majority of his constituents, but this was not indispensable. A man was once purchasing the representation of a place called Petersfield, and the price, which was being adjusted in pounds, was raised to guineas because he was on the wrong side of politics. The members who bought their seats sold their votes, and thus made their outlay reproductive."

The five years which had passed between the passing of the Reform Bill and 1837 had brought no small disappointment to the working classes. In the words of Goldwin Smith: "The working classes generally had welcomed the Bill, thinking it would bring relief to their sufferings, while the more democratic among them hoped that the ball of political change, once set rolling, would roll on. They, however, did not fail to see that this was a middle class measure, or to give vent to their class jealousy and distrust."

As a result of this disappointment Chartism, which had lulled in the high hopes raised by the Bill of 1832, revived again with an increased power and volume. Meetings were held throughout the nation, and the Charter of the People, with its six points, was declared. These were universal suffrage, vote by ballot, annual Parliaments, payment of members, equal electoral districts, and the abolition of the property qualification. One of these has been attained. We are getting near (1908) one or two others. These have been ever present to the Progressive mind. . Many steps forwards· have been taken, and every one has falsified the fears of the opposer. With the extension of political power there has come no doubt a broader spirit and keener desire to correct wrong and establish the reign of right. The axe has been laid to the root of many abuses. Institutions are not now honoured because of their age, but because of their fitness. We are told that the hoary head is honourable when found in the way of righteousness. Institutions are being tried by the same rule. Well doing is the guarantee of their existence. The progress made and the use made of our political power are encouragements to those who have taken up the work of the old Chartist to rest not until the whole of the charter and more has been realised, and an assurance to the fearful that the people of this country will have strict regard to justice in all their aims.

The Miner's Condition.

What was the state of the miners at the time? Their condition will be as instructive and interesting to us as that of any portion of the community. There are many sources from which we can draw our information. In S. Webb's "Labour in the Longest Reign" we find the following:—"Perhaps the most striking instance of improvement of social condition is that of the Northumberland coal miner. Two generations ago he was a helpless, degraded wage slave, utterly without the means of resisting the worst abuses of capitalist tyranny. The hewer of 1830, if we may quote a contemporary pamphlet, often received no more than 11s or 12s a week for 10 or 12 hours a day underground. The miners' delegate meeting settled the strike of 1831 on terms which included a minimum of 30s per fortnight for 12 hours a day. He was constantly cheated in the weight of coal drawn and in the food and other commodities that he was compelled to buy at his employer's 'tommy shop.' His yearly bond, enforced by ruthless magistrates, kept him in a position little better than serfdom, whilst the utter absence of any provision for education seemed to leave no ray of hope for any uplifting of his class."

In Walpole's history we find a statement more general in its character and more repulsive in its description. Speaking of the work of the Commission of 1842, he says:—"It proved that, in most of the mineral districts, children began work at seven, and that in many districts they were frequently employed at six, five, and even four years of age. Girls as well as boys, women as well as men, worked underground. The children had consequently often to work in the wet; they were kept at work in an atmosphere in which a candle would not burn. The smallest children were employed as trappers; but women and children (boys and girls) were also engaged as miners. Many of the seams were only 22 to 28 inches high, so that none but small children could pass through them. In some cases the car was pushed, in others the children, and even women, were made to draw it by a girdle and chain. The girdle was a band placed round the waist. The chain passed between the drawer's legs. Little children of seven worked for 12 hours a day harnessed like beasts by the girdle and chain, but, unlike the happier beasts of burden, subjected to the task before their growth was complete and their strength mature. Mothers worked at the same toil."

" The things which were done in the pit were horrible. No constable dared to trust himself underground in the company of the miners. Under such circumstances the lot of women working underground with men, the lot of children at the mercy of their masters or of the butties hardly needs description. No horse in an over-loaded coach, no donkey in a coster-monger's barrow, few slaves the property of a West Indian planter experienced the treatment which was the lot of many children in the mines."

In August, 1840, Lord Ashley moved for a Commission to inquire into the employment of children in mines. In a speech he made, he described the life of a trapper in words which stirred the nation to its centre. For the bene-fit of the present generation, who know nothing of that day, and who are apt to think that the conditions as we see them have always been, and who are apt to treat with careless indiffer-ence the memory and work of the men who initiated the movement for the amelioration of the conditions of child life in mines, I will quote at length from the report of the Commis-sion.

The Commission reported in 1842. It became a text book for " Continental and for English reformers and philanthropists, who studied its fearful disclosures with intense interest. A mass of misery and depravity was unveiled, of which even the warmest friends of the labouring classes had hitherto but a faint conception. It would be utterly incredible were not the testi-mony so overwhelming that in the most Chris-tian and civilised country in the world such enormities could have been permitted."

The evidence and findings of the Commission are set forth in two volumes. The Commis-sioners say " they were met at the onset of their labours by the general ignorance which pre-vailed in reference to the condition of persons employed in the mining industry into which they were to inquire. It was indeed notorious that in some of these occupations great num-bers of children are employed at very early ages. It was equally notorious that some of these occupations are among the most laborious in which it is the lot of human beings to toil; but no committee of the House of Commons had been formed to investigate the actual condition of this class, no attempt of any kind had hither-to been made to ascertain the ages at which the children in question really begin to work, the number of hours during which they labour, the exact nature of their employment, nor the im-mediate effects of such employment on their morals and health."

In the digest of their collected evidence they state: " That instances occur in which children are taken into these mines to work as early as four years of age, sometimes at five, and be-tween five and six—not unfrequently between six and seven; while from eight to nine is the ordinary age at which employment in these mines commences.

" That in several districts female children begin to work in these mines at the same early ages as the males.

" That the great body of the children and young persons employed in these mines are of the families of the adult workpeople engaged in the pits, or belong to the poorest population in the neighbourhood, and are hired and paid in some districts by the workpeople, but in others by the proprietors or contractors. In some there are a small number of parish apprentices, who are bound to serve their masters until twenty-one years of age, under circumstances of frequent ill-treatment, and under the oppressive condition that they shall receive nothing but food and clothing.

" That the nature of the employment which is assigned to the youngest children, generally that of ' trapping,' requires that they should be in the pit as soon as the work of the day com-mences; and, according to the present system, that they should not leave the pit before the work of the day is at an end.

" That at different ages, from six years old and upwards, the hard work of pushing and dragging the carriages of coal from the work-ings to the main ways begins—a labour which all classes of witnesses concur in stating requires the unremitting exertion of all the physical power which the young workers possess."

CHAPTER IV.—REPORT OF THE ROYAL COMMISSION, 1840.

The Report of the Commission appointed in 1840 contains illustrations of child and female labour in the mines. The trapper sitting behind the door; young persons of both sexes on hands and feet (all fours), dragging the tubs with a "soam," and women and girls carrying coals up the shaft. In Scotland the evidence of one girl (six years old) was that she had been coal carrying up the shaft for six weeks, and she had to make "10 to 14 rakes (journeys) per day, and carries full 56lb. of coal in a wooden bucket." This she did in company with her sister and mother.

There were no females working in the mines of Durham and Northumberland. We had long hours and other harsh conditions, but we were clear of that blot. In the words of the Report: "From the mines of this vast coalfield there is absolute absence of all female workers." We could not plead exemption on other points, and it may be instructive to look at a few of them as given in the Report. In respect to the age in South Durham: "In this district children are sometimes taken down into the pits as early as five years of age, and by no means uncommonly at six."

In North Durham and Northumberland: "In these districts many children begin work at very early ages. One case is recorded in which a child was taken into the pit at four years and a half old." Mr G. Elliot (afterwards Sir George, then head viewer at Monkwearmouth and Washington and Belmont), testified that he "is very much pressed and entreated by parents to take children at a very early age, from six years and upwards; has known boys of five years of age in some pits; could give names of boys of five employed in pits in Durham."

A Sub-Commissioner reported: "I visited the house of the parents of a little boy whom I saw keeping a door in Flatworth Pit. It was about seven o'clock on the Sunday evening, and the boy, Thomas Roker, was in bed asleep. His mother said he was about six years and seven months, and that he had been down the pit about a month or six weeks. The boy was at school at three years old, and his father wished to make him a better scholar before he went down. Always puts him to bed early, because he must get up every working morning at three o'clock, and he often rubs his eyes when he is woke and says he has only just been to sleep. He gets up at 3 a.m., and goes down the pit at four. He gets his dinner directly he comes home, about half-past 4 or a quarter to 5 p.m., and then he washes himself and goes to bed between six and seven." What pathos is in that mother's statement, and what a lesson for the boys of this generation.

What is the evidence as to the hours? The Report says of South Durham:—"In these districts the hours of work in all the well-regulated mines are never allowed to exceed 12. In many of these collieries formerly, and in some collieries still, when the hewers had cut down what was considered their proper quantity of coal, and had departed, the putters, the drivers, and all other persons were expected to remain until the whole of the coals were brought to bank, however long it might be, whether 13, 14, or 15, or even more hours. If, therefore, any defect occurred in the engine, or any other cause of delay took place, the people were detained below in consequence. Such is not the case now; when the hour comes the sound of "loose" is sent down the shaft, the glad tidings quickly reach the farthest workings, and all come up. But this is only true of the well-regulated mines. There are still in this district collieries in which the hours of work are extremely long."

North Durham and Northumberland.—"In these districts the regular hours of work are 12, being usually from four o'clock in the morning to four o'clock in the afternoon. But the children and young persons often leave their homes for the pit as early as one or two o'clock in the morning and stay to four o'clock in the afternoon." The evidence of a boy (Thomas Smithson) may be quoted:—"The caller calls him at half-past 2 a.m. He gets up at three, and starts down the pit at four; gets home at five; soon after washes himself and goes to bed about six or seven. He generally feels very tired when he comes home."

What were the wages? South Durham.—Two

paragraphs from the Report will suffice. "In this part of the kingdom, though the hewers be not employed at all, or only partially employed, the masters are bound to advance them at the end of the fortnight 30s for their maintenance. This is in addition to a house and coals. But when a hewer earns more than 30s in a fortnight the surplus above 30s is detained to pay off the sum advanced him in slack time, which sum, therefore, is to be considered as simply a loan and not a payment of money due. By this system the miner is always sure of the means of support, with 15s a-week, his house, and firing."

"The wages are paid once a fortnight, on the Friday afternoon, the reckoning being made up to the end of the preceding week. The trappers are paid in by far the greater number of instances 10d per day, but some are as low as 9d, and some even 8d, but very seldom. The drivers are paid 1s 3d a-day. The helpers-up, the cleaners of the tramways, the keepers of the switches, rank with the drivers."

Now, I fancy I hear some of my young brothers saying—Why were these things allowed to exist? Why were the men not united, and why did they not aim at rectifying these wrongs by the force of combination? To understand why, the men of to-day must imagine a state of things vastly different from the present. Then all sorts of impediments were placed in the way of workmen combining. The Act of 1825 had prepared the way for combinations, and although deficient in many respects received a qualified approval from the workmen, inasmuch as it recognised the right of combination, and it enabled them, without secrecy or dread of the consequences, to associate together for certain specific purposes. There were, however, numerous limitations, which hampered the workmen in their endeavour to unite for a common betterment in wages and conditions.

In order that the position of those who strove to bring their fellow workmen together and the dangers they had to face may be understood, and with he view to give prominence to the contrast between then and now, I will place on record the case of the Dorsetshire labourers in 1834. A society was formed in a Dorset village called the "Friendly Society of Agricultural Labourers." It was not in the least secret. The members went about their work in a proper manner. "The farmers took alarm, and induced the local magistrates on February 21, 1834, to issue placards warning the labourers that anyone joining the union would be sentenced to seven years' transportation." Within three days George and John Loveless and other four were arrested and lodged in gaol. "The trial of these unfortunate labourers," says S. Webb, "was a scandalous perversion of the law. The Lovelesses and their friends seem to have been simple-minded Methodists, two of them being itinerant preachers. No accusation was made, and no evidence preferred against them of anything worse than playing with oaths, which, as we have seen, formed a part of the initiation ceremony of the Grand National Union. Not only were they guiltless of any intimidation or outrage, but they had not even struck or presented any application for higher wages; yet the judge charged the Grand Jury on the case at portentous length, as if the prisoners had committed murder or treason, and inflicted on them, after the briefest trial, the monstrous sentence of seven years' transportation."

This sentence was approved by the Government of that day. The greatest expedition was shown to get the prisoners out of the country. They were sentenced on March 18, and on the 15th of April they sailed for Botany Bay. Great meetings were held, and numerous petitions signed. The agitation was kept up, but the sentence was not remitted until 1836. But owing to "official blundering it was two years later (April, 1838) before five out of the six prisoners returned home."

This is the most flagrant act of injustice, but not the only one. There are many alive to-day who, like myself in their working days, have seen men taken from their beds in the night, and like common criminals dragged to prison, the only offence chargeable being the part they took in seeking higher wages, resisting reductions, or striving for better conditions of labour. Those to whom I refer can remember Rebecca and her children personated by a band of the most stalwart and determined of the strikers, and dressed in garments borrowed from female relatives. It will therefore be seen that to be a union man, and especially in the front rank, meant something in those days.

Free Trade and Protection

In 1837 Protection was in its zenith, but the state of the people was at its nadir. There was a close cordon of protective duties. and Custom House officers drawn all round the nation. There was nothing left to protect, and, strange paradox, the condition of the people could not be worse. The mind of man could not conceive a worse state, and yet there are people to-day trying to persuade us to retrograde from the high comparative point in which we find ourselves down to the low depths of want and wretchedness of the period to which I am referring. The cardinal doctrine with them is "Protect, if you would be prosperous; shut out the products of other nations and the bountiful harvests of the world, and you will have plenty." That false and foolish teaching is being preached by educated men in the face of the sad facts of our history prior to the Repeal of the Corn Laws; and the first Gladstonian Budget, which swept away the soap duty, reduced the duty on 103 articles of food, and abolished the duty on 123 more, and in face of the fact that there are many men like myself whose memory retains still the pictures of those dark days of poverty and dear, poor food.

Readers of the Rev. Sidney Smith will be conversant with his description of that taxation period:—

"Taxes upon every article which enters into the mouth, or covers the back, or is placed under the foot. Taxes upon everything which is pleasant to see, hear, feel, smell, or taste. Taxes upon warmth, light, and locomotion. Taxes on everything on earth and the waters under the earth, on everything that comes from abroad, or is grown at home. Taxes on raw material. Taxes on every fresh value that is added to it by the industry of man. Taxes on the sauce which pampers man's appetite, and the drug that restores him to health. On the ermine which decorates the judge, and the rope which hangs the criminal; the poor man's salt, and the rich man's spice; on the brass nails of the coffin, and the ribbons of the bride; at bed or board, couchant or levant, we must pay. The school boy whips his taxed top, the beardless youth manages his taxed horse, with a taxed bridle, on a taxed road; and the dying Englishman, pouring his medicine which has paid 7 per cent. into a spoon that has paid 15 per cent., flings himself back upon his chintz bed which has paid 22 per cent., and expires in the arms of an apothecary who has paid a licence of £100 for the privilege of putting him to death. His whole property is then taxed from 2 to 10 per cent. Besides the probate, large fees are demanded for burying him in the chancel; his virtues are handed down to posterity on taxed marble, and he is then gathered to his fathers, to be taxed no more."

What was the state of the people? There are two or three testimonies to which we can turn. Macaulay in 1845 said: "Will anybody tell me that the capitalist was the only sufferer, or the chief sufferer? Have we forgotten what was the condition of the working people? So visible was the misery of the manufacturing towns that a man of sensibility could hardly bear to pass through them. Everywhere he found nakedness, plaintive voices, wasted forms, and haggard faces. Politicians who had never been thought alarmists began to tremble for the very foundations of society."

In 1885 Mr Joseph Chamberlain, speaking of 1842, said: "The whole of the labourers in the agricultural districts were on the verge of starvation. The poor rates were in some districts 20s in the pound. At the time of which I am speaking the large towns were described by eyewitnesses as bearing the appearance of beleaguered cities, so dreadful was the destitution and the misery which prevailed in them. People walked the streets like gaunt shadows, and not like human beings. There were bread riots in every town. There were rick burnings on all the countrysides. We were on the verge of a revolution when the Corn Laws were abolished."

Wages for agricultural labourers were seven and eight shillings per week. Men in the industrial centres were discharged in tens of thousands. Bread was a luxury, and turnips and potatoes a staple food. The four pound loaf was 1s, tea 8s per pound, and bad sugar 8½d per pound. Flour was more than double it is now. Taking the five years from 1837 to 1841 inclusive, the average price per imperial quarter was 64s 4d, while for the five years ending 1907 the average was 28s 8d—less than half in favour of the latter period. That Egypt must show brighter prospect before we retrace our steps towards it!

CHAPTER V.—EARLY RECOLLECTIONS.

Other Changes.

We are living in a different England from that of 1837. There is not a single aspect to which that remark does not apply. We are nearer our international neighbours. There was no telegraphic system at my birth. Neither was there the railway arrangements we have, with the powerful and speedy engines dragging such marvellous loads. In 1845 there were only 2,400 miles of railway in the United Kingdom. From the British Almanac I quote the following as being a very wonderful performance :—" On Saturday, the 5th of May, 1832, the engine called the Victory took 20 waggons of merchandise, weighing gross 92 tons 19 cwts., together with the tender containing fuel and water, from Liverpool to Manchester, 30 miles, in an hour and 34 minutes." Now we think we are travelling slowly if we don't do the distance in one-third the time. I was a year old when the first line of steamboats across the Atlantic was established. The postage was in the same crude state two years before my birth. If a letter was sent 15 miles the sender was charged fourpence. The charge was an increasing one until so far as a poor man sending one it was entirely prohibitive. The postage on a letter from some parts of Scotland to London was 1s 3d, the equivalent to a labourer's day's wage. There was no prepayment, and many were the dodges adopted by the receiver to escape payment.

Early Recollections.

There is great variety in all nature, and the lives of men and women are no exception. The conditions of life into which some are born are in every respect conducive to comfort, and were it not for the inherent tendencies of their own nature it would appear an impossibility for them to go wrong. Others meet at birth circumstances adverse in the extreme to all that is good and the possibility of attainment thereto, and are born into homes—

Where the new-born babe
Doth bring unto its parents' soul no joy;
Where squalid poverty
Receives it at its birth,
And on her wither'd knees
Gives it the scanty food of discontent.

Some, looking back upon their childhood and youth, can see bright scenes, and every incident is one of gladness; while others have no bright reminiscence, except those which arise from the impulses of early years, which find brightness in the darkest condition. Some find every rough place smoothed; while others are from birth the football of contentious circumstances, and their continuance and progress in life (if any comes) is no small miracle.

My birth was not only lowly, but the first event to which my memory will go was one of sorrow, when, at the age of four years and a half, I, with my two sisters—one two years older and the other two years younger—were taken to the bedside of my mother to receive her last embrace and kiss before she died. And now at 71, with an interval of sixty-six or seven years, I can see the poorly furnished room and the bed in the corner upon which I was lifted. And now as I write this the tears start to my eyes, and I can feel the close pressure to her heart, and the motherly affection on her lip as she kissed me. Since then I have been in many countries and scenes (some of which I would like to forget), but that picture and that feeling I thank God is with me still, and I hope will linger with me as one of my latest memories, and be one of the first which will open to my sight when I am called upon to lay down the burden and duty of life. She was small in stature (my daughter Maggie resembles her in face and form), but although unadorned by any of earth's ornaments, she is still one of the fairest and best women to me—as mothers should be to all men. She died at Chorley in Lancashire.

At that early point in my life I lost that which is of inestimable value to any right-minded man —the influence of a mother; that blessing to which men owe much, and in many cases prize too little. What boon can come to a boy, when his character is forming, equal to it? And how great is the darkness which comes to the life of a child when the mother is taken at a period when she is needed most; and especially if there be no settled home, and he is under the care of a father whose tendencies and necessities compel him to roam from place to place, and when at work his child is left to the care of strangers, which at best is cold, or to his own resources.

From the time of my mother's death until my father died at Stanhope seven and a-half years after, I don't think we ever lived six months in one place. My father being a navvy, and the railway system in this country being in its early development, there was a great demand for workmen at high wages, and he, being a strong, vigorous man, was sure of employment wherever he went. Being, however, of a very sharp temper, he would throw up his work at the first sign of harsh treatment or fault finding, and thus he and I were very often on the move, for I was his constant companion where possible. My two sisters were taken by my uncles, who were men of a different nature from my father, being tradesmen of good standing in the county. They would have taken me, but his desire to have me with him induced him to refuse, and as a consequence I made acquaintance with many parts of England and Scotland, and bore many hardships at a very early age. What this meant may be gathered from this outline. I remember on more than one occasion we travelled 30, and as far as 36 miles, in a day, and slept in a room where the gate was the door into it and the hedgeside or haystack the bed. In those circumstances my father would take off his slop or jacket, and wrap me in it, forgetting his own need in his desire to keep me warm. In those long walks, when I tired, he would carry me on his back, sitting astride on our earthly belongings he had stowed away in his slop, tying the bottom to make it like a sack. Ofttimes in these circumstances we were sore pressed for food, for when he drew his pay from the employment he was leaving he would not leave the locality until his money was all, or nearly all, gone. As a consequence we were oft in want for more than one day. On one occasion we were three days in that condition, and at dusk were coming from the North into Morpeth. Just before we entered the town I observed a small parcel lying on the road. In eagerness I picked it up, and on taking off the wrapper I found a large gingerbread cake. It was the sweetest meal I have had in the whole course of my life. We had an appetite with a three days' edge on it, and no time was wasted in ceremonious approach to the table or thinking of those who had lost the parcel. We were in a condition when the ethics of the transaction are apt to be relegated to a back seat. Whenever my good wife baked gingerbread (and she could to perfection), and when my daughters do (and they are motherlike), I think of the Morpeth treasure, for such it was of the most opportune kind.

When I was nine I was acquainted with a large number of our dialects, for let our stay be long or short in a town, I soon formed acquaintance, and, being quick in learning, I gathered up a few of the idioms of the locality. It might be "iggs" for eggs in Sussex; the "weal, vine, and winegar" of Norfolk; the "baggan" for tea of Lancashire; or the "laking" for play of Cumberland. I was at home with them all, and there are a few incidents impressed on my mind which lie in this period I would like to notice. The first in order after my mother's death was my attendance at a school kept by an old woman. This let me say to the credit of my father, he was desirous I should go to school, while on my part it took force to get me there. I never got a silver medal for never missing school. To play truant was my aim. I have so acted for three weeks consecutively. The school fee was given to me every Monday, but as I had been absent all the week the schoolmaster or mistress, whichever it might be, never saw the pence. That generally found its way to the sweetshop, although I knew what awaited me at home when I was found out. I pity the boy who receives such floggings as I got. The leather belt was the instrument, in the bedroom the place of punishment, and often no shirt to break the force of the stroke, given by a very strong arm. But this much I will say of my father, if he punished me the cause of it lay with myself. So long as I behaved as I should have done, he was as kind as his circumstances would allow. Although my knowledge of him was as a wanderer, yet he was to me the noblest of men. He was strong and vigorous, and at all times carried a proud heart, and I gloried in him, and do now.

I can see the old dame's school, but I have no recollection of the name of the town. We sat on rough forms, but what we learnt is to me unknown. It could not be much when we consider the school, the teacher, and the general state of education at that time, for the "Reading Made Easy" and Markham's Spelling Book were classics in such a school as I am speaking of, and the scholar who mastered them was looked upon with admiration, and the teacher spoke of such with pride. I remember I was the cause of much anxiety and trouble to the old lady. I cannot remember getting a prize for good conduct. She used to fasten me to her apron with a darning needle attached to the pinafore which I wore. It could not be on account of good behaviour (because if there was mischief I was in it), neither would my beauty be attractive (although, like all human kind, I conceit myself that my face is the best), and therefore it must have been to keep me under her eye, and to prevent me from creating a disturbance. Poor old soul, struggling to make a living by her simple instruction, I apologise to her memory and to all beside to whom I have been a worry in life, for I should feel a great deal happier if she had been the only one I had caused trouble to. But the yesterdays, whether filled with good or ill, live with us to-day, and maybe form the Banquos of our subsequent feasts. In this respect we are all Macbeths, and while it may be sorrowful it is a mark of Divine wisdom that we cannot obliterate the past at will. Heed to this would save our young men from regret.

CHAPTER VI.—SCHOOL DAYS.

The next event in the order of memory wears a darker shade, and the pride of one's heart might suggest a leap over it, but it is not one of the matters I need blush for. There is a break between the old schoolmistress and the full play for boyish mischief and the rigour and meanness of a workhouse. In what town it was situated, or why I was there (except as narrated below), I have no recollection, but this much I do know, I was there for six months. My dress and pinafore had changed to the small but manlike garb of jacket and trousers, and I chafed at the restrictions by which I was surrounded. I objected to the early rising, and longed with hungry expectancy for the announcement that it was meal time, and, Oliver Twist like, longed for more; for it was of this period and condition Dickens wrote in his "Oliver Twist." His famous character of Bumble did not dwell in fancy only. He lived and moved and had a being as many a poor orphan or forsaken item of humanity knew. There is now a more humane spirit abroad, and the great novelist did a great deal towards destroying the old and ushering in the new order of things in this as in other abuses. Whenever I hear tell of or see a kind workhouse master or mistress, to whom the children cling and don't run from, I thank them, it may be silently, but surely. The sorrow of the poor little orphans (either by death or neglect) is deep enough, and the outlook of their lives is black enough without having any unnecessary harshness to bear.

I was glad, however, when my father came for me, and the picture of myself running to him is not the faintest in the gallery of my mind; and well do I remember his rage and the threats he made in reference to the people who had placed me where he found me. It transpired (for what reason I know not) he left the place we were living in and committed me to the care of the people we were lodging with (for we were always at lodgings), and arranged with them that they should keep me, and he would repay them. This they failed to do, for what reason I know not. Maybe my wild ways were too much for them, for I am sure I would try them extremely. However, they placed me in the public institution where he found me. I cannot say whether he ever found the people again, but I have a vivid recollection of my own pleasure as I walked away with him from what to me had been a prison and place of punishment. It was a fixed abode, with its dreary yards and walls, and I preferred the wandering, if more precarious, life.

This happened to me before I reached the age of six, for at that age I find myself in a school kept by a master, and by him I was placed to teach some boys older than myself to read the New Testament. This may seem strange, considering the life we were leading, but I cannot remember when I learned to read. There was no other branch of learning to which I took except by force, but reading I took to it as easy and naturally as a duck takes to water. At the early age of which I am now writing I was conversant with the children's classics of that day such as "Robinson Crusoe," "Gulliver's Travels," and the round of fairy lore which to children is so real; and all my life the appetite for reading has been very strong, but I fear far too desultory. And, therefore, I was quite able to teach the letter of the New Testament (I don't vouch for the pronunciation) to those older than myself, but less eager to learn to read. It was by the utilising of quick children to teach others that many a schoolmaster or mistress carried on the school, and many were taught the mere rudiments of learning in such a manner.

I have given in outline, but yet I hope sufficiently detailed, an idea of what my existence was during the life of my father, but there are other two incidents in my school life which ought to find a place. One of them gives prominence to the tenacity of my memory, and the other indicates clearly the quick and heated temper which was in me then and which, I fear, still lingers and breaks out occasionally. At the school I attended in the South (but where, that is the question), when I was about eight, there was to be a public examination of the scholars in the Scripture class. The task was to commit to memory or acquire a sufficient knowledge of the first fifteen chapters in the Bible and the same in the Testament, to pass an examination through which we were put by the vicar or clergyman. The scholar who answered best made his way to the head of the class. When the proceedings closed I held that proud position. I remember the words of commiseration that were expressed by the audience, for while I was the superior in ability, I was the least presentable in dress. I do remember I had on a white smock, such as at that time was worn by agricultural labourers of that district. I can remember, too, the words of commendation spoken by the kind old clergyman, as, with one hand on my head, he presented me with the chief prize, a beautiful copy of the " Pilgrim's Progress," which brought me in contact with the grand old dreamer, and which I read with avidity. For the characters—

Christian, Pliable and Obstinate, Worldly Wiseman, Faithful, The Flatterer (oft seen in life now), Giant Despair, and Greatheart destroying things evil—were real men to my boyish mind; and I am thankful their reality still lives, and I hope it will never fade until I, too, with Pilgrim, pass over the River, assisted, like him, with the same bright, encouraging view, and cheered by the crowd of witnesses waiting to receive me when I land. Amongst whom I KNOW I shall see her whose companionship was mine for half-a-century, and from whom I parted a few months ago, and to whom I am confident I shall be again united in an eternal union when the messenger from our Father's home comes to call me.

Before I mention the other and finishing incident in my school life, which brings out the ugly side of my nature, I will insert a somewhat long journey I was compelled to take alone. From the Midlands, where the previous school experience took place, we tramped to Scotland. My father got work on the Caledonian Railway, which was then in process of making. Our lodgings were at Ecclefechan (Thomas Carlyle's village), a few miles north of Gretna Green. We lodged with a widow, who had one son, a weaver. He was the village fool, but at all times kind to me. On the same railway father worked near Lockerbie. He then resolved to return to England, and left me with some people, expecting they would look after me, and told them he would go to a railway which was being made from Whitehaven. Not long after he left they tired of their undertaking, and no doubt considered the best way was to clear me out; and although I was not nine years old, they took me to Annan, and gave me into the custody of the captain of a small vessel sailing to Whitehaven, with instructions to put me on to the end of the railway which was being formed, and there his commission ended. What was the size of the vessel or how long the voyage was I cannot say. This much I remember, I was dreadfully sick. I parted from the captain at Whitehaven, and set off on a journey which, to a boy of my years, was into the unknown, and was assuredly the uncertain. It was not the age of telegraphs and speedy and frequent delivery of letters, neither were there railways ramifying the country in every direction, as at present; and there was a great probability that father might have gone elsewhere, for he was a veritable bird of passage. I started on this plan: I kept the line of railway, and when I came to a gang of men I made inquiries if he were there, or whether they knew of him. Many times the answer was in the negative; a few times I came across a man who had seen him somewhere on the line a short time before. On I went, until just before the time to quit work, and when I was very hungry, I came to a number of men working in a deep cutting. As I stood looking down my father saw me, and, throwing down his pick, he made his way up to me. His joy at my presence, surprise at my adventure, and anger at the conduct of the people were all very great, and I should not have desired to have been that man if he had been in the locality.

How long we were there is outside my recollection, but I know that while around there we went to Penrith. I have many a time gazed with wonder when a boy upon King Arthur's table and the giant's grave, which are there. During our stay there the great riot between the English and Irish navvies took place. From all parts of the line both nationalities flocked to that centre. Armed with weapons of all descriptions—shovel and scythe, poker and pick, or with any other sort of instrument—these stalwart men made their way to the scene of action. I can well remember the soldiers being posted at all the approaches to the town, and searching every person who sought to enter for concealed weapons.

When I was a little more than eleven we found ourselves in Stanhope for the second time. My father was employed at the quarries. Here he found many men who, like himself, believed that game, be it bird or beast, was not created to be the special monopoly of one class. In this belief they were strictly orthodox, and fearlessly, day or night, asserted the justice of that natural doctrine. With them the right of property was with the man who caught the creature. This idea is clearly expressed in the old Stanhope song which was much sung in those days. The following are four of the lines:—

The bonny moor hen has gone over the plain,
When summer returns she will return back again ;
The miners of Weardale, they are valiant men,
They will fight till they die for the bonny moor hen,

Here I can well remember a Wesleyan Sunday-school anniversary, at which I recited two pieces—the hymn, "Oh, for a heart to praise my God," and the third chapter in St. John's gospel, and here the incident which finished my school days took place. I was sent to a school kept by a man of low stature. The school stood by the side of the lane, and on the high side of the town. The master was of a strict nature. That trait and my wildness did not harmonise, and I became the fly in the ointment to the old man, who credited me with all that went wrong. The climax came in this way: One day he had some business in the town, and he locked the girls in a room to keep us separate. This was too much, and the boys resolved to have them out. We had just achieved our purpose when suddenly the master appeared on the scene, and without inquiry he marked me as the ringleader (on the principle that if I had not been in mischief I would be), and gave me as much of the cane as his strength would allow. This was more than I could bear, and seizing an inkstand I hurled it straight at his head. It did not miss the mark, but caught him in the face. As soon as he recovered he took my slate and books and put them, with me, outside; and so ended my school days. However, he did not get clear of me so easily. There was a field behind the school which was nearly level with the window, and all the afternoon I went and played a tattoo on the panes, and whenever he came out I ran across the field. The result of that episode was my father got me work at the quarries where he was, and I soon found the difference between getting up to start at six after walking some distance on a cold morning, standing outside in snow and ice, and lying in bed until school time, and enjoying the warmth it afforded.

I have had the pleasure of talking to two men who remembered the above incident, and one of them added something I had forgot. My late friend, Mr W. Longstaffe, who was for many years secretary of Norwood Colliery, near Evenwood, and a member of our Miners' Executive, told me he was a boy at school at the time, and reminded me of a bull and terrier dog which was my constant companion, and would not allow anyone to touch me. A few years ago (1904, I think) I was speaking at a Co-operative meeting in Stanhope, when the chairman, about my own age, informed the meeting that he was one of the boys who with me were trying to liberate the girls on the day I mention, and he asked me if I knew what wages I had per day. I replied "No." Then, said, he, "You had fourpence halfpenny per day." The pay was not large, but I know the work was not pleasant. I used to stand alongside the small waggons, into which the men filled the soil off the limestone, and it was my duty to pick out the pieces of ironstone which were to be found, laying them to one side until there were sufficient to fill the tub or waggon. I desired to get clear of it again, but this my father would not permit.

CHAPTER VII.—MY FATHER'S DEATH.

I continued at the work described last week (picking out ironstone at the Stanhope quarries) and other boyish forms of labour until the death of my father, which happened on July 2nd, 1849. It was to me a sad blow, as it completed my orphanage, and left me at that early age face to face with the world. There was a romance about his death which, whenever I have related it, has caused people to look at me doubtfully, as if I was drawing the long bow, but I state with confidence that it is true as any event that ever was recorded.

I have said my father was a great walker. Let me illustrate that. One of my uncles (who told me this after I reached manhood) had arranged to meet him on the quiet at Bishop Auckland. This was necessitated on account of a transaction I have related earlier. When uncle reached Auckland he found there was a professional walker giving an exhibition of his ability, and father was walking by his side, and keeping pace with him. That will explain part of what I am about to mention. On Sunday morning, July 1st, he left Stanhope early, walked to Durham and back (21 miles each way) to see his brother, and was laid in his grave at 5 p.m. the next day, Monday, July 2nd. At that time the cholera was raging in Durham city and the seaports of the county. He caught the infection, and died, and was buried as I have said. There was another man who went to Hartlepool the same week end. He returned on Monday, and was buried on Tuesday. So much were the people afraid of the epidemic that no one belonging to the house in which we lodged, nor any of the neighbours, nor even the doctor, would enter the room. The doctor came to the door of the house, handed the medicine to me, told me how and when to give it, and during the whole of that weary night the only inmates of that upstairs room were a strong man (and he was strong) struggling with death and a sad hearted lad of twelve, who had to rub the legs or bowels when the fearful cramp seized the patient, and who feared the dread result might be a separation from one who loved his son with such a strong love, and whose correction (which was always justified and never unnecessary) was prompted by a desire for the good of the corrected. The end came in the darkness. The inmates were informed of the fact by the cries of the desolate, grief-stricken orphan upon whose life the shadow had fallen. A coffin was made as speedily as possible, and with all expedition the funeral was prepared for, and by five in the afternoon the father was laid in his grave. As there had been no time to inform the relations, the son was the only mourner, and he, without a full realisation of his loss or prospects, was called upon to face the realities of life.

My father when he died was 42 years of age. He was as fine a specimen of physical manhood as could be seen. When he left me on the fatal Sunday to go to Durham he was full of life and energy. Straight and tall; in movement like a well-trained athlete, and as fearless and bold as a man could be. Within thirty-six hours the pride of strength was gone, and he was laid in the churchyard at Stanhope. He was manly in all his actions, and loathed meanness, and did his best to stamp that side of his character upon me. In a boyish way I used to imitate men in the practice of what at that time was known as the "noble art of self-defence." So long as I defended myself it was all right with him, whether I was victor or not; but if I was the aggressor, and I was beaten, I invariably found the beating duplicated when the affair came to his knowledge. In that he was right, and from this distant date I look across the years and

2

subsequent events, and find my admiration for him is as strong as ever. True he led me through a wild, devious, and varied life, and oft brought poverty into my young life; but still he was MY bold and manly father, and I see him in no other light, nor desire to see him in any other.

He was buried on Monday, and on the Wednesday I left Stanhope to walk to Durham alone. I had on a new cap, which some kind neighbour had bought for me, while another gave me sixpence, and with that large sum in my pocket, and my meagre belongings in a bundle, entirely unacquainted with the route, except as generally described, but with a strong determination, and as good a heart as boys at my age and in my circumstances could have, I took the road with 22 miles of hard travel, and an unknown life before me. However, although young in years, I was old in travelling, and did not dread it as much as a boy would have done whose life had been spent in plenty and surrounded by maternal care and solicitude. I was used to roughing it, and a few of Dame Fortune's buffets extra would not matter much.

I set myself to my task with good will, and had made half my journey when I met one of my uncles. He was a shoemaker to trade, and it was to see him my father made the journey to Durham. He lived at the foot of Gilesgate for many years, and died there. He had heard the news, and in his anxiety for me was on his way to see what could be done, and kindly brought me back to his house and gave me share of whatever his circumstances would allow.

As soon as the rest of my uncles could be informed there was a family consultation to see what was best to be done with me. Right here I would like to express my gratitude to them for all they were willing to do, and tried to do, but which my wayward temper would not permit them to do. My father, wandering soul that he was, was the family favourite, and the affection they had for him was transferred to me. They found, however, they had a chip of the old block to deal with. They tried their best for a few months, and were baffled, as the following trade enumeration will show. I was sent as an errand boy to a grocer at the head of Easington Lane, to a butcher in Hetton in

the same capacity, to live with a John Wilson (a cousin of my father's, a blacksmith), whose house was on the Quay near Bog Row, in Hetton, and to an uncle of the same trade in Ryhope. While with him I had a narrow escape. Uncle sent me to Seaham Colliery, a distance of three miles, to order coals. I got on the buffer of a coal waggon at Seaham Harbour, from which I slipped, and my trousers catching the hook, I was dragged for some distance with my head and shoulders bumping on the ground. Luckily the cloth gave way, or I should have been bumped to death. From Ryhope I was sent to my uncle and godfather, John Wilson, who was a miller at Stranton, near Hartlepool, for whom I have to this day the greatest respect. As a last resource I was hired to a cousin of my father's, who kept the Tower Farm, near Ludworth Colliery. The main duty I was engaged for was to take milk morning and night in two barrels, one on either side of a donkey, upon which I rode, to Thornley, about two miles distant, and, of course, to do anything else I could during the day.

I had spent a few weeks there with my father prior to this hiring time, and therefore I knew the locality somewhat. On the previous occasion an incident occurred which illustrates the idea of witchcraft which obtained among the working classes at that time. There was a cattle disease prevalent, and G. Wilson, the farmer, lost 16 or 17 of his stock. The conclusion was that he was bewitched, and suspicion fell on the hind's (married servant's) wife. She had, it was said, an evil eye or some other means of bringing disaster upon those who offended her, and she used her influence to punish him. Why she should revenge herself upon the cattle was not considered. There was living in Newcastle a wise man, if I remember correctly, called Black Jack, and it was deemed advisable to consult him. He had no hesitation in saying there was witchery, and he gave the following advice:—"Take a young heifer, not diseased, and kill it. Then take the heart, and at 12 o'clock midnight fry it, and it will be seen who has wrought the mischief." I gathered that from hearing the older people talk about it, and was present when my father (who was a butcher to his trade) killed the beast and carried out the subsequent part of the proceedings. I was in the kitchen when preparations were made for the reception of the evil-doer, but before the testing hour arrived, tired nature had asserted itself, and I was in that happy state where witches and the wicked trouble not. I was told in the morning that my father walked sentry all night around the house, and I am confident if anything material or otherwise had appeared, they would have been used as a target. I was informed, too, that fearful noises were heard at intervals. Let that be accounted for as it may, it is a fact that the cattle plague was stayed.

I become a Miner.

One natural consequence of the farm being near the colliery village was the formation of comradeship with the boys who worked there. Their glowing, but highly coloured, acounts of of the life in the pit caught my fancy, and I resolved to seek employment. That and the love of change, which had taken deep root in me, formed the impulse which I could not resist, and in a few months I went and sought work at Ludworth Colliery. The first consideration was a home. That I managed, but such a home! This will be realised when I say it was in the family of the noted Tom Todd, who was then a boy about fifteen, and who for some years became one of the terrors of the east side of the county. The family consisted of his father, himself, and two sisters, the younger of whom used to work in the fields at the farm. I was often with her and others when they were at work. She hearing my openly expressed desire to start in the pit—and no doubt thinking I might assist in the family—induced her father to ask the manager. Leave was granted, and I accepted such lodgings as they could give me. My uncle Robert (the grocer in Ryhope), as soon as he heard of my intention to start in the pit, met me in Durham, where I had gone with some cattle to the fair. He did his best to dissuade me, and the good, kind heart shed tears when he saw how obstinate I was, and said I was the only one of the family to go to the mines. The miner at that time was not generally held in good repute by the classes outside his own rank. He now has more respect for himself, and respect is reciprocal. We have made a great advance in that direction. There is still room for further improvement. One of the lessons our young men especially should learn is this: "He who respects himself will assuredly be respected."

To the pit I went (a few months short of thirteen years), and made my home with the family I here named. The younger sister, Jane, as I have said, worked in the fields. The elder, "Nell," was the housekeeper. It will suffice when I say "Nell" was well-known in all the neighbourhood. Her escapades were many, and she had a mind full of mischief. I once saw her make the dumb speak. He was a beggar. She suspected him, and chased him with a brush, laying on until she loosened the organs of speech, and he cried out for mercy. Which she and all who saw it enjoyed immensely.

I did not stay long with the Todds, in which I see a special Providence. The next family who took me were from Cornwall, and were called George. After a short stay I was offered a home with a Wesleyan family, a thorough God-fearing people. Of Mr Catron it could be truly said "that man was perfect and upright, and one that feared God and eschewed evil," and he was not an exception in that good and generous household. I am sorry to say that the discipline obtaining, although not of the severe nor Puritanical order, did not harmonise with my ideas. I was working with a boy named Oxley, in whose family the conditions were of a laxer order, and more congenial to my taste; and, listening to his persuasions, to my own loss, I left the Catrons, in spite of their entreaties, and entered a social atmosphere charged with danger to a nature like mine. I had attained to the rank of a pony putter (it being about the time when ponies were being introduced). I was only fourteen; but age is relative in boy as in man. It is a question of aptitude and vitality, and I am thankful to God I have had a fair share of these, which has helped me where others less blessed might have failed, and which enables me at 71 to do an average day's work. My aptitude may be illustrated by the following: I was in a public-house with Oxley the elder, when he pointed to me and said, "That lad has made 30s this pay putting. Is it not good for his size?" These were not the days of big wages either.

I made a fifth home at Ludworth. This was brought about as follows: There was a decent family named Stabler. They had an only son about my age.   One Sunday we were sent to work in the 5/4 seam, and, strange as it may appear, we were the only persons in the seam. Our shift ended, we came to the shaft to ride. We rapped for the cage.   He was getting in first, when the engineman started the cage without the signal.   I retained presence of mind to seize his jacket and pull him back on to the flat sheet, and saved him, or he would have been cut to pieces.   When he got home he was ill with the shock (from which he died a short time afterwards), and he told his parents what had happened.   They sent for me and thanked me, and offered to take me if I was willing. When I saw the sweetness of the lady's face and the comfort of the home it was equal to an offer of Paradise as contrasted with where I was, and without hesitation I accepted, and removed with them to Sherburn Hill.   I was known there (and some of the old residents would speak of me yet) as Stabler Wilson.

Before dealing with my life at Sherburn Hill I would like to relate a narrow escape from death I had in the pit at Ludworth.   There had been an incline drift driven, and for some purpose the drift was laid with bricks in the bottom of the ways.   I was attempting to take a tub down the drift, and thought I could manage by going down before it, and pushing against it.   I had barely got started when my feet slipped and got under the tub.   I was thus pushed down, but my legs acted as a drag.   I was being taken down at an unpleasantly quick rate, and the great danger lay in my being dashed against some tubs which were standing at the bottom.   My shouts brought to my aid the waggonwayman, and he was able to stop me just in time.   If he had been a moment or two longer I should certainly have been crushed to death.   By his timely intervention the only damage done was a few days' soreness for me, and the outlay by my kind friends for a new pair of trousers, for the ones I started with from the top were partly left in the drift, and the remnant in rags hanging to me.

CHAPTER VIII.—AT SHERBURN HILL.

This will be a fitting stage to notice a point or two in the great change which has taken place in the life of a boy working in a mine between the time of my boyhood and now.   In every aspect the change is great.   How great only those who have worked in both periods can tell.   No amount of pen power, or word painting, can convey a proper idea of it to the minds of the boys and men of this generation. If they had a full appreciation of the change they would value more the efforts which have brought it about, and have more gratitude for the memory of the men who, with small opportunities, and in the face of great opposition, oftimes cruel to the extreme, but with an unshrinking determination, worked out the better day of the present.

Then the hours were long and conditions bad. Little regard was paid to ventilation, and there was often an ill-treatment of boys which is not practised now, nor would it be tolerated to-day. Take the hours.   There was no strict and precise loosing time such as we have in vogue now. It is true " lowse " or " kenno " was sent down from bank, but not given by the deputies as now at the flat, with an arranged travelling time of twenty-five minutes to the mile, and to be out at the minute.   Speaking of Ludworth, the time to be out was when all the full tubs were brought out.   If a driver was standing with his horse on an empty set of tubs, he was not allowed to unyoke.   He had to either go in to the flat or until he met the last full tubs coming out.   Then (and not till then) he unyoked and came out to ride, and at that point he started the next morning.   It will easily be seen what the consequence would be if there were any stop.   It meant a long day and a late return home.

In the winter time the boys hardly ever saw daylight except on Sunday, and then they were too sleepy sometimes to look at it.   I remember in my own experience at Sherburn Hill I lost an entire Sunday altogether.   I came home from work on the Saturday completely tired out, and kind-hearted, motherly Mrs Stabler persuaded me to go to bed.   I took her advice, and the next thing I realised was after they had their tea on Sunday.   The kind woman had been upstairs two or three times anxious about me, but when she saw me sleeping so soundly and peaceably she left me alone.   When I came down I thought they were at breakfast, and my surprise may be imagined when I was told they had finished tea.

In the matter of treatment of boys down the mine there is a complete change. In the days of which I am writing it was considered part of the training of a boy to feel the weight of the overman's yard wand, just as there was the frequent and necessary use of the cane by the schoolmaster, or the rope's end aboard a ship to quicken the apprentice. And it was an unquestioned prerogative of the official to punish when he thought fit. I will anticipate a little to relate a piece of very brutal treatment I received from the back-overman at Ludworth when I went to work there the second time. The reason why I went will be seen a little further on. I was at that time putting with my hands at that colliery, and travelling from Sherburn Hill. There were 12 of us hand putting. I was the least and youngest, being about 16 years and 9 months. We had claimed payment ("lying money") for waiting when there was a stop, but we were refused, and we unanimously agreed that when there was another stop we would go out. The opportunity soon occurred, and off we set in Indian file, I, on account of my youth and size, bringing up the rear. I felt myself secure (because many of the putters were much above 20, and big men), but I found it was not safe to put trust in putters any more than princes. On our way out we met the back-overman. He was a big, bad-tempered, brutal man, and a terror to all in the mine. As soon as those at the head of the file saw him they rushed back in-bye. I stood my ground. I can hear his loud voice now, as in loud, but not choice, words he asked if I was not going, and I replied, "No, I am not, except you promise to pay us." He then knocked me down into the middle of the way, and kicked me for some time. When he put the question again I answered, "You may kill me if you like, but I am not going in." What would have been the consequence I cannot say, for just at that moment a hewer named Quinn came out, and he stopped him and said, "Let the lad alone, you brute, or it will be you and me for it." The overman, like all human brutes, must have had a cowardly base, for he desisted, and Quinn helped me up and out-bye. I was in bed for three days. I then went to see the fore-

overman, who suggested that as I had collided with him I had better leave. This I did, as will be related further on.

As I have said, I left Ludworth and came to Sherburn with Mr and Mrs Stabler. He was a hewer, and I was started as a pony putter at Littletown, somewhat under fifteen. The overman there was Mr Henry Hepburn. He was a fine gentleman, who depended more upon kindness than ill-usage in his dealings with the lads. After I became a member of Parliament for Mid-Durham—and he was then turned eighty—he used to speak of me as one of his lads. No doubt he was surprised to find that such an unlikely youth had found his way to that high estate. I feel confident if anyone in his hearing (when I and a few others used to vex him and cause him anxiety by our conduct) had said such a thing would have taken place, he would have asked upon what they founded their assertion. The manager, Mr W. Crawford, gave me notice twice, and three times I stood before him in the office as a prisoner before the judge. He was an absolute ruler of that group of the Lambton Collieries, monarch of all he surveyed, and when an offence was committed there was an office trial. One of my earliest arbitrations, in 1874 or 1875, was at Sherburn Hill, and while we were taking the evidence I surprised Mr Crawford by saying, "I have been in this office before, sir." "When?" said he. "I have no recollection of you." He was amused when I pointed to where he sat and I stood, and related the cause of it.

My life at Sherburn Hill contains an event or two which I will insert here. The first in importance to me is my acquaintance with her who afterwards became my wife, and who was one of life's greatest blessings. Well do I remember when I first spoke to her. I was about sixteen, and she was nearly two years younger. No picture was ever depicted on canvas more vividly than that boyish scene is impressed on my memory now, and I hope it may remain as one of the last which faculties impaired by age may retain. There she stood with her long golden hair hanging down her back; and it was beautiful, as it was even to her death at 68, when time had changed its colour. Her face perfect as a girl, as all who knew her know it was when age had tried its marring hand on it. She was dressed in black with a white apron, and attracted me then as a boy, as she ever did, and never with greater force than when death laid his ruthless hand on her, taking one of earth's best array, and cutting asunder the ties which had bound us in a life-long heart fellowship; for ours was truly a union of hearts, and never was anything done by her to weaken that union. The first words I said to her were common place enough, but I have no hesitation in saying, at that moment was the tide in my affairs, and, taken at the flood, led me to a fortune before which that of a Carnegie, a Rockefeller, or a Peirpont Morgan sink into insignificance. I said, "Dis th' want a lad, hinny?" She started to laugh. That was enough for me, for one of the strong points in my character is to seize the skirts of happy chances, and not to hesitate when the occasion affords. I fastened on to that laugh, and never let go, and now the memory is sweet. I would not change it for all the wealth or honour the world could give.

The second event worthy of record is my first attempt at leading a strike and settling a dispute. I was sixteen at the time. The event had slipped from my memory, but I was in conversation a short time ago with my good and tried friend, Mr W. Robinson, J.P., of Hetton-le-Hole, when he reminded me of it, and I asked him to write it out for me. This he did without any hesitation, and the following is the letter he sent. I give it in his own words. All who know him can depend upon him.

"46, The Avenue,
"Hetton-le-Hole.
"4th December, 1908.

"Dear Mr Wilson,—The following is what I remember of our young days. In the year 1853, about the middle of the year, we as pony putters were very dissatisfied with the wages we were earning for twelve hours' hard working—from two to three shillings per day, but seldom the latter. At that time our score price was 8d per score. We agreed to see Jacob Ellis, the overman. Not being satisfied with his answer, we, after talking the matter over, decided on the Monday morning not to go down the pit, but went to Littletown instead. The putters there joined us, and we held a meeting behind the pit heap, when it was agreed to go to Sherburn House, but before we could get there the lads had gone down, and we went to the Lady Durham, which they were just commencing to sink.

After spending some time we agreed to go back to Littletown to see Mr Crawford, the manager. When we got there an old man named Grey, who looked after the horses, told us it was too soon, and advised us to go home, which we did.

"In the afternoon of the same day, while playing at ball at the top of the Single Row, the overman came up from Littletown and told us that Mr Crawford had sent him to tell us that if we went to work the next day he would give us an advance of one penny per score. While he were considering the matter he went into Jack Walker's public-house. You then got on to the ash midden at the Row end for a platform. You said the advance of a penny per score was very small, but we could put three score or more, and that made threepence per day, or two and ninepence per fortnight. After a good deal of consideration we agreed to accept the offer. Someone was wanted to tell the overman. No one seemed willing. You asked me to go. I went to the public-house, where he was sitting with a glass of ale and smoking a yard of clay, as it is sometimes called.

"We went to work the next day. So far as we knew all was right, but to our surprise in a day or two you and I received a month's notice. During the time I expect my father went to see Mr Crawford. He said you and I were the ringleaders, and but for us the pits would not have been idle. After some time he said to my father, 'Your son can start to hew at Little town, but Wilson will have to leave; I will not have him here.' I suppose you never went to see him, but got work at Ludworth Colliery, and travelled from Sherburn Hill. Some time after you came back to the Hill, as I remember we hewed beside each other down the 'Old Back' in the West pit. Some time after I think you went to Broomside Colliery with Tom Dove. I lost sight of you for a time. I am not sure whether this was when you went to sea; I know you were there for a while.

"In 1862 I moved to Hetton, and did not see much of you until 1874, when I was sent to Wheatley Hill, where you were at the time, to ask you to arbitrate for us in fixing a price in the new pit. From then till now we have had a close acquaintance.—With regards from

"W. ROBINSON."

It is true, friend Robinson, we have been close together, but not too close. You are a man with whom one need not be afraid to hunt tigers, for you will not skulk when there is danger about. Your worth has never been properly estimated in the county. There has been little of the showiness of the demagogue in you, but all the solid substance of a man. When you are weighed in the balance you will not be found wanting. Your letter will let the lads of to-day see the hours we worked, the pay we got, and the treatment meted out to those who desired to amend the conditions of labour. Their salvation has come to them through self-sacrifice of men like you.

Being refused employment at Sherburn Hill,

and not being inclined to leave the village and my good friends, I sought and obtained work at Ludworth as a hand putter, at which I continued for nine months. It was a trying time. I had to leave as early as 3 a.m., or shortly after, to go down at four. I was thrown into competition with young men who were strong and robust, while my physical strength at that age was not very great. I had to make up for a weak body by the self-will and determination of which I had a fair share. It was at the termination of these nine months that I received the ill-usage from the back-overman to which I have already referred, and which was the cause of my return to the Hill again.

CHAPTER IX.—AN APPARITION.

During the time referred to last week (my stay at Sherburn Hill) there were two incidents to which reference may be made. The second of these arose out of the first. There was at this period a travelling theatre known as "Collett's." It was located often in Sherburn Village just where the four roads meet. The pieces they were going to perform were announced by the orchestra, which consisted of a clarionet played by George, the brother of the proprietor. He was a very strenuous performer, if not musically accurate—so much so that the common remark was that George was trying to blow himself through the instrument. The tragedies he announced were of the most blood-curdling nature. The more horrible the better they were appreciated. And we youngsters left the booth with hair on end and flesh a-creep. The choice pieces were of the "Maria Martin" and "Hallgarth Murder" type. I remember my then, and always, sweetheart and future wife and I were down seeing the "Hallgarth Murder." It was a fine, clear moonlight night, not a cloud to be seen, still and bright. The place was packed, as the theatre was only about a mile from the scene of the actual murder. We were among the gods. All went well until Clarke had been tried, and was brought out for execution. Everywhere was silent expectation, when just at the crucial point there came a gust of wind, "a mighty rushing wind," which carried away the canvas top of the structure, except certain portions. These cracked like

great whips. The women screamed, and there was a universal rush for the doors. Mrs Collett, who had been killed as Mary Ann Westgarth a short time before, stood on the stage wringing her hands and crying. We, occupying an elevated seat up in the gallery, were about the last to get out. Strange to say, when we did reach a position out of the crowd, the wind had subsided, and the moon was shining as clearly and silvery and the heavens were as quiet as when we went in. The people explained the occurrence by saying it was a judgment shown because of the proximity to Hallgarth Mill, where the murder was committed. For myself I have never sought for a solution. I state the facts, and vouch for their accuracy.

The consequence of a nightly repetition of these dreadful tragedies was a fear to go to work at the early hour in the morning. Since then I have read somewhere that Napoleon said there were few men who had the two o'clock in the morning courage. Whether that be so or not I cannot say. I am confident, however, there was one youth who used to be short of courage at three. Like the character in the play, I whistled aloud to keep my courage up, and thought every bush was a ghost. Now there arose out of that mental state a serious situation, with a ludicrous ending. At that time to the inhabitants of Sherburn Hill (I don't know it may be now) there was one haunted place. On the road to Haswell, and just at the end of the "Wide Lonnen," there were, and are now, two gates, which formed the entrance to a bridle road leading down to Ludworth Colliery. The generally accepted idea was that one of these gates used to open and shut with a bang as the result of some supernatural agency.

One morning I went to work with less courage than ever. The night before I had seen "Maria Martin," with all its horrors, and I saw her everywhere. All went as well as my fear would permit until I got a few yards beyond the haunted gate, when, as Burns says:

"I there wi' something did foregather,
  Which put me in an eerie swither."

At that moment the gate went to with an awful clash, and my hair stood on end and my flesh was all a-creep, while on before me, to my highly strung imagination, there appeared horrible and fantastic shapes. I wanted to go to work. I had about a quarter of a mile to go on the turnpike before I took the field road across two fields to Ludworth, but I durst not face the fearful objects. There was one way. If I could get through the ghostly gate and trespass over a field and a half I would pass those dreadful beings and strike the field road, and so on in safety to the pit.

I took heart and got through the gate, and set off to the bottom of the field. These fields were part of the Ludworth Farm, where I was the milk-barrel boy some three years before. There is a peculiar lie of the land; one field is much higher than the other. On the side of the hedge where I was it was high, while on the other it was quite low. I was making my way as I best could, congratulating myself upon my cunning in having outwitted the appalling figures I had left in the road, when suddenly I heard the clink of a chain. Awful sound! Terror stricken I looked up, and there I saw a great head, and what appeared to me a pair of horns partly over the hedge. There was no need for a starter to cry "Go" to start me in the race. I off at full speed across the two fields which lay between me and the pit, and crash over the hedge came the being to which the head and horns belonged. At that time I could realise the feelings of Tam O'Shanter when the spectral dancers of Alloway Kirk burst out after him, and with the same desire for safety that he made for the "key stane o' the brig," so I made for the pit. As Tam 'oked back and saw "Nannie" and her col-

leagues, and as a consequence urged on his "grey mare Meg," so in my case close upon my heels I heard the clink, clink of the chain, and when I cast a backward glance I saw the two straight horns, and put on an extra spurt, until just when my strength and wind were giving out I managed to get over the rails, and then came a total collapse.

When I recovered consciousness I was alone. I went to work, and as I returned I thought I would take the same road back, in spite of trespass, as I had a desire to see, if possible, if an earthly explanation could be given of the circumstances. Just about the point where the chase began, there, looking over the hedge, I saw a donkey with a chain and clog to his leg. And audibly I addressed him as follows:— "Hello! it's thoo, is't? If thoo hed catched me Aa deserved it, for Aa learnt the te run after folks and bite them if thoo could." It was a retribution. This was the donkey upon which I used to ride with the milk barrels, and my own spirit of mischief taught him to run after people viciously, and I believe in the end he was to kill. I came near suffering for that act of cruelty, for I have no doubt he would either have killed or hurt me seriously if the chain had not hindered him and given me a chance to escape.

"Chalking On."

There has been a change in the mode of keeping count of the tubs which the men filled and the putters brought out since that time. Now the hewer and putter put the "tokens" on, and they are counted at bank. At the time of which I am writing it was kept by a system known as "chalking" on. The process was as follows:—At every flat there was a boy or man who was known as the "chalker on," whose duty it was to keep an account. He had a board varying in size in keeping with the number of hewers and putters engaged at the flat. Down one side of the board the names were written. When a putter came out with a tub he shouted "Chalk on." The question was put, "Whe's the been at?" The reply was the name of a hewer. The initials of the hewer who had filled the tub were marked on the outside of the tub, as, for instance, if John Smith had filled it, J. S. would be the sign. The mode of keeping the account was four downward strokes and one across, which stood for five—a mode which is adopted in many cases of counting in other matters to this day.

The tokens inside the tub and the abolition of the "chalking on" was introduced by the employers to save themselves from a system of defrauding to which they were subject, as, it will be obvious, the system exposed them to. There were three modes in operation in defrauding. The "chalker on," if he were so inclined, could mark more on than the man had filled or the putter had brought out, if he had a favourite, or "blood was thicker than water." Sometimes, when a putter came out and got the tub marked down to a man, he would quietly draw the tub back, and, resting awhile, would come up against the set with a bang, and shout out, "Chalk on," and another name. On a Saturday, if the "chalker on' wanted a short day, he would get to know by some process how many tubs each hewer wanted to fill, and in a short time the putter would be informed to tell the men they had the requisite number on the board, and they were enabled to get home early. On a "baff" Saturday there was no "loose." At Pittington, where I "put" a short time, the putter always told the hewer when it was his last tub.

After I had been travelling to Ludworth about nine or ten months, and I had received the ill-usage from the back-overman, as I have related, Mr Stabler thought the manager (Mr Crawford) at Sherburn Hill might have relented and be inclined to overlook my first effort at trades union leadership, and he went and asked him to allow me to start again. For a long time he refused, but finally he said, "He may start to hew in the West Pit at Sherburn Hill, but he shall not commence again as a regular putter. If he does there will be no peace among the lads, for he is a born agitator."

CHAPTER X.—FIRST CAVIL.

I accepted the offer to start hewing in the West Pit at Sherburn Hill, and at the age of sixteen years and nine months I got a cavil up the "Drop," and in some of the hardest coal ever was hewed in this county. My "marrow" was young, like myself. His name is N. Turnbull. I speak of the present because he is still alive, I think, and living on Sherburn Hill. There is a great change in the conditions of hewing. The hours were fully 50 per cent. more in the pit than they are now in the whole workings. There was no "loosing" in the face, as is now the custom. The fore-shift man went down at the latest at 2 a.m., but some went much before that hour. If a man in back was later than 6 or 6.30 a.m. he was late. As soon as a man arrived on the pit heap in the back-shift he, with his picks, was put into an empty tub and sent down, the signal to the engineman being a call from the banksman, "Men on." In the working face there was an overlapping of work, not as now putting on the clothes as soon as the back-shift man comes in. It is safe to say that there was fully two hours to work together before the fore-shift man left. It was customary for a man to take a jud off across the four yards for an ordinary day's work. If his working place was two yards wide, then two juds was the ordinary quantum for a strong man. And (which makes the contrast greater) the working place was to "nick," cut up the side with the pick, and it can easily be imagined how heavily that would press on the shoulders. In respect to youths like myself, or weak men, the full day's work could not be done. The following would be the mode of procedure: The fore-shift man would knive and nick and fire a jud. He would fill as many of the coals as possible, and get the second jud commenced. When the back-shift man came in they would work together as best they could, and when the second jud was got down, then he would go home. In a word, if he got his sump and a place cleared for his marrow to start he did well. I have used our pit terms. The miners will appreciate the change, and to those who are not miners it will be clear that the hours were very long, and all will admit that we have not merely lived over half a century, but a wonderful change has been wrought in the conditions and hours. It is worth something to look upon the change, and to feel one has not been a drone in procuring the change.

There was one evil effect of this taking a

place in the ranks of men to me. Forcing me to hew lifted me out of the category of boys at a very early age. If the years and strength were short the desire to be a man was strong. In Cassell's Popular Educator there are two rows of figures, the high and the low. The starting point is a boy, and the question asked is, "What will become of him?" Will he take the road to mental culture and respectability, or will it be that of neglect and a disreputable life? At this point of my life I was at the parting of the ways. The trend I received in youth, combined with the opportunities, gave me the bias, and with sorrow and regret I confess I took the low road. How far I went or what was done on it will be of no material benefit to any person to know. There are things I keep to myself, and, with Burns, will not tell to anyone. It will suffice as an index if I say that I fixed my mind upon the wrong ideal of manhood, set at nought good counsel, formed the wrong companionship, and devoted my spare time to a wrong purpose, and I feel the loss now.

Sherburn Hill at that time was the gathering ground at the pay week end for gamblers, drinkers, and fighters from the neighbouring collieries. Its pay was on the "Little Pay," and as a consequence the "Big Pay," or alternate collieries, sent their contingent of men ready for any and every mischief. To be like these was the goal of our youthful ambition. We used their vocabulary and followed their example. The more adept the man was, the greater our admiration for him, and the more ardent our desire to be like him. There were men in the village who were as eager for any sport or bout of fisticuffs as the visitors, and therefore the occasion was not far to seek or long to wait for.

It will therefore be easily seen what impressions these circumstances and surroundings would have on a mind such as mine, largely prepared to receive them, and on a nature ever eager to be in the front rank. Those impressions were not allowed to have undisputed sway, for my good friends, Mr and Mrs Stabler, did their best to counteract them. They were not church or chapel goers, and therefore the example was wanting, but they used to do all possible by giving me good advice and by sending me to Sunday-school. For a short time I was thus brought under the influence of good men. I feel confident they were grieved many a time by seeing conduct both in and out of school which was directly opposed to their life and teaching. Good Mr W. Robson, the leading singer, and Mr G. Suggett were two of them. Their teaching was not lost; it was only hid. And my attempts to preach the same Gospel in the same chapel some years after, in their presence, was proof thereof, and I believe cheering to them.

The result of this conduct on my part created friction between Mr Stabler and myself. There was none on the part of Mrs Stabler, for if ever mother was kind to and bore with the waywardness and wildness of a son she loved, that kind heart was, and did to me. I was like many today who at seventeen think they know more than a man of years, who chafe at the restraint older and wiser heads would place upon them and who will have none of their counsel, and set at nought their reproof. I cannot give an estimate of the grief which was in those friendly hearts; but I have a full knowledge of the great loss it was, and is at the present, to myself. I left as sweet a home as ever boy or man lived in, I care not whether he lived in palace or cottage, and I entered on a course which wasted twelve years of my life which, if devoted to mental culture, would have fitted me to fill with greater ability any sphere in life where reason is the deciding force. So far as I am concerned regrets are useless, although I have oft had bitter regrets when I have felt myself cribbed and confined and hindered for want of the knowledge I should have gathered in the spring of life. My object in recording it is in the hope that some young man at the parting of the ways—the diverging point of right and wrong, or, to alter the figure, when a life of usefulness or waste is in the balance—may be led to seriously consider and make a wise choice. The spring time of life is the period of preparation, and mental waste is not only the greatest, but the most fatal and least remediable.

A Strike and Curious Wage Settlement.

My next lodging was with a family named Dove. I was at my own hand, and was fairly thrown upon my own resources. There was no lack of ability to earn more than my needs required, but the surplus went to the wrong bank, where the only interest was destroyed health and character, and the banker kept the principal. The variation from that was an endeavour to get other people's money without working for it by the many and diversified methods in vogue at the time, except stealing. At that I am thankful I always drew the line, unless it was giving expression to the boyish idea that we had a proprietary right to the produce of everybody's garden. The old people on the " Hill " a few years ago believed that such an idea had a strong hold on me. It was oft made manifest, for if such a depredation had been committed they generally credited " Stabler Wilson " with it. Where I did it full apologies are tendered.

The family with whom I now found myself were very decent, respectable people. They took me to lodge because of the companionship there was between their son, about my own age, and myself. There is nothing worthy of note during the year I was with them at Sherburn Hill except a strike which took place, and a somewhat peculiar settlement of a request for an advance in wages made by the hewers. There was no union at the time, and as a consequence the stoppage of work was sudden, and the proceedings somewhat turbulent and erratic. There were some men who went to work, and I saw two of these very seriously ill-used. One of them was standing against his own door, at the top of what was then the Engine Row. He was making insulting remarks to the crowd of angry men and women. The sight of him was sufficient to inflame, but his words added fuel to the fire. Suddenly a strong, powerful Welshman broke out of the throng, and before the " blackleg " was aware he ran and struck him a fearful blow with his foot on the breast. The impact was so great that door and man went crashing into the house, and for some time it was feared it was a case of murder. The other case was a poor, innocent elderly man (names withheld) whom the whole crowd of strikers met on his way from Littletown to Sherburn Hill. He was surrounded where there was a large pool of water. He was not struck, but hustled until he was got down, and then he was literally danced on by many of the young men. In connection with the strike, Rebecca and her children were out at night on mischief bent, and there was a collision between the men and the police near Littletown. The largest bulk of those who kept working lived there, and as a consequence the attention of the strikers was given to it. The rows were made a nightly marching ground, and any loose property (such as scrapers and rain water tubs) was taken away or destroyed. The authorities silently prepared for the conflict, and one night when the men went down as usual they found a cordon of policemen standing in silence awaiting them in the dense darkness. When the crowd, unaware of their presence, got close up, at a signal, the whole of the police lanterns were uncovered, and a blinding light flashed upon them. There was immediate confusion and a general stampede, and the swiftest runners got the quickest away to safety. I spoke some years after to a man who was there. I said, " Did you run?" " Yes, I ran a bit," he said, " but there are some who have not stopped yet." There were many men apprehended, some of whom were in bed at the time, and some were taken out of their beds, not because they were in the disturbance, but because they were taking part in a strike, for at that time there was one law for the employer and another for the workman. It was criminal for a workman to do that which his employer could do with impunity. He could arrange with his colleagues to reduce wages, and lock men out if the terms were not accepted, and turn them into the street to compel acceptance. There was no law to interfere with him. Let the workman want a higher price for his labour, he was liable to find the machinery of the law ranged against him, and there was a class connection, if not an open compact, between the magistracy and employers.

The request for an advance, which had a peculiar ending, was not connected with any strike. Some of the hewers thought they should have an advance, and a meeting was called. The matter was fully discussed, the necessary deputation picked to go and place their request before Mr Crawford. He had one strong trait in his character; he was one of the best promisers. If promises to inquire into a matter would have been of service none who went to beg a favour would have come empty away. This deputation did not come away without a promise. The meeting was waiting to receive the report. It was something after the following:—"We've seen the maister. He's very sorry he cannot give an advance, but we can gan in half-an-hour suener, and that will be as good." And the meeting broke up in admiration for the kindness, although some of them were at that time going to work in the fore shift at one o'clock and shortly after six in the back shift. I would like to see the faces of the men in a meeting now if the same offer were made as an equivalent to an increase in score price. There is a change. It comes from the use and application of a force which many to-day are tardy in their desire to accept.

CHAPTER XI.—SEAFARING DAYS.

I lodged with Mr Dove at Sherburn Hill for about a year, when we left at the "bindings," and went to live at Carrville, our home being near the east end of the Long Row. We did not leave Sherburn Hill because of any desire for a change, but because of a general edict which Mr Crawford issued. In the years 1854 and 1855 there was a great tide of emigration from Durham to Australia. The gold fields were just opening out. They were the El Dorado. Once there, and a fortune was assured. The conversations at the rendezvous, corner-end, or public-house were largely interspersed with the names of the clipper ships—Blue Jacket, Red Jacket, etc., the Red Jacket being the favourite; or of Ballarat or Bendigo, the centre of the gold deposit. Some men in their eagerness to get there went off without getting leave from the owners, and were followed to Liverpool, and brought back to work on the colliery until the next "binding." When the yearly "binding" came round in March of 1855 Mr Crawford refused to employ any members of a family whose father intended to go to Australia. Mr Dove, the man with whom I lodged, was one of the intended emigrants, and his son and nephew were as a consequence compelled to seek work elsewhere. If I would have left them I would have placed myself outside the edict, and remained on the colliery. To leave them was the alternative; but I elected to be loyal to my friends, although it meant leaving behind the sweetheart—that wonderful attraction to a young man, and to me much so. It was the loadstone which drew me many a time from Carrville to Sherburn Hill, and compelled me to make many a late journey, which I would cheerfully make now if the same attraction was there, although with a slower step, but with affection as warm.

We got work at Broomside Colliery, and removed to Carrville, near the end of the Long Row. At that time it was a vastly different place from the present. The Grange Collieries were going, and so were Belmont and Broomside, and the men who worked at them were as lively and ripe for mischief as any that could be found in any part of the county. There was at that time a much greater cleavage between the townsmen of Durham and the "Geordies." Seldom we hear that term applied with the same opprobrium now as then. There was a bitter feud, too, between them. On Saturday nights, when turning out time arrived, there was sure to be a sort of running fight, commencing at the Market Place and extending to the gate at the top of Gilesgate; and woe to the straggling or belated miner if caught by the weaver bodies. They would have got the same measure meted out to them as they would have given to any of the weavers if found at the same time of night in one of the neighbouring villages. I saw a few of these struggles, but as I am, and have been, a prudent man, foreseeing the evil and hiding myself, I was never far from the thick of the fray, and close to men whose names were a terror, who to my youthful mind were heroes of the first water, and who were a sure rock of defence in any attack that might be made.

The "Geordies" could be identified by the peculiarities of their dress. Now the distinctive class garb is gone, but then it obtained to a larger extent. I was in the Assize Court at that time when an effective use was made of it by John Davidson, who was defending three men who were charged with highway robbery. The person robbed was my uncle, and the place between Carrville and Rainton Gate. It was very dark. My uncle was positive in his identification, but the defence set up was the darkness of the night and the uniformity of the miners' dress. The jury accepted the defence, and the three men were acquitted.

Happily the difference in class feeling and dress are gone, and there is a blend of town and country and weaver and miner, of which all must approve.

I lived at Carrville a year, working half of it at Broomside Colliery, when, owing to something happening—I forget what—we were all taken to the Lady Seaham, near Pittington Station, where the second half of the year was spent. Nothing worthy of record occurred except two close shaves I had of ending my life early. In the first half while at Broomside Dove's son and I were hewing in the " broken," and the timber began to crack, indicating the pressure which the strata was putting upon it. We made our way out as best we could. I was the furthest in. If the stone had fallen straight down we should both have been caught. It was a squeeze. When I got to the outer edge running backward, it was so near that it took the lamp out of my hand, and would certainly have crushed me to death if Dove had not seized me by the belt and pulled me back into safety. It was as close a call as any man would wish, and for a deliverance therefrom he would feel very thankful.

The other near acquaintance I had with death was of a different character. At the period of which I am speaking what were known as " women's feasts " were much in vogue. They were held in some public-house, and were in connection with the breaking up of the women's funds. There were generally three nights' dancing to celebrate it. I never could dance much, even to this day, but I enjoyed it. And when a late hour arrived, and the fun became fast and furious, I was as eager as any for taking part in it. It was a dangerous practice when the weather was cold. Towards the end of the year I spent the greatest part of three nights at a feast at Sherburn Station. The room being very warm, and the weather cold, and not sufficient care being taken, two days after the finish of the frolic I was laid into bed with a raging fever. More tender nursing could not have been given to any person. Mrs Dove had a pure mother's heart. She watched over me night and day. On New Year's Eve, about the coming of the New Year, anxious watchers were at my bedside in keen sympathy with me in the dread struggle; and just when the New

Year's welcomes were being shouted a strong constitution triumphed, and the road to returning health was entered upon, but it was weeks before the goal was reached. Well do I remember the first time I ventured out. I was led to the door by my good old friend, and with hands pressed to the wall (as I was not able to go without support) I managed a few yards and back, increasing strength coming with every morning's effort.

(Photo. of Mr Wilson, age 19, taken just before going to sea.)

I worked the year out, and then at the " bindings " of 1856 we returned to Sherburn Hill. The second residence there was not long, for I resolved to try the sea. This came about as follows: My elder sister, who was living in service at West Hartlepool, became engaged to, and ultimately married, the mate of a ship, named W. Beatey. Whenever the ship was in the North I made one of the crew; and, only seeing "life on the ocean wave" from the shore and its pleasures, I became enamoured of it, and I secured a berth with them as an ordinary (very ordinary) seaman at the extravagant wage of 30s per month. The vessel was a brig, her name the Sussex. She hailed from Shoreham, and she was a coaster in the coal trade. The port of lading was invariably Hartlepool, but that of discharge depended upon circumstances. Sometimes Shoreham, and other times "The Pool," just below London Bridge.

The first voyage was nearly the last, and would have been if I durst have faced ridicule. I resolved to make myself proficient, but a collier brig did not afford much opportunity. I practised the art of sculling a boat or going up the rigging in the dark, as there was the dread of people seeing my clumsiness and jeering. I learnt the points of the compass in the taproom of the nearest public-house to the Shoreham harbour. The compass was stamped on the side of the beer jug, and my brother-in-law offered to bet a quart of beer I could not commit to memory and repeat the points of the compass in twenty minutes. He lost, and we shared the stakes. After the wager was decided the barman wanted to learn who I was, and he put the question. He was told I was a pitman. (Miner is a more modern term.) Pressing for more information he inquired how long I had been down the pit. "Seven years," was the answer. In most surprised tones he said, "Have you not been up until now?" I was surprised at him, and replied, "Yes, every day except on rare occasions." "Why, I thought you pitmen lived down there always!" said the querist. It was not long before I gathered from many other quarters that he was not alone in his ideas, for there was a generally held opinion that the coals their ships brought home were dug out of the bowels of the earth by a class of people who were little removed from barbarism, and whose home was down in the eternal darkness.

To corroborate my experience, and to show that the mine-dwelling idea was widely held, let me relate a portion of the experience of another man. His name was W. Palmer. He lived at Sherburn Hill in my youth, and I got into his company as much as possible. It will suffice to say that the tricks and dodges he did not know were hardly worth gathering up. He not only knew them, but could practice them

expertly. He was one of the twelve apostles who went from the North in the 1844 strike. He used to go off with his nut basket, and on one occasion found himself in London. Seeing some red-herring in the window of a shop, he entered, and in a vernacular strange to the tradesman he said, "What's the reed-herring, mister?" Both tongue and description of the article were puzzles, and he was asked to explain, which he did by pointing to what he wanted. "Oh!" cried the shopkeeper, "they are Yarmouth bloaters," and, turning to Palmer, he asked, "What are you, and where do you come from?" "I am a pitman, and I come from the county of Durham." That increased the surprise of the Londoner, and he requested the Northerner to accompany him to a tavern near by, and took him into the parlour, where a number of gentlemen were sitting, and made Palmer walk round like a horse showing his paces at a fair, and the general cry was, "Why, he can walk as straight as ourselves. We thought those pitmen could only walk in a doubled-up posture owing to the cramped condition of their work and their continual residence underground."

I have said that my first voyage was nearly the last. We ran to Hartlepool, but off Flamborough Head we found ourselves in a terrible storm, and as we neared Hartlepool the waves were running fearfully high. We lay "hove to" for 23 hours, and then the captain ordered preparations to be made for an attempt to reach the harbour. The wheel was unshipped, and a tiller fitted in. My brother-in-law, who was a good sailor, and the strongest of the able seamen were lashed to it, one on either side. Before taking his place he came to me and lashed me, with my knife in hand, to the foot of the rigging aft, and told me to remain there until the worst came, and then to use the knife. The two steersmen then took their places. The captain then took his position, and the ship's head was pointed to the harbour. The smallest deviation from a straight course meant dashing on one of the piers or the rocks lying to the north—the Middens, from which no vessel was ever saved if it got on in a storm. The seas were tremendous. The pilots were crowded on the pier, afraid to venture out. Along the cliffs, and at every point of advantage as far as the lighthouse, thousands of people were gathered to witness the struggle. Sometimes we were buried in the trough of the sea, then perched like some huge sea bird right on the crest of the wave. When we were in that elevated position we could see the handkerchiefs and hats waving. This was repeated every time we rose up, for there is no doubt but when we were hid from view they gave us up for lost. For myself, I looked in an anxious manner in the direction of Sherburn Hill, and I hesitate not to acknowledge that if it had been possible I would have transported myself to that village again. I did resolve that if I was only safe ashore I would return to hewing again. Three things were in our favour. We had a stout ship, good men steering, and a captain who knew the coast and the harbour as well as the best pilot connected with the port. We neared the piers, and under the skilful pilotage of the captain we went straight in between them. As soon as we were in a pilot sprang aboard. The anchor was let go. The ship was brought up as quickly as possible, because the way on her

would have run her ashore, and then the captain relieved his mind by swearing at the pilot, who took charge as soon as he was on deck. The oaths were tremendous. He must have felt considerably relieved when he got rid of his feelings, even on the wings of an oath. They were sweet music to me. I remember hearing one as I was loosing myself from the lashing. It was well rounded and loud. "Go to ——, you ——; we don't want you now. You durst not come out when we were in danger." It is on record somewhere that a Bishop, being at sea in a storm, was alarmed, but the captain gave him assurance by saying, "There is no danger. Listen how the sailors are swearing." A short time after he listened again, and broke out in tones of fervent thankfulness, "Thank God they are swearing still, captain." Whether that be true or hypothetical I know not (it is not Bishop like), but I confess here and now that those oaths of our captain were in my ears like a pæan of victory and a song of assurance, which drove away my fears completely.

CHAPTER XII.—LIFE AT SEA.

With safety I lost the idea of the danger of a seafaring life and the resolve to go back to the pit. Like all persons who make pious resolves when at death's door or in serious danger, I felt my courage rise as the distance from danger increased, and when the ship was loaded I was as eager as the rest for sea again. This eagerness must not be credited to my love for the sea, or any excess of boldness on my part. No; it arose from moral cowardice. I was afraid my companions and acquaintances at Sherburn Hill would jeer me and call me the one-short-voyage sailor. I could stand a great deal, but that was too much for me. The facing of a storm was nothing as compared with the curl of the scornful lip.

The poet who wrote the "Life on the ocean wave" had never spent much time in a coasting collier of that period, or he would have been bound to confess that there was more poetry than reality in his idea. It was as far removed from the glorious life he described as it was possible to be—crowded in a dark forecastle, no seats except your sea chest, the food of the

roughest kind, the beef and "spuds" and duff brought down in "kids" or small tubs. The mode of cutting the beef was to take hold of the piece you were going to eat, and slice it off with your sheath knife. That was the sacred, inviolable rule, and he who violated it was in great danger of getting a slash across the knuckles to remind him of the etiquette of the situation, and to teach him manners. Often the rations were short, for the captain in many cases having so much allowed to provision the vessel, would scheme to save, and by giving light weight and short measure to the sailors make profit for himself. There were no inspectors of weights and measures aboard the ships, and it was therefore safe to use false scales, weights, or measures.

The cleaning of the forecastle was the work of the apprentices. They took turns week and week about to scrub the floor every morning, and to sweep up after the meals were over. The forecastle was generally near the room where tar barrels, tarpots, brushes, cork fenders, and articles of a cognate character were stored. The smell which arose from close contact with that room was unpleasant, and the endurance arose from the familiarity which breeds contempt. The entrance to the forecastle was down a perpendicular ladder, into a darkness illumined only by a stinking oil lamp, the light of which only made the darkness more visible in the corners, and the smell of which was not that of eau-de-cologne. From floor to ceiling the height did not leave much margin above the head of a six foot man, while along the ceiling were the hammocks slung on hooks. The only scrap of comfort, especially in a storm, was sleeping in them, because they swung with the motion of the ship. They were comfortable after you learnt the art of getting into them, which was not easy at first, for at the first attempt you might easily find yourself, like vaulting ambition, on the other side.

There is a great change in this. Plimsoll and J. Havelock Wilson, with his colleagues, have not lived in vain, and sailors have a right to be thankful they have lived. There is another change, speaking of the collier vessels, which is the application of machinery to the discharge of the cargoes. These were discharged by a process known as "whipping," which was extremely laborious. This was done entirely by the sailors. Two or three of these went down into the hold to fill strong wicker baskets, which held a few hundredweights of coal. To the basket or hamper a rope was attached. This went over a pulley. At the other end the rope branched out threefold, like a cat-of-nine-tails. Then there was a large gate six or seven feet high, and somewhat wider, having, say, five or six bars. This was raised in a slanting position. Three sailors, each holding an end of the rope, run up this gate, and when the large hamper was full they would spring off, and their weight and a few hand-over-hand pulls would pull up the coals. When starting from the top, of course, the work was comparatively easy, but when the floor of the hold was reached, and the basket was to fill under the combing of the hatchway, it took a heavy and united haul. In that case thorough harmony of pull and jump from the third or fourth bar to land the load was needed. The whole effort was done as if set to music in the following order:—The three men were on the bar they leap from; the hook was attached; then three hand-over-hand pulls

and a spring to the deck, the combined weight bringing up the load with a jerk. As soon as it was landed, up they went to the jumping bar again, and repeated the same process without variation, except a change at certain intervals with the fillers below. It was pure hustling until the cargo was out. Now the machine has been happily substituted for that unsailor like and arduous manual labour, and the insensate, untiring servant of man does the work of days in a few hours.

There were two specially dangerous circumstances through which I passed while in this coasting. The first of these was on the night the Royal Charter was lost, on October 25, 1859, off the coast of Wales. She was supposed to be the richest vessel that had ever left Australia for England. She was near home when caught in the storm to which I now refer, and all hands were lost except a few, who were saved by the bravery of one man, who swam out in face of the waves with a rope, and if the ship had held together all might have been saved. We were on our way from Hartlepool to Shoreham, when we were caught by the storm on the "Deeps," which are between Flamborough Head and Cromer Point. We struggled across safely, but were compelled to anchor under the lee of the land between Cromer and Yarmouth. The land was low, the wind howled and roared, and the waves broke with fury upon us and covered the deck. For thirty-six hours everything was battened down. We were all on deck the whole of the time, except in a lull of about five minutes, when we dashed down below and snatched a few biscuits. It was but a temporary respite, for again the storm burst upon us with an increased force. Repeatedly the angry and hungry water rushed over and covered everything. We could see nothing except one sheet of tossing waves, snarling and snapping. Twice we took to the rigging, but the ship, like a strong man under a burden, groaned and recovered herself. We had need to bless the honest shipbuilder who built her so stout and strong. If not she would have broken, and we should have been lost to a man. To add to our difficulty, the pumps were to keep going. When not pumping we fell asleep up to the waist in water. The song the "Bay of Biscay" fit us exactly. For near two nights and a day we were tossed about, wet, cold, and hungry. "There we lay on that day."

The wished-for morrow breaking through the mirky sky brought no relief. It was a sad and dismal view. During the second night the storm abated, and we were able to set our sails and make the homeward passage in safety.

The second of the near escapes we had while in the Sussex was in Yarmouth Roads. It was a close call, and a dangerous incident. We were at anchor, with a strong wind and a heavy sea running outside the sands. The ship strained at her anchor like a dog trying to get clear of the leash. The wind was straight from the seaward, and whistled through the rigging. It was my watch from 10 p.m. until 12. Shortly before my watch was up the mate (my brother-in-law) came on deck, and after some conversation he asked me who relieved me, and I told him an able seaman named Beck. " Tell him to get the other anchor ready lest this should give way." I gave the order, and bidding him good-night I went below. Divesting myself of my wet outer clothing I got into my hammock. I heard Beck at work clearing the other anchor, and was composing myself for a sleep when I heard a loud snap—the anchor chain had parted —and a cry " All hands on deck." We tumbled up without any more clothes or head-covering. The captain had sprung to the wheel to keep her clear of the other shipping which were at anchor around, and the lamps of which could be seen through the blinding rain. " Let go the anchor," cried the captain. " This is for our lives; so smart's the word." We needed no other word of exhortation. We were driving stern first, and not much margin to work on. The order received its answer in our united " Aye, aye, sir," the plunge of the other anchor, and the rattle of the chain as it rushed through the hawse pipe. The anchor seized the ground and held. The ship was brought up suddenly, and, as a young unbroken colt pulls at the halter and swings round in a circle, so the ship pulled at the anchor and swung her stern round, describing a half-circle. In her swing she caught the bow of a brig, the Mary Ann, of Shields, and carried away one side of her bulwarks and rigging. We remained on deck all night, pumping occasionally; but the crew of the vessel we struck were at the pumps continuously. They had our sympathy, which was all we could extend to them.

In the morning we saw how true were the captain's words that the speedy letting go of the anchor meant safety. We were within two or three hundred yards from the dangerous Barber sands. A ship once on those sands has little if any chance of ever coming off again. It would have taken but a few minutes to have driven us on to them, and with such a storm as we were in (which could snap a thick anchor chain) and a furious sea dashing upon us the ship would have been broken up in a short time. In those circumstances the chances for the crew would have been small indeed. I might add here, although outside my own experience, that my brother-in-law joined another ship after that voyage, and she ran on to those sands, and the whole crew were lost. The people on shore saw them washed off the rigging, and could not assist them. The news of the sad affair reached me in the East Indies some months after.

There was a pride of caste among the sailors then, as there may be now. The man who had been across the line and around the Cape considered himself one of the elite of the trade, and looked down with contempt upon the man who had simply served in the coasting trade. After I had acquired a proficiency in steering and reefing and splicing ropes I thought I would try to rise to the higher grade, and ship for a Southern voyage, and in company with a young man about my own age I went to London, and signed on for Kurrachee, up the Persian Gulf. The ship was a barque of about 500 tons, one of the slowest ever launched. If there had been a prize for a slow ship when she was built, the builder would have been an easy first. Of that there can be no doubt.

The captain was on a par with his ship. He was little more than half-witted. He must have been either one of the owners or belonging to the family, and was given that berth either to secure him a living or to get the insurance for a lost ship and cargo. I quote a few words from a book by Sir W. Runciman which describes the situation in that respect at the period of which I am writing in better words than mine :—

" The whole system of dealing with seamen was a villainous wrong, which stamps the period with a dirty blot, at which the British people should be ashamed to look. Ships were allowed to be sent to sea in an unseaworthy condition. Men were forced to go in them for a living, and scores of these well-insured coffins were never seen or heard of again after leaving port. Their crews, composed sometimes of the cream of manhood, were the victims of a murderous indifference, that consigned them to a watery grave, and the families who survived the wholesale assassination were left as legacies of shame to the British people, who by their callousness made such things possible. Whole families were cast on the charity of a merciless world to starve or survive according to their fitness. The people were content to live under the rule of a despotic aristocracy, and so a devastating game of ship owning was carried on with yearly recurring but unnoticed slaughter. In one bad night the billows would roll over hundreds of human souls, and no more would be heard of them.''

It was in those conditions that I sailed in the Ennerdale, of Whitehaven, with a captain below par. The first mate was a gentleman, and the second mate a bully of the worst type. Our cargo was composed of rails for the new railway, with the necessary fish plates for the joints, and hogsheads of ale and porter and bottles of Allsop's Pale Ale in casks. This portion of the cargo was very much less when we landed than at the start. Some of the barrels in which the bottles of Allsop were packed at the commencement only contained a few instead of dozens at the finish, while the great hogsheads had a large vacuum in them instead of being full. Many a time on the voyage the old captain could be heard saying, "Where do these men get the drink? It is a puzzle to me." I could have told him of a long clay pipe stem, through which the porter was sucked after a hole had been bored with a gimlet into the top of the hogshead.

I have said the first mate was a gentleman, for whom the men would do anything. The second was a brutal bully, whom all hated, while many feared him. It was customary after a ship was out into the open sea to divide the crew into two watches or shifts. They were all mustered before the mates, and then the selection began, the first mate having first choice of a man, and so on alternately, the second mate selecting the second man, until the division was complete. Fortunately I was selected by the chief mate. If I had been under the other I fear there would have been a collision—as there was on one occasion, which I will relate later.

After we left the Thames we met stormy weather at the start. The vessel, having such heavy, dead weight in her, rolled and plunged, and the cargo shifted. The rails were lying athwart the hold, and would soon have drilled a hole in the side. The fish plates (about a foot long and three inches broad) were on ledges, and they began to slide on to the rails beneath with every heave or roll, and to us made a terrifying sound. There were two sailors who had earned credentials of authority by their sailings round the Cape, and to whom we paid great deference. They filled us with alarm by asserting the ship would never live to see the end of the voyage. The consequence was a resolution to refuse to work unless the captain would promise to put into some port and have the cargo secured. He refused. Immediately every man went down below. I was steering. We were off Beechy Head, and with a stiffish wind and a rough sea. The captain came aft to where I stood at the wheel. "Are you going to promise to part the cargo right?" I said. "I will see you all ―― first." "Then you take the wheel," I replied, and let go, and went below to the others. That made him give in, and in a very few minutes the mate came and told us the captain wanted to speak to us. In a body we went aft, and, after some little bluster, he promised if we would work the ship down to Plymouth he would put in and have an overhauling. I went and took the wheel for the rest of my time. The others took their places. The old man tried to deceive us, for when we got off Plymouth he tried to trade upon our ignorance and sneak by. We were too wide awake, and we threw up again and struck until he signalled for a pilot. It took a week to make all safe. The two sailors who had told us of our dangerous condition refused to proceed with the ship, and they were sent to prison for six weeks, and two fresh hands were shipped in their stead. One of them was a Russian Finn, named Abraham, a splendid sailor, about 50 years of age, warm-hearted, and full of good nature. He fell into the watch I was in, and, although there was such a wide difference in our ages, we were drawn together by a mental gravitation, and in our night watches we walked the deck together, and he told me of his adventures and escapes until, in my imagination, I was taking part in the same stirring scenes. Good old

Abraham! You carried a great kind heart in your weather-beaten and storm-scarred body. You will have made your last voyage, and have entered into the great harbour, but I am sure you would have the Pilot aboard when you crossed the Bar, and would find good anchorage within the vale. To rub shoulders with you was to come in contact with goodness of the highest order, and for a young man like me to be in your presence and hear your somewhat broken English was to receive an inspiration towards a nobler manhood. I never inquired about your creed, but I know your character was sound, and that is the best trade mark.

We left Plymouth, and were nearly five months before we reached Kurrachee. The full length of the voyage from London out was five months and a week, but we were so heavily laden that we had water on our decks, except two days, the whole time.

One voyage was sufficient in a vessel like the Ennerdale, but there were things which made the voyage unpleasant apart from its length. Our cramped situation in the forecastle was one of these. There were 16 of us boxed up in it. It was certain that, except we were all very mild mannered men (which we were not), there would be a conflict of temper, to say the least.

CHAPTER XIII.—SHIPMATES.

The food we had to eat at sea was death to a man's digestive organs, and conduced to scurvy. There was a continuous round of salt junk for dinner, except on Sunday, when, as a counteracting influence against the scurvy, we had a mixture of meat and carrots, which the sailors called "soup and bouilli." This was fresh and partly cooked. On that voyage, outward and homeward, we had some salt beef which was making its third voyage round the Cape. The lean of it was as hard as wood. On more than one occasion I saw one of the sailors carve out a small box from a piece of it. Before we got home the biscuits were in a state which I will not describe, as it would be too repulsive. This much I will say, in many of them there were objects which to look upon would have played havoc with the appetite, and which had made for themselves a home and habitation in cavities in which they burrowed. They were not weevils, which are small, but were large and well fed. There were two ways of dealing with these objects. One was to eat them in the dark, so that they were lost to sight, although unpleasant to the taste. The other process was to place the biscuits and their inmates between two clean pieces of canvas and pound them with a hammer or marlin spike until they were like oatmeal, and then, putting it in a basin, pour boiling water over it, and make what we in the North call a "crowdy." That was a favourite way with me. The condition of the biscuits

arose from the following cause. When they were provisioning the ship for the voyage and taking in the stock of biscuits, they never took out the old ones and cleaned out the locker. The new ones were thrown in front of the old. We, of course, making a long voyage, were compelled to use up those which had made many voyages, and, as a consequence, they acquired the condition I have mentioned.

Another point in relation to the food may be mentioned here, and which had great influence in preventing an outbreak of scurvy. Every day at 12 the crew were called aft for lime juice. Every man carried his pannican, or some other small vessel, containing some drinking water. The captain or some of the officers served out to each one a certain amount of the cordial. The measure was in shape like a tailor's thimble, and held about a tablespoonful. It was a very pleasant drink, and no doubt very beneficial from the point of view of hygiene, for without some counteracting influence we should have been in a fearful plight.

In addition to the lime juice, we oft had opportunities of catching fish, especially when we got into the warmer latitudes and in the track of the flying fish. There was both health and amusement in the sport. It helped to break the monotony and to secure good, wholesome food. In regard to the flying fish, these, in their spring out of the water and out of the reach of their natural pursuers, the dolphin and the albacore, which prey upon them, cannot swerve in their flight. They make an arch, and when they are descending, if a ship is in the line, they drop on deck. As soon as they do that the welcome sound of their flap, flap, is heard, and, bucket in hand, the sailors rush around after them. In size about like a herring, they afford a rich and acceptable treat to men, who, but for their timely arrival, have no prospect for dinner except salt junk.

Then, the fishing for dolphin and albacore. This was different. They were not so much heaven sent. There was more work, but they were none the less acceptable. The following was the process. Say the ship was about becalmed. Going along very slowly—and we never went quickly—it would have taken a hurricane to have driven us six or seven knots—there was a gentle swell, with a slight rise and fall of the vessel. The fisher would go out on the bowsprit with a stout line in his hand, at the end of which was a fish hook. This was got up to represent a flying fish by attaching two pieces of white cloth having the resemblance to its wings (or fins, which bear the name). The line just reached the water. When the bow of the ship rose the bait had the appearance of a fish leaping. The pursuing fish made a dart at it, and soon found its mistake. Then the struggle commenced. They are about a foot and a half long, and very thickly built, and consequently were a good weight hanging on the arms of a man with his feet on the foot rope and his breast across the bowsprit. At his first cry for assistance, it was afforded, because the catch was too great a luxury to lose. The flesh resembled lean meat, and was a beautiful change from the salt junk, which was always in view, and looked the better the further it was off, and consequently every opportunity to defer it was embraced.

There were other two forms of fishing. Those were not for food, but amusement. One was for Cape pigeons when in the locality, and the the other for sharks, whenever the chance arose. The birds were caught with a slender line, a very small hook, and a little piece of pork. It was allowed to trail over the taffrail. Flocks of these birds follow the ships, picking up food for days together, when off the Cape. They were, therefore, soon down at the hook, and if they swallowed it were soon landed on deck. On some occasions the one caught would be decorated with red cloth, and let go. In a few minutes he was surrounded by the rest of his kin, and picked to death. It was sport for us, but death to it.

The shark fishing was a greater undertaking, yet equally amusing, and with a different object in view. Of all created things the shark is most feared and hated by sailors. They are his natural and sworn enemies. Given the chance, and he will receive no mercy at their hands. The measure he metes out is given to him. To catch him you wanted almost a calm sea. Then get a line like the one used for drying clothes. At the end of it attach a few feet of chain, with a very large hook and about two pounds of pork. This, like the hook in the pigeon catching, was allowed to trail in the wake of the vessel. Presently you would see the pilot fish, which is supposed to bear the same relation to the shark as the jackal does to the lion. Then you saw a dark fin of the shark sticking just above the water. As soon as he gets near the bait he, like a flash, turns on his back to swallow the attractive morsel, and is caught. The top jaw of the shark protrudes over the bottom one, and so long as he is on his belly he cannot bite. When he was hooked two or three men hauled on the rope until his nose was level with the taffrail. Then a running bowline was slipped over the tail. This was drawn up until both head and tail were level. The shark was then dragged on board broadside on to the deck. Then the work of torment would commence. Taunts would be hurled at him, and he would look out of his vicious, cruel little eyes, and make efforts to slide along to his tormentors. We had two sailors who did not object to eat a bit, and they would get a log of wood, put it under his tail, and slice pieces off with an axe. These they would cook, and hold a slice against his nose while he was alive, with the expression "Have a taste, Johnny." The next stage was to turn him over on his back, and cut him open. Dissecting his stomach to see what it contained was the finish. After an examination of the contents (if none of the sailors wanted his backbone or jaws) he and they were launched over the side. On one occasion we had eight of those terrors of the sea on the deck at one time. These, after being tormented, were invariably cut open and thrown back into the sea. In that state they would show indications of their cruelty.

We had as officers a most wonderful contrast in character and conduct. The captain was a crank, pure and simple, and his moods were as variable as the wind. He was not cruel, but whimsical, and as a consequence nobody cared for him or what he said. Sometimes he conceived the idea he was an orator, and, like all men who pride themselves on that qualification, he was ever seeking an audience. This he would secure by seizing upon the time when the lime-juice was being dispensed, and all the crew were on deck, and give us an harangue upon some subject neither he nor we knew anything about, and about which we cared nothing. He and I were very good friends. We never different except once. I was at the wheel, and my nose itching, I took one hand off the wheel and rubbed it. He saw the action, and yelled out, "Let your nose alone; why are you rubbing it?" I quietly replied, "It is my own, and I will rub it when I like, and neither ask you nor anyone else." That was sufficient. I collided with his idea of dignity. He raised the spying-glass he held in his hand, and said, "I will knock your head off if you give me any impertinence." To that, in a somewhat louder tone, I said, "I have given you no impertinence. I, with you, must rub where we itch, and the best advice I can give you is don't use your glass, because neither you nor any other man in this ship shall strike me and not be struck back." That led him to a reconsideration of his intention, and he walked away along the quarter deck having a talk to himself, which was safer than striking me.

I have indicated the great difference which was between the first and second mates. The first was a gentleman throughout, while the second was a compound of bully, brute, and coward. The former was gentle and slender made; the latter was coarse and strongly built. Early in the voyage the mate took a liking to me. It arose out of the following incident: When I shipped in that ship I was equal to any man in steering or reefing, going aloft or any of the ordinary work of a sailor, but I was a bungle at sail-mending. A few of us were sitting with a sail trying to patch it after we had been out a month or so, when the mate came and stood looking at us. I could see he was amused at my attempts to sew. After a few minutes he said to me. "Did you ever serve your time to be a sailmaker?" I replied, "No, but I lived in the same street with a sailmaker once." He walked away laughing, and then shouted, "Come here; I want you." When I got to him he smiled and said, "That was a smart answer you gave me. I think you have something in you. If there be anything you want to know come to me, and I will teach you." He was as good as his word, and before the voyage was over he taught me something more than the rudiments of navigation, and until we parted in London with a warm shake of the hand and mutual good wishes he was a kind friend, and there was nothing, no matter how dangerous, but I was ready to do if he requested me, and to oblige him I was in one or two situations of that kind.

What a contrast to the second mate! With us there was gentle but firm rule and ready obedience. In the other watch there was a perfect reign of terror. He was a past master in the arts of punishment and the working up of his men, and he did cruel things to men bigger than himself, against which they made no protest. They often complained when we foregathered on deck in the dog watch. It was a mystery to me how they bore it. My chum was in his watch. A kind, soft nature he had. He told me that the brute had struck him two or three times, and it maddened me, and I resolved that when the opportunity afforded I would repay him. It came. I was at the wheel from 10 to 12 p.m. A dull-headed apprentice belonging to the second mate's watch relieved me. I gave him the ship's course, and left. When the second mate came on deck he found we were on the wrong course, and inquired who gave it. The answer was "English Jack"— meaning me. The word was passed along to the forecastle that I was wanted. As I went out my friend, Abraham (the Finn), followed with his sheath knife in his hand, and to encourage me he said, "If he touch you, Jack, me knife him." "No, Abraham," I said; "leave him to me. I can manage him." Going aft along the weather side, although it was dark, I could see Abraham creeping along by the bulwarks on the lee side. On to the wheel I went, and was met by the second mate with the query, "What course did you give this man?" I replied, naming the point of the compass. In a passion he called me a liar. "How do you know?" I said. "You were not here, and my word is as good as yours or his." Thinking to terrify me he said, "Say that again, and I will give you a clip under the ear." Laying my hand on his shoulder I said, "I have been waiting for this. Don't make any noise so that the captain can't hear, and come on to the main deck, and you will soon see who can clip the best. Get your jacket off as soon as you like." He hesitated. "You bully, you struck Harry Parsons two or three times. You are a coward. If ever you put a finger upon him again you and I will settle it." Like all bullies he was soft, and that protest cowed him and changed the atmosphere of his watch, and removed the fear of physical force from the men. He still used his tongue in a foul and vulgar manner, for he had a vocabulary of sea slang terms full, if not choice or elevating. On two or three occasions, egged on by the others, an attempt was made to induce him to quarrel, but it was unavailing.

CHAPTER XIV.—EXPERIENCES IN INDIA.

One of the greatest wants at sea, so far as I was concerned, was the want of books. I borrowed all I could, and read them and re-read them. So strong was the appetite for reading that I turned to the Bible, not on account of its sacred character. It would have been a blessing for me if I had gone, because of its grand moral and spiritual principles, but (with regret I write) such was not the case. I read it through about five times. There was this good result seen in after years; when the turning point came I was not a stranger to the general outline and historical portions of it. If my time were to begin again I should not turn to it as a variety and break in the monotony of a long and tedious voyage, but because to me it is the lamp to the feet and the light to the path of men as they journey through life. It has no compeer. All others, the greatest works of the greatest minds, are but dim uncertain lights when compared to it.

Everything comes to those who wait, and our voyage ended after lasting five months and a week. If ever men were buffetted by storms we were. On three successive Sundays we found ourselves by the reckoning off the Cape of Good Hope, and on every day at dinner time we were met by a hurricane, before which we had to run almost under bare poles; but in the end we reached Kurrachee, and lay there for about two months and a half.

Our arrival there was not long after the Indian Mutiny, and there was a remnant of the smouldering hate still in the hearts of some of the natives, which made it somewhat dangerous to be ashore after dark. We were not fully alive to it, and ventured ashore when the darkness was very dense. So dark, that one night, while we were in the narrow streets, we had to get a boy about 12, who was dressed entirely in nature's garb. He was void even of Mark Twain's proverbial necklace. One of us had to take him by the shoulder and walk along in close Indian file. On another occasion a few of us went to the canteen among the soldiers. When we left to come down to the ship we "were na fou', but just had plenty" to make us merry. Passing through a wood I found myself at the head of the file. Before I was aware I struck a wall or palisade about half my height, and over I went into a ring of natives, who were sitting just over the obstruction. They scattered like rats, but when they realised who we were they took us on to the road leading to the harbour; but before we got down we tried to get into two very dissimilar places. One was the gaol and the other a Parsee Temple. The sentries at the former told us they did not want any "bobbery," and the people belonging to the temple were persistent in their attempts to keep us out, which they did, and we were informed that it would have been a bad job if we had forced our way in. It was a mad, useless prank.

I was very often ashore with the captain. My work was to clerk for him when he went to buy anything. Part of our cargo on the homeward passage was saltpetre. This was bought from the Parsee merchants. They are the fire worshippers. It was necessary to test the saltpetre by fire, but the Parsees would not allow us to do so by their fire, and the captain and I were compelled to take the sample of saltpetre and walk along the street until we came to a fire, then submit it to the test, and walk back to the merchants to conclude the bargain, if the captain was satisfied.

In these buying expeditions there were many opportunities of seeing the different castes into which the people were divided, and the lines of separation which are seldom, if ever, crossed. The stately Parsee, clothed in a white long flowing dress, whose manner indicated the superiority of his class. The Hindoo, or clerking class, who were the writers, and who carried their letters in the hollow of their head dress. The lithe and straight Lascar, dressed in a tunic and trousers of check, with long black hair, his head covering being in shape like the Turkish fez or smoking cap. Those were the sailor or waterman class. Then there was the coolie class, who, by the fiat of their social arrangement, were born to the rough and lower forms of labour, out of which they had no hope of rising. They had, however, one very strong trait of character. They knew how to make work last. If a baulk of timber was to be removed three of four of them would range themselves alongside, and every process of stooping and lifting and carrying was set to music. They had some droning kind of song. They would commence it, and then at a certain part stoop in keeping with the tune. Then take hold, lift, and walk off as a well-drilled band of dancers, and they took good care that the music was not of a lilting "Weel may the keel row" kind, but more in harmony with the "Old Hundred." On the principle that the workman's arm keeps step with the tune he sings we can very easily measure the speed at which they worked. The wages they received were low, and consequently the quantum of work was proportionate, proving (if it needs proof) that low-priced labour is not the cheapest, for if any of us wanted a day ashore we were compelled to engage two of these coolies each to take one of our places in discharging and loading cargo. The prices we paid were two annas (threepence) per labourer. Even at that rate of equivalent or compensating labour the captain would grumble loudly, because he considered himself robbed in the exchange. There was one

custom obtaining among those labourers. They used to shave their heads as clear of hair as the faces of men who use razors, and yet go around in the sun with impunity, although it was so hot that one of our crew (strong on figures of speech) said there was but a thin paper partition between it and the hottest place the mind of man ever conceived. For myself my invariable dress was a flat topped canvas cap, similar in shape to that worn by some of our soldiers now, a pair of low shoes of the same material, thin dungaree trousers, and flannel body shirt, without sleeves and a low neck like a lady's evening dress. And then I would have gone with less if the proprieties would have permitted it. From the shoulder down to the fingers, and from the edge of the shirt up over neck and face, I was as dark as many of the natives.

There were many incidents to enliven our stay in the harbour. There was the playful, bantering, bargaining with the bumboat men, who came alongside the ship in the same manner that a general dealer drives from door to door in the street. They brought off fresh bread and fruit (besides curios), which was a very acceptable change from the fare provided in the ship, but which was purchased at the sailor's own cost. The bumboat men were at all times chary about allowing any of the young sailor's to get down into their boat, and did their best to keep clear of the side, and they had need to fear. There were occasions when there was a slight swell, and the mast of the boat leaned over towards the ship. Then an opportune spring on to the mast and a slide down landed you safely among their merchandise. At once there would arise a noise compared with which the Tower of Babel was a solitude.

Then the praying of the Mahomedan workmen was another source of amusement. They had stated times, but it was possible to incite them to do it at other than those fixed periods. All that was necessary was to throw water on them, and that was sure to bring about a praying bout. They would down with their carpet, and go through the whole series of their bendings of body and bumpings of the head on the ground. If we wanted to prolong their devotions all that was required was to stand and look at them. Then their words would flow with greater rapidity, and their genuflexions would be quickened as if sanctity depended upon speed, quantity of words, and evolutions. They were a complete illustration of the Saviour's description and warning, "When thou prayest thou shalt not be as the hypocrites are, for they love to pray standing in the synagogues and in the corners of the streets, that they may be seen of men." "Use not vain repetitions as the heathen do, for they think they shall be heard for their much speaking." They got plenty of opportunity to show off before us both at regular and irregular times, although our action was prompted by a pure spirit of mischief.

Turtle hunting at night was a source of amusement and profit. The sea turtle lay their eggs in the sand above high water mark. They can do very well swimming in the sea, but on land their progress is very laborious and slow. From the edge of the water to the place of deposit they scoop up a ridge resembling a row of potatoes in a field. The hunting party kept along the water's edge until they struck one of these rows, and then followed it. This had the double advantage of keeping between the seas and the turtle, and affording an easily followed trail. If the turtle was still inland it was captured with ease, and turned over on to its back. Ropes were attached to its legs, and it was dragged along the sand on its shield. There was an amount of danger either from disaffected natives, who might look upon us as lawful prey, and attack us in a larger force; or from wild beasts, as we were compelled to go some distance from the harbour. We were fortunate, although we heard often the roar of the lion at a distance, which to our unaccustomed ears was sufficiently terrifying without the presence of the roarer. Distance lent an enchantment to the sound which nothing else could give.

I had one very pleasing experience, although it had a somewhat rough commencement. I had been ashore with the captain, keeping accounts for him, and had left him, and was making my way to the ship. When I got to the landing place there were two English sailors and a native boatman quarrelling. I went up to them and inquired what was the matter. The boatman, in his broken English, explained that these men had engaged him to bring them ashore from their ship, but when they were landed they refused to pay the amount agreed upon; in fact, refused to pay anything, and were threatening what they would do if he persisted in asking for payment. A love of right led me to join myself to the weaker, and, what was more, the right side. The consequence was the sailors saw the error of their ways, and showed their change of heart by handing over the money. The further consequences were good to me. The boatman, whenever he saw me, pointed me out to the members of his caste as his brother John. He was ready at any time to row me without charge, and there is no doubt but many an act of kindness shown to me by others was the result of it. On the day we sailed he was alongside with his boat, and I told him we were starting for England. The tears came to his eyes, and in every way he could he expressed his gratitude for what at best was but a small matter.

CHAPTER XV.—HOME AGAIN.

The voyage home from Kurrachee was just a month shorter than the outward one. There was the salt junk a little salter than it was, and the biscuits a great deal worse, because we were compelled to go further into the dim recesses, and seldom explored corners of the lockers. There are only two incidents to which I will give a place. The first is in relation to a close call I had from death. When we first landed in Kurrachee there was a European doctor resident there. He gave us advice as to our diet. His warnings were most emphatic in respect to drink, and his opinion was that a very large percentage of English sailors who died was in consequence of drinking, and especially liquor. His advice was good, but it fell on heedless ears. On the principle that a man thinks all men mortal but himself, without exception we thought his teaching might find fitting application to the case of others, but not to us, for on the very night, with his kind and wise words fresh in our minds, we accepted an invitation to join the crew of another ship which was there before we arrived, and, like Tam O'Shanter :

" Kings might be blest, but we were glorious,
    O'er a' the ills o' life victorious."

We forgot the length of the voyage; the storms and hardships were less than dreams to us, and there is not one who was there, if there be one alive, who could tell how he got aboard his own ship, but we all had vivid recollections of it next day.

Beyond the ill-effects of next day there were no evil consequences seen until we had been a few days out homeward, when " the fairest of our gallant band " (which was myself—the conceit will be forgiven) was stricken by Yellow Jack, from whose clutches few escape. We were passing through the Mozambique Channel, which lies between the South African coast and the Island of Madagascar, when I was at the worst, and it was a bad worst. My shipmates were the essence of kindness. Every day I was carried up on to the quarter deck, for we had beautiful weather. I was laid under an awning which was rigged up for my special use. Rice water was kept handy, and at the least sign (for my voice was reduced to a whisper) anyone nearest would run and minister to my wants. My strength was so nearly gone that the hens (which were kept for the captain's use) would with impunity sit on my breast regardless of my efforts to drive them off. The only doctor I had was the captain, who dozed me well with calomel (so I was told after), and whose knowledge of medicine and its administering was very elementary, and contained in some stereotyped prescriptions. However, in spite of the captain's crude ideas of medicine, and with the aid of a good constitution I managed to pull through, although I carried with me for some considerable time the effects of his doctoring and the illness.

Our voyage home was on a different route from the outward. On that occasion we never saw land from the time we lost sight of England until we neared Kurrachee, except a bare outline of Madagascar; but on our return we kept close in to the South African coast, and round the Cape of Good Hope, passing near to St. Helena. We ran down the Trade Winds in a slow but pleasant manner until we crossed the Line. We were no sooner out of the North-east Trade Winds than we struck a most severe storm, and I have no doubt had we had the same dead-weight cargo we took out we should have made the acquaintance of Davy Jones. If I had the pen of a Clark Russell I might describe the waves as tney ran like great hills, tossing, tumbling, and rearing their great white crests above us. I went to the wheel at twelve noon, and as I walked by the captain he said, " Wilson, you lash yourself securely to the ring in the deck just behind where you stand." I objected. He persisted, and it was well he did. A stout rope was placed around my waist, and one end made secure to the iron ring. I had not been at the wheel above five minutes when it gave a heavy kick, which would have thrown me over it, and either against the bulwarks or overboard, and in either case sufficient time would have elapsed to place the ship at the mercy of the waves, and she would doubtless have foundered with all hands. The captain kept me at the wheel for six hours, although two hours made the usual " trick " (or time) there. He did it because he had confidence in my skill in steering, for whatever I might be deficient in I was equal to the best and the superior of many at the wheel. There I stood, and I have never seen such an awful sight as that day presented to me. The position of the ship was like a continuous tobogganing. One minute we were climbing up the side of a great mountainous wave, and then sliding down the other side. Anyone who has been on the toboggan, and on the hind seat, will have some idea if they will enlarge the toboggan to the size of a vessel with three masts and look up as slowly and laboriously it climbed, or down as it rushed the watery slope. I can assure them there was no poetry in the saying that the seas ran mountains high. Many a time I took a quick look back, and saw the huge wave towering right above us with a great curl on its crest ready to engulf us in its watery and deadly embrace. Looking at it from this distance, our escape was a miracle, but the old ship, if she was slow, was stoutly built, and we came safely through as severe a storm as ever was encountered, and nothing but the buoyancy of her cargo and the stoutness of her timbers brought us into better weather and smoother sea. Whenever I am at the seaside in a storm, and see a ship labouring in a heavy sea, or whenever I read of the terrible storms which some-times spread havoc around our coasts, strewing them with wrecked vessels and sending brave crews into eternity, I need no stretch of imagina-tion to evoke my sympathy. It is always at hand.

That was the only serious storm we had. There were others which were the ordinary oc-currences of a sailor's life, which to a landsman might appear great, but to the crew were very minor indeed. Old, slow, but sure, our vessel ploughed along. There was nothing of interest except in our crossing the Gulf Stream—that mysterious flow running across the ocean from the Gulf of Mexico, with its accompanying field of seaweed, the heavy darkness like a dense black thunder cloud, and the flitting balls of fire or electricity, about the size of a man's hand, which leap from spar to spar like so many will o' the wisps.

After a passage of four months and a week we sailed up the Thames. The crew, and especially those of the second mate's watch, were not satisfied that he should go free after his per-sistent brutality, and it was arranged that be-fore we reached the dock he should, if possible, get part of his own back. The lot to "bell the cat" fell on me—at least I was asked to do it. The task was congenial, and everything was done to provoke him to quarrel. Insulting re-marks and open and flagrant refusal to obey his orders, challenges to fight which no man of spirit would have refused, insinuations made by two or three who would gather beside him; but all to no purpose. It would have played into his hand to strike, be-cause that would have brought severe punishment. The project failed as the result of his own cowardice. We moored in the London Dock, left the old captain and first mate with a hearty shake of the hand and good wishes for their welfare (although any of us would have been very loath to ship in the Ennerdale again), but not a man amongst us had a farewell word for the bully, who had done his best to make long and in many respects unpleasant voyages more so, and some of the crew who remained in London did their best to find him ashore, but he discreetly kept out of their way.

My stay on shore, like that of many more sailors, was limited by the length of time the money held out. I did not stay in London near the docks, where crimps and worse creatures do abound even now, but did in greater numbers and impunity then. The female members of the gangs of these investors of Ratcliffe highway would, by their allurements, decoy the unwary sailor into some den, where he was soon robbed of all his wages and ready to take the first ship he could get. The locality is greatly improved, but then the Jew clothes dealer, the low public-house kept by colleagues of the crimp, and therefore useful in drugging the unsuspecting seaman, and the undisguised brothel, from which men have been turned stripped of money and nearly nude, were side by side, and many and various were the tales which were told of and by men who had been so treated.

This my "chum" and I managed to escape. We kept clear of those professional "friends." He was a native of Shoreham, where my sister, then a widow (having lost her husband during my absence), lived, and, being desirous of see-ing our friends, we went directly there. After a few weeks ashore I shipped in a brigantine called the Isabella, hailing from Shoreham. I was careful not to sign on as an A.B., but took 5s per month less wages, and was classed as an ordinary seaman. My object was to keep in that category until I could take my place as proficient as men who had served their time as apprentices to the trade, and thus avoid reflec-tion on the part of the officers, although I could do more than some who were classified as able seamen. My stay with the Isabella was not long—in all about six weeks. I left under the following circumstances. We went from Shore-ham to St. Peter's, on the Tyne, with timber; then down to near Shields, where we loaded for Hamburg. While in that port I was seized with an inflammation in the right side. I struggled on until we reached Sunderland. Seeing my state, the captain asked whether I had friends in the North. If so, seeing the state I was in, he would suggest that I should go and stay with them until he made another voyage, and if my health was better when he returned, my berth was there for me at any time.

My mind turned to young Dove, with whose father and mother I lodged when I was at Sher-burn Hill, and who in the meantime had got married. He willingly took me in to lodge at Haswell Colliery, and I drew my discharge from Captain Billinghurst, of the Isabella. It bears date May 9th, 1860, and has been framed and preserved by my good wife, and by her placed in a prominent position in our house. Its intrinsic value is not much, but to her it was priceless. I had a great liking for the old captain. He was rough, but kindly. When in a storm he chewed tobacco at a great rate; and the snap of his box could be heard with rapid frequency. He was no shirker, and as a consequence had a repugnance to all who did shirk, but the man who did his duty had at all times a friend in him.

The doctor whom I called in told me what disease I had suffered from and the medicine I had taken. " You have had the yellow fever, and you took calomel for it, and it is remaining in your system yet." The course of treatment was sufficiently severe to draw or drive anything out of the system—medicine very unpalatable, but no doubt very necessary; twelve leeches on the side one day and the next day a fly blister over the same place. I was blessed with a nurse. My sweetheart had removed with her sister to Haswell, and lived opposite my lodgings. Her heart was kind to all who needed help, but when the sick one was the object of her love, above his deserts, her care and attention increased. It is only fair to say that neither the skill of the doctor nor her nursing had a fair chance. There is a forgetfulness in bad habits, which in this instance was no exception when the circumstances permitted. But we will let that rest in forgetfulness.

I never saw Captain Billinghurst or the Isabella again. I have no doubt the generous old weather-beaten soul has found safe anchorage in his last harbour, for he did his best to make as pleasant as possible the life of the crew under his care, and at a time when the law had not been thrown around the mercantile seamen as it has now. The old song set forth that there was " a sweet little cherub which sat aloft to watch over the life of poor Jack," but the doubt is that he never got on to the deck. There were two sayings in relation to the sailor's life: " There is no Sunday where there are nine fathoms of water," and then an addition to the Decalogue, " Six days shalt thou work as long as thou art able; on the seventh thou shalt holystone the deck and scrub the chain cable."

CHAPTER XVI.—BACK TO THE MINE.

By a combination of influences I shook off the liking for the sea, or at least there was a stronger counter-attraction set up. These influences were: Old associates and habits; the contrast between the dingy, confined forecastle and the comfort of home life; and, strongest of all, the persuasion and presence of her who within a short time became my lifelong partner in the battle of life. Without her the others might have failed, for the rambling spirit was strong, but with her in support I resolved to take to the mining life again, and I commenced to hew at Haswell. The manager or agent there was Mr R. S. Johnson, who was shortly after succeeded by Mr W. F. Hall, with whom I came much in conflict in after years.

There are a few events which occurred about this time, and although I took little if any part in one of them, they are yet worthy of note. The first in order of these was the struggle between Gladstone and the Lords over the repeal of the paper duty. My last discharge bears the date May 9, 1860, and on the 21st of that month his Budget was introduced, which abolished a number of indirect taxes and reduced many others. It was accompanied by a Bill for the repeal of the paper duty. This went up to the Lords. There was great excitement. What would the Lords do with it? In the words of Sir W. Molesworth: " As the Bill involved a remission of taxation the attempt to reject it raised a great constitutional question. It was admitted that the Lords had no right to amend a money bill so as to change the amount of incidence of taxation in the smallest particular." That position the Lords denied, and although the Lord Chancellor urged them to the contrary they threw it out by a majority of 89. On the 15th of April, 1861, Mr Gladstone introduced the Budget again. From the date of their action when the Lords threw out the paper duty Bill until its reintroduction as a part of the Budget there was great anxiety and interest in the country. There was an extraordinary desire to secure a place in the House to hear the statement by Mr Gladstone. Crowds of ticket holders were in attendance at half-past eight in the morning, and a long stream of people were there on the chance of getting in. The paper duty had been dealt with in a separate Bill, but now it was included in the Budget. This was an effectual, and, under the circumstances, legitimate circumvention of the House of Lords in its hostility to the proposal for the repeal of the paper duty. Bitter opposition was shown to the course adopted in the Commons, not only by Conservatives but by one or two on the Liberal side. This came especially from Mr Horsman, who charged Mr Gladstone with giving the Constitution a mortal stab. To him and to that charge he made the following reply:—

" I want to know what constitution it gives a mortal stab to. In my opinion it gives no stab at all, but so far as it alters, it alters so as to revive and restore the good old Constitution which took its root in Saxon times, which groaned under the Plantagenets, which endured the hard rule of the Tudors, which resisted the Stuarts, and which has now come to maturity under the House of Brunswick. I think that Constitution will be all the better for the operation. As to the constitution laid down by my right honourable friend, under which there is to be a division of function and office between the Commons and the Lords with regard to fixing the income and charge of the country from year to year, both of them being equally responsible so far as that constitution is concerned, I cannot help saying that in my humble opinion the sooner it receives a mortal stab the better."

The Budget passed the Commons by a majority of 15. In the Lords its rejection was moved by the Duke of Rutland, but was not pressed to a division. The Lords were defeated, and the era of cheap books and newspapers ushered in. It was customary for five or six persons to take a paper in jointly and read it in their turns, but after the repeal there was not only a free but a cheap press. I would like to set this forth in the words of one of our most eloquent modern historians, Justin McCarthy. In his history of our own times, and referring to this period, and speaking of the opposition

Gladstone had to meet and the great work he effected, he says:—

" In spite of all this, however, Mr Gladstone succeeded in carrying this part of his Budget. He carried, too, as far as the House of Commons was concerned, his important measure for the abolition of the duty on paper. The duty on paper was the last remnant of an ancient system of finance which pressed severely on journalism. The stamp duty was originally imposed with the object of checking the growth of seditious newspapers. It was reduced, increased, reduced again, and increased again, until in the early part of the century it stood at fourpence on each copy of a newspaper issued. The consequence was that a newspaper was a costly thing. Its possession was the luxury of the rich; those who could afford less had to be content with an occasional read of a paper. It was common for a number of persons to club together and take in a paper, which they read by turns, the general understanding being that he whose turn came last remained in possession of the journal. The price of a daily paper then was uniformly sixpence, and no sixpenny paper contained anything like the news or went to a tenth of the daily expense which is supplied in the one case and undertaken in the other by the penny papers of our day."

The pressure of the paper duty fell heaviest on the poorer class of the people, who were most in need of cheap literature, and least able to procure it. They were deprived of learning in their youth by being compelled to commence work at a very early age, and those who were wishful in their manhood to make up that deficiency were prevented by the high price they had to pay for books and newspapers. To use an expression from a speech by Mr Joseph Cowen, " they were prevented from access to books, and then charged with being ignorant." " On dear books," said Mr Gladstone in 1860, " which are published for the wealthy, it is a very light duty; on books brought out in large quantities by enterprising publishers for the middle and lower classes it is a very heavy and a very oppressive duty." This great boon to the working class, opening out to them the avenues of learning and mental culture, was only one among many for which they have to thank him and hold him in grateful remembrance.

In 1862 the whole of the kingdom was startled

and saddened by the dreadful calamity which happened at Hartley Colliery on January 16th. The accident was unique, the death roll extremely large, and it evoked sympathy from all quarters and every class, for there was not a house in the village upon which the blow had not fallen. The accident was caused by the breaking of the great pumping beam. There was only one shaft, but, as was customary at that time, it was bratticed in the middle, and thus for working purposes formed the coal drawing shaft and the pumping shaft. When the massive beam fell, it carried the separation brattice with it, and in consequence the shaft, the only way out for the men and boys, was completely blocked. There were 204 in the pit at the time, and in spite of every effort they were all lost.

I need not detail more as to the accident. The sorrow which followed and the heroic deeds performed are all well known to us, and will be so long as the mines last. There were two beneficial outcomes which are with us yet. These are the great Permanent Relief Fund, covering the whole mining area of the North of England, Cleveland, and Cumberland, and stepping in with its rich provision whenever death enters the family by accident in the mine, or the bread-winner is shorn of his strength by the same cause. The second is the compulsory two shafts in all mines. These are great benefits operating upon separate and distinct lines. The two shafts were demanded with a view to life saving, and the great relief fund was formed to provide for those who might be left behind to mourn, and, without such a provision, to struggle with poverty. Both the demand and idea have been realised. The movements in the direction of attainment of both objects were started on the eighth day after the accident. A public meeting was held in the Guildhall, Newcastle, and the day after in the Lecture Hall, Nelson Street, Newcastle, when two resolutions were submitted, the first requesting the workmen in the two counties to arrange for collections at the collieries, and the second affirming the desirability of petitioning Parliament to appoint a committee to inquire into the accidents in mines, and expressing the opinion that no colliery should be worked without two shafts having been first sunk for the security of the workmen.

These were both realised, and are with us, but not without some opposition. The establishment of the fund received great assistance from some of the employers, such as Hugh Taylor, Joseph Pease, and Lord Durham, but there were certain quarters where it was met with coldness, if not with active opposition. To some, and especially some managers, it was thought to be the thin end of the trades union wedge, and that was sufficient to evoke opposition. However, there were a few determined, right-minded men at the head who had set their hearts upon the success of the undertaking, and they kept pressing forward until finally their persistency bore down all the obstacles. Not only had they the opposition arising from fear, but they had the indifference of very many of the workmen, who were not sufficiently filled with the spirit of forethought and regard for their families as to induce them to pay their contributions in a voluntary manner. Let me anticipate and say that by the adoption of the system of deduction at the colliery, which took years of effort, for some managers refused, the families of every workman—man and boy— find themselves provided for when by accident death deprives them of the bread-winner. These Northern counties owe a great debt to men like Thos. Weatherly, Alex. Blyth, John Howie, G. Parkinson, C. Haswell, W. Steele, C. Graham, T. Gascoigne, J Bones, and J. Leithead, who was the first treasurer, and who for nearly half-a-century acted in that capacity. Happy is the community which has men so disinterested and large hearted in its midst, and who, in the face of obstacles varied and many, press forward the good object. They are the true benefactors and reformers. I am happy in the remembrance that at a later period I had the honour to take a small part with them in the promotion of their good work, and although, like the apostle, born out of due time, I had some share in placing the fund upon its present basis, and know somewhat of its early struggles. I have a full knowledge of the time and energy it required to get the contributions deducted from the pay at the colliery office, and I was no stranger to the gathering of the data to form the superannuation department, which has proved such a boon to the aged and worn out miner and his partner, if he is blessed by having her by his side.

CHAPTER XVII.—MARRIED LIFE.

I fancy that the ladies who have done me the honour to accompany me in this rambling journey will be wondering when I crossed the line from single life into the state of matrimony. I am sorry to have kept them in suspense so long. It is a little cruel, but I will now enlighten them. I made the venture on the 5th of October, 1862, in Shotton Church. It was Houghton Feast Sunday. I can soon describe the company and carriages. We walked from Haswell, and there were four of us—a nephew of the bride, the uncle of the bridegroom, and the happy couple. This world would be a much happier place than it is, and we should be saved so many of the fearful exposures in our law courts, if every man drew such a prize as I did on that day, and found such a real helpmeet as mine. I will not say I got the best of her sex, but I will say no man ever took to himself a better wife in every sense of the term. The words of the wise writer of the Proverbs could with safety be applied to her: " She openeth her mouth with wisdom, and in her tongue is the law of kindness. She looketh well to the ways of her household, and eateth not the bread of idleness." She fulfilled that description to the smallest particular. For near forty-six years we were joined together in the closest and the most loving and helpful ties, which with the nine years of sweethearting made fifty-five years of companionship. If from the first I had taken the advice she gave and kept the course she urged me to take I should have saved a few years that were wasted, and worse than that. She never reproved nor complained; the reverse was her policy. She strove to attract by making our house a bright and cheerful home. There was always " a clean hearth stane " and a cheery welcome. We were in the storm and stress of life often, but the burden was a mutual one. She never did anything to make it heavier, but much to lighten it; and oft I have received inspiration and strength when, without her, there would have been darkness and doubt and failure. As I write these words, with the memory of that happy marriage day—better for me than I ever imagined—still living in my heart in its most minute detail, I am buoyed up and cheered. Time did not lessen her beauty, but enhanced it, for at 68 she was admired. Although there has entered into my life a loneliness unrealisable to any but myself, and although I long for " the touch of a vanish'd hand, and the sound of a voice that is still," the memory of the happy 46 years of married life and the assurance there is in my heart for the future are sources of strength to me. When the battle is going against me, receiving extra force from my own weakening and ageing state, I can feel the soothing and inspiring influence she has left deep-rooted in my heart, and am thankful that ever we laid the foundation of a happy, helpful married life.

There were a few prophecies as to what the result would be to her. Some said " she was a bold woman. To say the least, I was a rolling stone." There was one old woman who held a different view. In her opinion there was better metal in me. Her reply to my wife's eldest sister and other fearful souls was, " You are wrong: he will make a lady of her." Many a time in after years, when the turning point came and steps were taken to a higher and better life, we had a good laugh over the matter, and it afforded me opportunity for some little chaff when I reminded her of the prophecy, and told her what a hard and difficult task it had been to bring about its fulfilment. All the time it was the easiest thing in the world. She needed no making; she was a lady from the commencement. The improvement in our circumstances was only increased opportunities for her ladylike nature to be seen and felt wherever she went.

We started housekeeping in the Long Row at Haswell. The houses were of the back-to-back kind. There were two rooms—the kitchen and the room upstairs, with a straight up ladder as the mode of reaching it. There was not over much room, but there was plenty of happiness, which with us was the main consideration. More progress from every point of view might have been made in that small house, but there was one foolish person living in it, and that was not the wife. She was from the start a housewife in the best sense of the word. Discreet and saving, but she was "unequally yoked," and consequently very much impeded.

Preparing for America.

We were not long in this comfortable home of ours, nicely set up, until the spirit of change seized me again, and America was the goal. There are natures who are always at the antipodes of the fortune they are in search of. Like the child chasing the rainbow, it is ever ahead of them, and they follow the ever fleeting phantom when the substantial is by their side. Such, I fear, up to this point was my state, and it was assisted by the glowing accounts which reached us from America. The Civil War was raging there, and men were in great demand at very high wages. After we had been married a year we began serious preparations for the journey. She was inclined to stay at home amongst her friends, but when she saw how I was set upon going she gave way, and it became, as all else in our married life, a mutual concern.

During the time we were preparing, the spirit of trade unionism took hold of the miners of the two northern counties again. The lead in the matter was taken by Northumberland. Durham at that time was a hindrance rather than a help; a hanger-on more than an equal as at present. This is plainly seen if we turn to Fynes' history of the miners of the two counties and the strong remarks which are found in a speech made by E. Rhymer in a delegate meeting held in Newcastle in 1865. The following are the words:—

" With respect to the county of Durham, he was sorry that they appeared as a black spot in England respecting the Miners' Association. They numbered about 1,000, but there were only 74 represented at that meeting. The hours of the men were eight hours working, the average daily wage being from 4s to 4s 6d. The hours of the boys on an average were fourteen per day. The system with respect to the boys was the most wretched in the civilised world. They never saw the light of the blessed sun from Sabbath to Sabbath. He had authority to tell them that the district which he represented begged of them, through him, to send help to save them from starvation and misery."

The spirit pervading these words is sombre, and forms for this generation surprising reading. It is not merely a long way back, but a great depth from the apex of trades unionism upon which we find ourselves now. They were stated a year or two subsequent to the year I am dealing with. In 1863 an attempt was made to form a union for the two counties. With that end in view a delegate meeting was held in February of that year. Mr W. Crawford was the secretary, and was appointed to draw up a code of rules.

There was a National Conference of miners held in Leeds in November of that year (1863). To that conference Mr Crawford, with other delegates, was sent to represent the united counties of Durham and Northumberland. Fynes, in his history, gives in outline the subjects which were deemed suitable for special consideration as being of interest. I quote that portion:—" (1) Better supervision of inspection, the amendment of the present Mines Inspection Bill, and the appointment of one sub-inspector for every 4,000 men employed in coal mines in the United Kingdom. (2) That where coroner's inquests were held over persons who had lost their lives in coal mines the jurymen on such inquests ought to be operative miners. (3) That a Ten Hours Bill for boys in the coal mines was highly necessary, and ought by every legitimate means to be sought for. (4) That no boy ought to descend a coal mine sooner than six o'clock in the morning. (5) That it was indispensably necessary for the safety of coal miners that only properly qualified persons should be appointed to responsible situations in coal mines, and that all agents should undergo an examination before some disinterested person competent to the task."

The wave of unionism struck Haswell, and along the east side of the county, as it did throughout. Amongst the many meetings which were held one was fixed on the Sherburn Hill side, just above what is known as the Pit Row. Large processions came in from the neighbouring collieries. Mr Crawford attended on his way back from the Leeds Conference. The chairman of the meeting was W. Palmer, whom I have referred to earlier. The speakers, in addition to Mr Crawford, were R. Walton, G. Par-kin, and J. Julian. Each of these dealt with a special subject or phase of the miners' life, resting their remarks upon the necessity there was for a close and compact union, embracing every workman. Whatever were the wrongs to right or the improvements to make, by that force alone could they hope to attain them. There were on one hand freedom and equality, the birthright of all men, or simple and gross slavery on the other. I was not the most careful listener. The truths I had complete faith in, and was ready to dare and do a great deal for them, but there were other matters (less useful) which claimed my attention, and, I am sorry to say, got it. Yet I can remember the outline of their speeches. Walton dwelt upon the necessity of the careful working of the mines. His great fear was the danger in driving places too wide. The greatest width should be four yards. We may wonder what he would have said now in the days of the " Welsh stall " and "long wall " systems. Parker was of a philosophical turn of mind, while Julian, who was a Primitive local preacher, took his watch (which he held in his hand) as an illustration of the power of union. From Mr Crawford we had a report from the conference, and a full explanation of the questions dealt with there. It was the first time I had seen him. He, too, was a local preacher, and was dressed in full ministerial garb, which at that time was (except in rare cases) vastly different from the present. It was peculiar and unique, and the wearer could be classified anywhere without much effort.

We returned from the gathering, and a meeting was called. It was resolved to form a branch of the young association. To that there was no demur. When the officers were being appointed I was proposed as secretary. I took two objections. First, I was preparing for America. The second was, in my opinion, a more fatal one. I have always held the view that in the selection of lodge officials something more than mere clerking ability or power to declaim are essential. Regard should be had to the bent and tendencies of the life of the candidate or person selected for the place. That is my opinion. It was then, and on the strength of it I refused. I was willing to do all I could to establish the union while in England, but the idea I have mentioned being to me the right one, I objected.

The choice fell on an instrument ready made to the hand of the manager, the late W. F. Hall. It cost a large sum to keep the union out of Haswell; but finally the free drink system and the action of the soulless prevailed, and those who were wishful to root and ground it were compelled to acknowledge they were defeated, and the darkness and consequent harsh conditions resulting therefrom were supreme. It mattered not to those who sold themselves. They were favoured above the good men on the colliery. The condition was congenial to the meanness of their nature. Give them beer and let them feel the approval of the official, and they had no longing beyond. With the true men whose souls burned within them at the wrongs they were called upon to bear, it was vastly different, and they were ready to cry out, " How long are we to bear these things? Is there no hope? To whom shall we look for succour if we are thus false to ourselves?" Still they hoped on, and in a few years their desires were realised, and their sufferings laid the foundation of an association which has no superior in the whole of the trades union world, and few equals.

CHAPTER XVIII.—OFF TO AMERICA.

The end of the year (binding year) came early in the month of April, and my good wife and I, having realised all we could for our goods, sailed from Liverpool on the 10th of that month. We did not burden the ship with our luggage. We sailed in the National Line steamboat Pennsylvania, and were three weeks on the voyage, and for seventeen days of that time in the teeth of a heavy gale. We were part of about a thousand people who occupied the steerage. Six hundred of these were taken in at Queenstown. I wish I had powers of description strong enough to enable me to set forth what was meant by going steerage in those days. It is no use forming our conclusions from that class of accommodation which is provided now. There is now some provision of cabin and berth, as in the first or second cabins. Not so well-fitted and furnished perhaps, but similar in shape. Then there was no attempt at comfort. There was a crowding and herding together, with no regard to privacy. Twenty-four people entered one door, and the sleeping accommodation was on the principle of the comic picture postcard, "When father says turn, we all turn!" The only attempt at separation was carried out by keeping the single men at one end of the ship, while the single women and married couples were at the other. These were subject to the further separation which gave the single women a section to themselves.

The steerage emigrants had their own beds to buy and bed clothes to provide. Those were available for use on land, when the new home was reached, except the mattrass (bed), which was thrown into the harbour or sea either just before or just after Sandy Hook was reached. The beds cost about 10s 6d each, and nearly filled the shallow cavity, so that the space allotted to six people was nearly a flat surface. In addition the outfit to provide included a knife and fork, a tin plate and pot, which were to wash after every meal, or to be used in the dirty state. In fact, every utensil for domestic purpose had to be provided at the passenger's expense. The food was of the coarsest kind, and served out in a manner on a par with its quality.

In this condition we were for ten nights with the companionways fastened down. This was done for a twofold purpose: to keep the water from flooding down below, and to keep the fear-stricken passengers out of the way of the sailors. There needs no stretch of imagination to supply an idea of what would be our state at night, when the fear was increased to a great extent, and when every danger known to the sea was fearfully magnified. Sometimes the tins which had not been too well secured would start a journey with every roll or pitch of the vessel, and when the stern rose out of the water the great screw would miss, and there would be a loud burring and a terrible shaking of the whole of the great fabric. Then would set in a dreadful dread of danger. This was indicated oft by the attitude, and oft in lamentations. I was looked upon as being a guide by the party with whom we were travelling, because I had some

acquaintance with the sea. Betimes I could keep them quiet, but there were occasions when that did not avail. This was most conspicuous one night. The water could be heard rushing about on deck (we found in the morning the panels had been washed out of some of the doors). Some of the passengers seized their boxes, and were dragging them towards the steps. In answer to my question, "What are you going to do?" they replied, "Sure, she is going down." "Then," said I, "it will take you all your time to save yourselves." My good wife kept confidence in me as long as possible, and then she said in quiet tones, "We are gannen very canny to the bottom." We had two friends who left Haswell with us, Mr and Mrs Noble. They were (with Mrs Wilson) in a greater fright than they liked to show. I was lying on my portion of that misnamed a bed, and called out, "Come to bed." The reply from Mrs Noble was, "It's nowt to thou; thou's used tid."

We landed in New York on May 1st, 1864, at the Castle Gardens, which was at that time the receiving station for the steerage passengers. It is now an aquarium, and the emigrants are taken to Ellis Island, which is in the mouth of the Hudson river. The American alien law was not so strict then as it is now. We passed a turnstile, and answered a few formal questions as to name, age, occupation, and destination, but none of the long list of questions which now confronts the lowest in the rung of the emigration ladder. There is a difference between to-day and when we landed. Now the emigration laws have reared a high prohibitive wall around the shores of America, and in many cases a man's merit depends upon the amount of money he has in his pocket, as if these were exchangeable terms. One of the most curious questions asked to-day is "whether he is in possession of 50 dollars (£10) or not, and if less, how much less." The logic of it is, if you have 50 dollars your virtue is up to par, but if below then every dollar below that figure detracts from your appreciation and acceptance. The real essentials of a man are not in the calculation, except a man be a known loafer or rogue.

In 1864 conditions were different. If the present day law had been in existence then, my good wife and I would have been turned back. Our tickets were good to Pittsburg by the emi-

4

grant cars, but we were some considerable distance off 50 dollars as a combined capital. When I got a place to work on the Monongahela river we had three English sovereigns left, and the Chancellor of the Exchequer of our little republic stuck to them in fair and foul weather. When we had plenty, and when we were not above but on the poverty line, as we were more than once, she kept her hold of them.

At the time when we touched the American shore their motto and desire was: "Let them all come, and no questions will be asked." The Civil War was nearly in its last year, and the country was in a terrible strait. It is a well-known fact that a large amount of the fighting force of the North at that time was drawn from the emigrants, and these were not got by the purest means. Large recruiting fees were paid to the crimps, who crowded around the landing place or waylaid the unsuspecting in the street. They were not choice in their methods. There were three in use; cajolery, force, or drug, and many a young fellow at his landing was met by one of these human sharks, fattening on his kind, and before he was much older he was entered as an American soldier and on his way to the front, and his friends never heard of him any more. They mourned for him, while he filled an unknown soldier's grave.

They tried their wiles on me, but it was of no avail. I was under a good caretaker. She considered me the best of her earthly possessions and assets. Those who read this may say she had not got much then. That is admitted. However, after staying a day in New York, we cleared for Pittsburg, and I soon found that every native American did not love his country sufficiently well to stay at home and fight for it. When the ballot was drawn in many cases those whose names came out were either to seek the next morning or had bought a substitute, and there were big prices paid for one. The process of ballotting was something like the following. When the call came from the central authority that a draft or ballot was to be made, say for ten in every hundred of the citizens, all the names of the males between two ages as a minimum and maximum were placed in a ballot box. Then every tenth name was hung out on a list at the public building. This was eagerly scanned the next morning, and in many cases the owner of the name was to seek, but

not in the direction of the battlefield. There were many who knew the road to Canada. Many a time I was asked if I would enlist, but my invariable reply was in their own variegated vocabulary, "No, sir; this is not my funeral." I was working at Broadtop, near the borders of Maryland, when the Confederates made a dash for the Pennsylvania Central Railway, and the farmers came past our house driving their stock before them. Their haste was so great that they had not time to speak about the weather or bid a friend "Good morning." There were five hundred miners in the line of the expected march, and there was a rifle sent for every man, but mine was never claimed. It no doubt lay there until, like Rip Van Winkle's, it rusted, lock, stock, and barrel.

As I have said, we were booked through to Pittsburg. There were plenty of chances of work, because at that time labour was in the state of having two masters seeking one man. Men were precious in those days, and commanded good prices. We had arranged to go to Mrs Wilson's brother's, who had been out about a year and a half, and was at that time, as we thought, working at Limetown, on the Monongahela river. We had quite an adventure and a disappointment at the start. The adventure arose from the fact that we got to the wrong station at Pittsburg. We had been requested to call at the "Old Folks At Home" Tavern to meet the brother. He was not there. We went direct to the station, as we thought right, but as it turned out wrong. Our correct route was by boat up the river. We took the train up the riverside to McKeesport, about 15 miles. I learned there was a Bishop Auckland man called T. Clark who kept a tavern near the riverside. So, hiring an old darkie, who had a mule and cart, we placed our box (not boxes) in it, and went down to Clark's. He and his good wife were kindness itself. They cheered us up with cheering optimistic reasons for the miss at Pittsburg, and made us free of the house for the night. In the morning I left Mrs Wilson at our good friend's, crossed the river, and walked up to Limetown. It was a long walk of some 12 or 15 miles, and I landed there just as the men were coming out of the drift. The custom was then for the hewer to sharpen his own picks, the first man out getting the anvil. I made for the pick shop, as being the most likely place to either find our lost relative or learn of his whereabouts. Leaning over the half-door of the shop, I asked for him. One of the men came forward and said "he was here until two days ago, when he left for the old country." He had been going out of Pittsburg as we entered. He saw the disappointment on my face, and, in cheery tones, he added, " Never mind, my lad, it will be all right. Wait until I sharpen my picks, and I will look after you." His name was Sydney Gardner, a native of Somerset, but he went from Thornley Colliery. We formed a close friendship, which was never broken while I was in America. Afterwards I repaid Sydney in a striking way. We had to pass the house of the boss, and he readily gave me a start. I had tea with the Gardners, who offered us a room in their house. Shortly after tea I hailed a steam-boat, and set off with the good news to my wife. We caught the midnight boat up, and reached Limetown about one in the morning.

As I have said, the Gardners let us have a room in their house, which to us, in our circumstances, was a very great kindness and of great assistance. It removed from us the idea of strangeness, and saved us from the anxiety of house seeking. The only thing we had towards housekeeping was a new " bed tick " brought from home. The next day Sydney and I went to a farmhouse and filled it. I have been asked what kind of feathers they were, and my invariable but truthful reply was, " They were long ones; so long you could have lain on one end of them and picked your teeth with the other." There was no fear of being hurt if you fell out of bed, for it was one of those known by the classical name of " shakydown."

CHAPTER XIX.—LIMETOWN.

I commenced work the second day after we got to Limetown. There were two reasons which prompted me. The first and immediate one was we were not millionaires when we left home, and we were a great deal further off when we reached our journey's end. There were not many dollars between us and the border line. The second reason was the employment on the river was divided into four periods. The river was low because of the drought in summer, and in winter there was no traffic owing to the frozen state of the river. During the latter period no coals were sent away, and no work was done except in the case of men who went in and stocked their coals in their working places, and then worked long hours filling them when the " run " commenced. The periods when coals could be sent away were known as the " Spring and fall runs." From these two causes there evolved the application and appreciation of the proverb, " Make hay while the sun shines," or in another form " Use your opportunities while they are near you."

We did not stay long at Limetown, but there were two or three incidents which may be noted. The first gives an idea of the difference in the state of feeling as to the cause of and continuance of the war. There was a rough shanty of a tavern a mile or two up the river, which was a favourite, if not a very pleasant resort, for the " jolly good fellows " of the locality, who generally left, walking with more eccentricity and less erectness than they went with. Sydney Gardner was a great politician when he had got over the line which divides sobriety from intoxication. Like many of this day, he could right all wrongs, and fully explain the ethics of all questions when so inspired. While we were in on a certain day he reached the oratorical point, and of course the war, with its causes, being the all absorbing topic, he launched into it without hesitation or qualification. In his opinion the real and only cause why the country was rent in twain and thousands of men were being slain was to " free a nigger." He reeled around the room and landed up against the bar. The landlord, who was a staunch democrat, and therefore in opposition to Lincoln's policy, had just received the sad news that his son, who was fighting in the Northern Army, had been killed. The declamation of Sydney hurt his feelings, and when the orator collided with the bar the landlord seized him by the collar of the coat and pulled a revolver from a shelf. This he thrust

against Gardner's cheek and said, " If you say
again my son was shot to free a nigger I will
blow your brains out. He was not shot for that,
but to maintain the Union." As a result both
the intoxication and oratory ceased right at
once. There was no peroration whatever to the
latter.

A Mine Explosion.

During the short stay at Limetown I had my
first experience of exploring after an explos-
sion. The drift in which I worked (and close
to which we lived) exploded in the early morning when the men were going in. I was sitting
getting breakfast when it took place. There
were in at that time six men and two boys.
These were the sons of one of the men. The
other men were an Irishman named Leonard,
and four Englishmen, J. Allan, of Six Mile,
Northumberland; John Adams, from Wingate;
E. Taylor and Rogerson, from Trimdon Grange.
These four were in the habit of going to work
together. They took in a waggon (tub), which
two of them would push in and the other two
with the picks in on alternate mornings. On
the morning of the explosion they were doing
so. They had presence of mind to throw themselves in the end of a place which was "stop-
pened" off. They saved the full force of the
blast, but were affected by the afterdamp. We
managed to get to them and get them out.
They were so much affected that holes were
dug in the soil, into which their faces were put,
and as they recovered they were laid upon our
"shaky down" bed and left to the tender care
of the women. Leonard had been pushing a
waggon (tub) in himself, having his picks inside. He was further in than the others, and
when found he was in the tub with one of his
picks stuck in his side. There was another
marvellous thing in connection with him. The
sole of one of his shoes was cut as clean off as
if someone with a sharp knife had been at work,
and every toe nail was gone off his foot. Those
who have been in exploring parties will know
that there are many cases which, if not strictly
similar, are inexplicable to the unscientific
mind.

The search after this was for the father and
sons, and these we found just through a door
through which they had gone with their naked

lights, and receiving the force of the explosion
they were in a terrible state.

There was great excitement in the neighbourhood, and as usual on these occasions some men
showed their sorrow by getting drunk. It is a
poor way, but it is theirs. For myself, I had
enough without seeking the tavern. I did get
a little brandy, which would not have fallen to
my share if it had not been for my wife. There
were only three or four of us in the mine exploring. She was one of the anxious ones outside. There was a noted character named Wild
Pat, part of whose wildness lay in keeping safe.
He got hold of the brandy bottle, and with it in
his hand he would rush into the drift mouth as
far as the daylight would reach and out again.
This to him was such a brave thing that he
must needs have recourse to the bottle. This
was too much for my lass, and she took it from
him, saying " Give me that. I want it for those
who dare go in and not play about as you are
doing." And she got and kept it until we came
out.

An Amusing Incident.

Sydney Gardner was one of those whose grief
was in proportion to their drinking. He spent
the greater part of the day in the tavern, and
was in a far advanced state both in drink and
consequent oratory. He, with a man named J.
Wilkinson, who went from Trimdon, was coming down the river in a boat. Wilkinson was
rowing, and Gardner was using the boat as a
rostrum and declaiming to the people on the
banks as they passed along. The house we lived
in was only separated from the river by a horse
track. Mrs Wilson and I stood at the door
laughing at the antics and words of the orator.
Just when the boat got opposite the house our
mirth was suddenly turned to terror, for he
gave a lurch and went clean overboard head
first. His companion sat paralysed with fear,
and made no effort to seize him. A boat was
lying convenient right in front of us. I rushed
to it. Fortunately the oars were in it, and I
reached the spot just as he rose to the surface
for the second time, and was able to grab him
by the collar and hold him against the side of
the boat I was in. I asked and urged Wilkinson to assist me, but he was nerveless; and although brave ordinarily he confessed after-

wards he could not move. I kept my grip until assistance came, and we got Sydney brought round and into bed, and thus I was able to repay him for his great kindness to me when I first arrived there and afterwards, and drew the bonds of friendship closer than before.

The explosion had one useful effect. It drew the public attention to the danger which had never been suspected, and induced the miners to demand greater care from those in charge. One item of their demand was the appointment of examiners, analogous to those obtaining under the Mines Regulation Act with us now. Many meetings were held, and the qualifications of certain men for the post were canvassed. Out of one of these meetings arose a rather curious incident, which had a somewhat humorous ending. Our meeting was at the drift mouth. The two questions before it were the desirability of an examiner being appointed, and the most fitting man for the position. The merits of various men were discussed, and at last an American rose. His object was to plead his own cause. A part of his speech has never left me. "Gentlemen," he said, "I guess I am the man to be appointed to that place." There was a natural and general query why he should be selected. His reply was, "Wall, I know a lot about gas. I got my knowledge by working six months in a gashouse down at Pittsburg." The meeting did not hold the same views as he did, and he did not get the post.

The choice fell on me, but I refused, because I had made up my mind to leave the locality as soon as I could. I was urged by the workmen and the boss. He offered large inducements. One old Northumbrian, a miner from Seghill, who had been out in America about eleven years, gave me some good advice in peculiar phraseology. "When I first came to this country I was continually hearing of good places some distance from where I was, but I have come to the conclusion that you are always fifty miles from the best place in America." The advice was as sound as true, but unheeded, I am sorry to say.

We removed to Plymouth, in Lucerne county, on the eastern side of Pennsylvania. There were some people living in Plymouth who had left Haswell a few years before, and to whom we wrote. The distance (without being strictly accurate) was some three hundred miles. It is in the anthracite region. The work differed widely from the bituminous seam on the river. There it was similar to that at home, all pick work. At Plymouth the pick was seldom, if ever, used. The whole process was with heavy jumper drills, and great charges of powder. There was another difference. Those who got and filled the coal in the anthracite were divided into two classes, the man who owned the "breast" and the labourer. The former got the coal down, and when this was done in sufficient quantity he went home, the latter remaining until the coals were filled away. On the river every miner had his own working place. This was like the old country, and therefore more in harmony with my habits. I could not get a "breast," and as a consequence had to take a labourer's place. This was against my feelings on two grounds. It was inferior, and that was very galling, and it compelled me to remain after the other man had left and gone home. I therefore resolved to leave again.

Before dealing with our next locality it may be interesting to note a little joke which was unconsciously played upon myself and Mr Bones, the man with whom we were staying, by Mrs Wilson and Mrs Bones. They went to the store, and amongst other items of domestic use they wanted some salt. They asked the storekeeper if he had any, and were told he had, but it was in sacks. "What is the price of a sack?" They were told it was twenty cents (tenpence). They concluded salt was cheap, but the sack would be too heavy, and they would therefore pay for it and send us down for it. The man smiled, but made no remark. We were living about a mile from the store. When they returned they told us what they had done, and sent us off for the sack they could not carry. When we got to the store I went in and asked the man for the sack, expecting we should have a load to carry back. He laughed loudly, and placed a small sack on the counter which I put with ease into my jacket pocket, and was not the least inconvenienced thereby.

Difficulties of Shopping.

The difference in the names of articles of home use between England and America is very confusing to the housewife when she first goes out there. We had as a neighbour an old lady who had left Tyneside some years prior to our acquaintance with her. She gave me an account of her first attempt at the store. I may say she had never changed her dialect, but spoke the pure Wallsend, with the burr untouched. She described to me the many misunderstandings which arose between her and the storeman until she came to the last article, which was treacle. In unadulterated Northumbrian she said "Aa want some treacle." "I don't understand what you mean, madam." "That in there," she said, pointing to the tall boiler-like receptacle. "That is molasses." "That's what Aa want, give me a pund of it." "We don't sell it by the weight, madam; we sell it by measure." In complete surprise the old lady exclaimed, "Good God, dee ye mean to say ye sell treacle by the yard in this country."

Our resolve being formed to leave Plymouth, the question arose to what part we should go. We learned that S. Gardner had gone to Broadstop, in Huntingdon county, and we fixed upon that locality. I knew vaguely the direction, but the precise point was a mystery. However, with that faint knowledge I set out, leaving Mrs Wilson, and dividing our money, which was a great way off a Rockefeller's fortune, as will be seen. My route was by way of Harrisburg, striking the Pennsylvania Central there, thence on to Huntingdon, where I had to change for a branch line, the whole journey being between two and three hundred miles. When I reached Huntingdon I went to the ticket office and asked for a ticket for Broadtop. "Which station do you want to go to, for Broadtop is a wide extent of country?" And he then in true railway official style mentioned a number of names. "Look here, boss," I said, "book me to any station you like. Take your choice, for I am careless about it." He looked at me in surprise, as if he had run up against an idiot who needed a caretaker. Then finally he said "I will book you to Dudley, which is as far as the train goes." "Right, let me have the ticket to Dudley."

When I reached Dudley it was nearing dusk, and right opposite was a tavern. I had two bundles; one of them contained my pit clothes, and the other underclothing for home wear. I went across to the tavern, in which there was as rough a crowd as ever I saw, and I had before that seen a few. I very soon made up my mind

to clear out as soon as I could without giving offence. Getting to the door I struck the road up through a large and thick forest. I hope the roads have improved since then in the country districts of America, for they were very bad at the period of which I am writing. Not only were the roads badly kept, but they were made worse for a stranger in a wood in the dark, by their mode of cutting down the trees in the line of the track. The stump of the tree was left about breast high. These could be avoided in daylight, but in the dark, made denser by the shadows of the trees, the consequence was a continued counter with the tree stumps. My perplexity was increased by the uncertainty which awaited me when I got through. There were three questions: How far was it through? and what should I find when I got through? and where was I to lodge? After about a mile of the rough and darksome road I emerged, and then there was a strange climax to a strange journey. Just where I got into the open country were three houses. They were standing on a bankside, back from the road a few yards, and coming down to one of the houses were a man and a woman. The man had his miner's oil lamp stuck in his cap (which is the method in use in the mine), and he was carrying a baby. It was Sydney Gardner, the very man I was in search of. Here was a chain of fortuitous circumstances. The ticket clerk at Huntingdon gave me a ticket at hazard for the right station. If I had remained five minutes longer in the tavern or left five minutes earlier I should have missed him. There he was. The sight of him was a pleasure. I gave them time to get into the house, and then I went up to the door and knocked. He answered the knock. When he opened the door I said, "Are you taking any lodgers in here?" He started back, exclaiming, "Good gracious, it's Wilson." "Yes, Sydney," I said, "I have been seeking you all day." He seized me by the hand, crying out "Where have you come from? Come in, for you are welcome."

A Postmaster's Surprise.

There needed no second invitation. Never did any benighted traveller accept hospitality with greater eagerness than I did. The next day he went with me to the boss of the mine he was working in, who readily gave me work. I wrote at once to Mrs Wilson, telling her of my good fortune, and asked her to come directly. I had to go rather better than a mile down to Dudley Station to post the letter. When I reached it I found myself in a fix. I was not rich enough to buy a stamp. I put on a bold face, and went into the post-office, which was a general store as well. To the postmaster I said "Look here, boss, I am in a fix. I have left my wife in Lucerne county, and I have written a letter to her, but I have not money enough to pay for a stamp. Will you trust me for one?" He looked up smiling, "Yes," he said, "I will; there it is." Mrs Wilson came four days after. I met her at the station. Beyond the usual loving greetings (and they were loving), my first words were, "Have you any money?" With her usual cautiousness she answered my question in the Scottish fashion by asking what I wanted with it. I explained the circumstances. "Yes," she said, "I have a dollar." It was one of those wifely fibs which are allowed the careful housewife, and which the recording angel never notes. They are virtuous evasions which need create no dread of the future. I with dollar in hand went to the post-office, and, as proud as if I was a millionaire, said, "I have come to pay for that stamp, boss." He was knocked all in a heap, and cried out, "You don't mean to say you have come to pay for it? Well, you are a strange man, for I never expected to see you again." He saw us many a time after, for a large amount of our household requirements were got in his store during our stay in that locality.

In going to Broadtop we struck a good place. Money was plentiful, if there had been sense in the earner. The place was not large, but we had good neighbours, both English and American. Being young, and lively, and social we took part in all their frolics and dances. The frolics were many—apple peeling, corn shelling, and others of a similar kind in which the principle of neighbourly feeling predominated largely. When any of these functions took place, say, apple peeling, there was a gathering from near and far. The barn was cleared, the apples placed in the centre, while with knife in hand the helpers sat in a circle. The same would take place when the Indian corn was to shell. The work over there was supper and a

dance with its master of ceremonies, whose duty it was to call out the various changes in the figures.

We were primitive people, but while we were away "from the madding crowd" of a great city we were not in the least bound by its conventionalisms. The squire (or magistrate) was elected every year by the popular vote of citizens. In a community like ours the highest citizen was not a long way up. There was no need for a social telescope to see him. In the parish just above us the squire was the picksharper, while at Dudley, on the other side, he was a small storekeeper. In one case marriages were made and justice dispensed at the anvil. That was the altar. In the other case the little office of a very small store was the court of justice, and the place was solemnised for marriages. The latter in both cases did not stop the picksharping much or prevent a customer from being served in the store. Marriage was not a ceremony over which they wasted many words, nor was it an ordeal about which any man needed to be nervous. The most solemn compact of human life was easily made, and dissolved with the same ease.

The dispensing of justice was done in a crude manner, for the squire knew little of law, and the procedure in the court was on the principle of go as you please—a sort of catch as catch can. A case in which I, with a few others took part, will illustrate. There was a family living in the locality named Booth. They emigrated from Washington Colliery. There were the father, a son, and two daughters. One of the girls was housekeeper to a miner. He charged her with stealing eleven dollars. For this she was taken before the squire. Like all other people from one part of England, we from Durham were clannish. The result was we went down with her, and we resolved to have her acquitted. As we made our way down my companions said to me "You will have to be the pleader." This was said, not because I knew anything about law, but because my tongue was a little more glib than theirs. I was a long way from a lawyer, both in knowledge and dress. My garb was a slouch hat, a woollen shirt void of collar or tie, neither jacket, waistcoat, nor braces, and my pants inside my top boots. We were not a large crowd, but we were noisy, and the Durham twang was predominant. Our strong points were confusion in court, and perplexity in the magisterial mind. We were successful in both. Every time the prosecutor attempted to state his case I did not rise to a point of order, but of disorder, until eventually the old man did not know which way to turn. The dilemma did not arise entirely from the noise, but from the Durham patois, which filled his ears with strange sounds and left his mind a blank so far as any intelligent grasp of what was meant was concerned. That was the psychical moment (as the writers say), and I went close up to his chair, and in a quiet tone said " Squire, you had better acquit this girl." It was the best American I had at command, and it fell pleasingly on his ear, and he replied " I guess you are right, she is discharged." That placed me in the proud category of successful lawyers, for I had never lost a case, that being the only one I ever had up to that time. I conducted another of a somewhat different kind which will be related later.

CHAPTER XX.—BROADTOP.

Our time at Broadtop was happy and prosperous. The precise portion of the locality where we lived was a short distance below Broadtop City, and was known as Friendship. The city was on a par with many others in America, consisting of very few houses, and not seen until you were right in its midst, and you wondered by what rule it was dignified by the name of city. Here our daughter Dorothy was born, and although social comfort was a great way from that in England, we were as happy as possible. I am no cabinetmaker, and therefore the class of furniture we had will be easily imagined when I say I made it all myself, except a few chairs. My principal tools were an old saw, a plane, a small axe, and a hammer. I would like to give a description of the bedstead. It was four poled, but these were not made of mahogany. They were props from the pit, and about five feet high. The mode of construction was as follows:—In addition to the props I got four planks. Through these were bored holes about six inches apart. We had no augur, but a red hot poker made a good substitute, and effected the purpose. Through these holes a stout rope was run and crossed, and formed a good mattress, upon which our bed was placed. The bedstead when set up in its naked form as it left the maker was rough, but my grand partner in the domestic firm was well skilled in all the details of housewifely hypocrisies by which things are made to appear what they are not. In the hands of the good wife " things are not what they seem." Amongst the other articles I made were a " long-settle," couch-like, strongly built, and admired by all who saw it, and a fabrication which puzzled the neighbours for some time. They concluded we were going to keep hogs, and that it was intended for a feeding trough. There was little if any symmetry about it, but with a pair of rockers on it made a very good cradle. There was one thing in our favour: the furniture did not suffer much by comparison with that of our neighbours, for in every case it was for use and not for show.

Life in the country districts and in the villages differed from that we had left in England. There was more latitude and freedom in roaming around the fields or woods. People were not confined to roads, turnpike or footpath; neither were they subject to the interference of the man who called the farm his. If a miner or other workman kept any stock, such as pigs, hens, or geese, these had free run of the forests, and oftimes were not seen for weeks, while the geese were plucked at seasons alive, the same as sheep were sheared. This was done to procure live feathers. It may have given additional value to the feathers. Of that I am no judge. What was clear to me was that it was cruel to the birds, and gave them a naked and a very miserable appearance as they wandered around entirely featherless. One of the most striking differences was the rendezvous or congregating places for the miners after the day's work was over, or during the spare time. In England it is the corner ends, or some other open resort. There it was and is the village store. In summer they sat around outside, and if thirsty walked in, and up to the bucket of water and got a drink; and if there were no water they would inform the storekeeper (not in tones of apology) of the fact, and he was expected to bring some as quickly as possible, even if the person asking had never spent a cent. in the place. If the weather was unfavourable, or in winter, then they crowded inside and sat on the counter, or anywhere else, or around the stove (which he was expected to keep warm), and swap yarns or experiences, the competition being as to who could tell the tallest story. The more improbable it was the more it was relished. With chair tilted back, feet elevated, and oft seeing which of them could send the tobacco juice the furthest, the store was looked upon as common property, and in many instances they would sample the biscuits or apples without offering payment. When I was over in America in 1904 I was the guest of a Mr Hibberd, who kept a large store in Westmoreland City. I found the same custom prevailing. He told me he objected to the community of goods. He had no objection to them sitting around upon the porch or inside, but he had to their eating his goods, and he placed a notice above the apple barrel to the following effect:—" It is said the Lord helps those who help themselves, but the Lord help the man who helps himself out of this barrel."

When we went to Broadtop the Civil War was raging, and the North was putting forth every effort to finish it. Their repeated draftings had either got their strongest men to the front, or they had "made tracks," or bought a substitute, as in many cases was done if they could find an eligible one in the person of some young emigrant. In the Northern States localities differed very widely and acutely in their feeling. In ours the Democratic party was largely in preponderance, and it was not at all times safe to offer a word of praise of Lincoln. The sympathiser, if not sure of his company, need not have been surprised if he was called upon to look into the barrel of a revolver or rifle. A single instance will illustrate. For a short time we had two young men living with us, one of whom was Mrs Wilson's nephew. One of them was washing himself in the "shanty" on his return from work on a certain day. To amuse himself he was singing part of a song, the chorus of which was to the effect "We would hang Jeff Davis on a sour apple tree." I question if he knew who Jeff Davis was, or what relation he had to the war. That did not matter, for suddenly there appeared in the doorway an infuriated democrat with a rifle, who, full of anger, threatened to shoot the singer if he did not desist. There is no doubt but he would have done so, but the singing stopped suddenly, and the singer bolted into the house, half-naked as he was. It therefore behoved all who in the least believed in Lincoln or the emancipation of the slaves to exercise great caution, and keep their mouths as with a bridle. If they were of the other school they could make as loud a noise as they thought fit, and denounce him to their heart's content.

Our stay at Broadtop covered three very important portions of American history of that time, and we therefore saw a great deal of what I thought then, and what I think now, was very unpatriotic conduct. These were Lincoln's second election, the conclusion of the war, and his assassination. He was elected for the second time on November 8th, 1864. For some months before that day, although the country was in one of the most critical and anxious periods of the Civil War, requiring all the care and forethought of those in authority, and the issues of one of the greatest questions that ever engaged human attention or taxed the resources of any nation were in the balance, yet he, who was the moving spirit in the initiation and the consummation of the righteous project, was on the eve of its realisation made the object of vile threats and slanders. The Democratic party were clamouring for a policy of peace at any price with the South. To that policy Lincoln was in direct opposition. He was ready for peace, but on the following terms:—" While the rebels continue to wage war against the Government of the United States, the military measures affecting slavery, which have been adopted from necessity to bring the war to a speedy and successful end, will be continued, except so far as practical experience shall show that they can be modified advantageously with a view to the same end. When the insurgents shall have disbanded their armies and laid down their arms the war will instantly cease."

Stern, indomitable " Old Abe." There was no compromising or evasion with him to catch votes and secure another term of Presidential office. Equality and the love of human right and a recognition of the fundamental truth that the colour of the skin ought not to differentiate the human race weighed more with him. Freedom was with him an eternal principle; to live in the White House was temporary and fleeting. Speaking to one of the regiments at this particular and important juncture he said: "I happen temporarily to occupy this big White House. I am a living witness that any one of your children may look to come here, as my father's child has. It is in order that each one of you may have, through this free government which we have enjoyed, an open field and a fair chance for your industry, enterprise, and intelligence; that you may all have equal privileges in the race of life, with all its desirable human aspirations—it is for this that the struggle should be maintained, that we may not lose our birthright. The nation is worth fighting for to secure such an inestimable jewel."

A draft of half a million men was called for, and his friends urged upon him to suspend it until after the election. His reply to their urgings was characteristic: "What is the Presidency worth to me if I have no country?" As the day of the election drew nigh it was deemed advisable to send soldiers to the points of danger, and especially New York and Chicago. In the country districts, as in the one we were living in, the opposition was very violent and dangerous to the voter who favoured the return of Lincoln and the continuance of the war until the complete surrender of the South. Those of us who were unnaturalised spent our time as observers of the agitation and the disturbances on the election day, and we saw not a few chased and ill-treated by the spiteful majority.

During the whole of this turmoil the war was proceeding slowly but surely. Grant had shut Lee up in Richmond, and doggedly held the position until Sherman made his great march to the sea, and so cut off Lee on the other side, and compelled his surrender. It is well-known that Lee was America's greatest soldier when the war broke out, and that both sides were eager to secure him. After much consideration he decided to throw in his lot with the South, and as a consequence his Arlington estate, near Washington, was forfeited, and is now, and has been since the Civil War, a soldiers' cemetery. I remember a conversation I had with some Northern soldiers who were on their way home in the cars in which I was riding. As souvenirs of the war they had pieces of the tree under which General Lee gave up his sword to General Grant. They said that within a very few minutes after the surrender the tree was cut down, and cut to pieces and gone, so eager were the soldiers to get a piece to take home with them. When speaking of the generals, and especially when comparing Lee and Grant, they hesitated not to give the former the chief place in their estimation.

CHAPTER XXI.—THE MURDER OF PRESIDENT LINCOLN.

Before the war was finished the annals of American history were stained by one of the foulest deeds ever done in that or any country. Lincoln was murdered on April 14th by G. Wilkes Booth in the theatre at Washington. There is no doubt but the deed was prompted by two motives. Booth, like many of the Secessionists, was disappointed at Lincoln's re-election, and, like them, too, was of the opinion that if he were removed the war would be ended on terms favourable to the South. Booth was only twenty-six years of age, and was an actor. Yet, young as he was, he was at the head of a conspiracy formed for the purpose of assassination. So great was his fanaticism that when much younger he assisted at the capture and execution of John Brown. Three murders were planned: Seward, who was the Secretary of State in Lincoln's Government; Andrew Johnson, who was Vice-President, and Lincoln. The last Booth reserved for himself. He learned that the President intended to go to Ford's Theatre on the 14th, and immediately laid his plans. He, being an actor, had the run of the theatre, and was therefore no stranger to its construction and passages. He knew exactly the position of the Presidential box. In order to guard against interference when he effected an entrance he, by the help of some accomplice on the theatre staff, arranged for a wooden bar to be so fixed that the door could not be opened from the outside, and a hole was bored in the door in order that he might shoot through the door or observe the position of the occupants. He had a fleet horse ready at the door, in the charge of one of the employees. To facilitate his entrance he procured a card or permit, and was allowed to enter. The President and his party were intently watching the play. Booth fastened the wooden bar, and noiselessly approached with a knife in one hand and a pistol in the other, which he placed behind Lincoln's head and fired. One of the party seized him, but dropping the pistol he stabbed the attempted arrester in the arm, and leaped from the box on to the stage. In that act his spur caught the folds of the flag with which the front of the box was draped.

He fell on the stage, and by the fall broke his leg; but, as if he was not hurt, he turned to the audience, and, holding the knife in his hand, he shouted the motto of the Virginian State, "Sic semper tyrannus," and while the people were struck with surprise he ran and leaped on the horse at the door, and so for the time got clear away, while the murdered President lingered until next morning. The piece of braggadocio enacted by Booth as he rushed across the stage led to his identification. In his flight he was accompanied by a young man named Harold, who was one of the conspirators. In his endeavours to escape he was assisted by rebel sympathisers, but his broken leg was so painful that he was compelled to seek shelter. If he had been in health he might have kept clear of his pursuers for some considerable time. For a week he was hid in the house of an adherent to the Confederacy, although detectives were watching near his house. In order to prevent discovery their horses were killed, lest they should neigh, and thus betray them. By the help of this man they were able to cross the Potomac river, and with the assistance of some Confederate soldiers they were able to find shelter in a barn, the property of a man named Garrett. Here they were found by a party of Northern soldiers. When asked to surrender Booth refused, and said he would fight the whole party at a hundred yards. The young man who was with him came out and gave himself up. Then the barn was set on fire. By the light from the flames Booth was seen taking aim at the officer in charge through one of the crevices of the logs, when he was shot by Boston Corbett, an Englishman, who was a sergeant of the Northern cavalry. The bullet struck him behind the head near the place where he had shot the President.

Thus ended, so far as the direct assassin was concerned, one of the most useless as well as one of the foulest crimes ever committed. There could no gain to the country accrue from it, for the war was virtually at an end, and the Cabinet and Vice-President were imbued with the spirit of Lincoln, and resolved to effect the object for which the war was commenced. The results which arose were twofold. It afforded the localities such as where we lived an opportunity for rejoicing, of which they took advantage, and it filled the whole civilised world with horror at the foul and disgraceful deed. Lest anyone should think I am speaking without authority when I say there was rejoicing I will record a matter which is fresh in my mind to-day. One of the Democratic comic papers parodied the murder by giving a mock inquest over the body. One of the witnesses supposed to have been called was an Irishman, who said he was in the theatre at the time. He was asked to describe what he saw and heard. The reply given was: "I heard a shot fired. I saw a man jump on to the stage, across which he ran with a knife in his hand shouting aloud, 'I am sick, send for McGuinness.'" And that piece of despicable journalism evoked many a laugh where there ought to have been universal sorrow for the dead, and regret that America contained a monster so cruel as to commit such an act.

My only object in mentioning that disgusting thing is to give an idea of the feeling prevailing in some localities in reference to President Lincoln and his work, and to show that not only had he to meet the Southern Confederacy on the battle field, but there were bitter enemies at home thwarting his designs where possible, and hindering him in the grand and glorious work. Speaking now of him (as I believed then), he was a hero of the highest type, and one of the world's greatest men. Although he was the head of the American nation, yet the world had a share in his nobility. It is a wise arrangement that the influence of a good man's life cannot be bounded by arbitrary and national lines. It is as wide as the world. No man could have lived a more lowly life or commenced life's struggle on a lower rung of the ladder, and yet by the force of his splendid qualities he forced his way to the highest position in one of the greatest nations of the earth. He was a lover of right, and his determination in support of his belief was unswerving. He was a man full of a noble purpose, and he counted his life as nothing if only that was attained. There never was a grander soul found in the human breast. It has been said that his life could be summed up in three words: "Toil, triumph, and tragedy." Toil against narrow and disadvantageous circumstances, triumph in a great and noble cause, and tragedy in the hour of that triumph at the hand of a man drunk with fanaticism.

Those manifestations of rejoicing at his death were confined to certain districts. Throughout the country there came great mourning to those who on the fatal day were filled with joy for the great victory right had achieved over wrong by the Northern Army. Everywhere there had been signs of gaiety. Flags and decorations were in profuse display, but the sad news of the sudden and awful calamity which had fallen upon the nation turned the gladness into mourning. The funeral procession was taken from city to city—Baltimore, Harrisburg, Philadelphia, New York, Albany, Syracuse, Rochester, Buffalo, Cleveland, Columbus, Indianapolis, Chicago, and Springfield, Illinois, his own city, where he was buried at Peak Ridge. I was in New York at the time the body was there. The sight of the draped city, with a continuous stream of people thronging Broadway on their way to the City Hall, was most solemn and impressive. All classes were vieing with each other to show their respect. The rich with costly wreaths, and the poor with flowers they had twined themselves, for they felt that the nation had lost its greatest citizen. The sorrow expressed was not confined to his own land, but from every country there came tributes to his worth and the loss the world had sustained by his death. Queen Victoria wrote to Mrs Lincoln "as a widow to a widow."

CHAPTER XXII.—BRIEF STAY AT MORRIS.

The result of President Lincoln's death to trade was disastrous. It was as if some mysterious force had suddenly changed busy activity into dead stagnation. I speak of the mining industry and of the district where we were living. For about nine weeks very little, if any, work was done. We remained there about six months afterwards, when we decided to remove to near Peoria, in the State of Illinois. There was a family or two living at Wesley City with whom we had been very friendly at Haswell. I left Mrs Wilson with some American neighbours at Broadtop (and very kindly they behaved to her), and I started some 800 miles. Work was brisker there, and after a few weeks she followed. Winter had set in, and she, with the baby, had a very rough journey, being snowbound about four days. We had hardly got ourselves fixed in a little house, standing in the middle of a field, until a strike took place. It was rough while it lasted, and this was the only place where I saw pistols used as arguments to persuade blacklegs not to work. I knew four men who went inside the drift a few yards, where they could see anyone who came in without being seen themselves. Their determination was to shoot all who entered with a view to working. Luckily no one came. A day or two after some of the blacklegs got in, but they were brought out by men who held pistols to their heads, and taken to the pick shop, and compelled to promise they would not go to work again so long as the strike lasted.

Our stay was very short at Wesley City, for after the strike very dull times set in. We resolved to move again, and this time as far back as we had come. Our aim was to reach Morris Run, near Blossburg, some forty miles from Buffalo. The route to it from where we were was through Chicago, and along the lake shore railway to Buffalo. I am not sure as to the exact distance, but I should say not far short of 900 miles in all. We knew there were some people from our neighbourhood, so that shelter of some sort was certain.

We were not there five minutes before we

realised that we had got from bad to worse, or, as our proverb has it, " out of the frying pan into the fire." The day before we arrived forty men had been discharged for depression of trade. The party with whom we had left Peoria consisted of Mrs Wilson, myself, and other three men, one of whom was T. Pearson, who hailed from Trimdon. We were in a fix, but I learned there was a man there seeking about forty men for some mines in Cameron County. It was this chance or nothing, because we were not very rich. So we went in search of the man, and engaged with him to start that (Friday) night at twelve. He had two sleighs to carry our picks and other belongings. The whole country was covered with snow and ice. We were six miles from the station we wanted to reach. It was the roughest journey I have ever tackled. We were nearly five hours on the road. When we arrived the boss was very wishful to know if any of us could buy our own railway tickets, but he found he had struck the most moneyless crowd he had ever seen or heard of, for according to our admission there was not a dollar in the whole number. His motive was to get us bound to him by this purchasing of a ticket, and we were as much determined he should not. So far as I was concerned I was dubious about the whole matter, and if it were not bona-fide the dollars would be useful in taking me to Pittsburg. Without any collusion we were all like-minded, and put forward a strong plea of poverty.

He therefore had no alternative but to buy tickets for the whole number. At 6 a.m. we started, and were travelling or being shunted until near twelve midnight, when we landed at a very wild looking station which civilised comfort had never come near. Our bags were taken into the luggage room, and we set off for a two mile walk as straight up a hill as any vehicle could go through an immense pine forest. Pearson went on ahead, but I stuck to the boss, and put him through a cross-examination as to the reason why he was seeking men. " Was there a strike?" " No, there was not a strike; it is simply a scarcity of men." At last we reached the top of the hill, and I heard Pearson shouting my name and urging upon me to go to where he was. My answer was for him to come and show me the way, as it was im-

possible to find it. He did so, and brought a lantern with him. He took me and six others to a house, where he said he had got lodgings. He had done so in the following manner: When he reached the top of the mountain he saw a door open, and he walked in. A man was sitting by the fire. Pearson took off his coat, and spread it on the mat before the fire, and lay on it. As he did so he exclaimed, " I am going to lodge here." The man in surprise and anger cried out, " If you are not out of here pretty quick I will kick you out." " I tell you," said Pearson, " this is where I am going to lodge, and there are other seven beside me." The woman, who was in the pantry, came out and said, " Where does thou come from?" " If I am not wrong," was the reply, " not far from where thou comes from thesel'. Aa belang Trimdon." It transpired that she had left Castle Eden, and her husband dying, she had married this man. Her explanation soothed him, and it was arranged that she would put the eight of us up for that night at least. It was a log house, consisting of one room as a kitchen, and another upstairs. There were eight of us, and therefore four beds were necessary for us, and there was only the one they occupied themselves in the house, and that stood in the downstairs room. She was a woman of expedients. Four " battins " of straw were got, one of which was placed in each corner in the upper chamber, and all the spare bed clothes and wraps were improvised, and we passed a not uncomfortable night. I have experienced much worse and slept less soundly in much more luxurious surroundings.

The next morning was Sunday. As soon as it was light we went out to see what the locality was like. To me it was awful as a place to bring Mrs Wilson to. I could have roughed it very well, but I had too much regard for her comfort to bring her there. In the village there were thirteen log houses, and a large boarding house. It stood on the brow of the high hill. The large pine trees had been cut down, and afforded building material. The ends of the logs jutted out beyond the end or sides of the building, and the branches were thrown up in heaps promiscuously, without any regard to order or arrangement. The pathways between house and house were as intricate as the runs of a rabbit warren. The intricacies explain the reason why I could not find Pearson the night before. One of the party, named Peter Allan, who left Illinois with us, had rushed for the large boarding house (in which there were sixty boarders before our arrival), and while our landlady was getting breakfast ready we decided to have a look at Peter and see how he was faring. Sunday morning as it was, there were a number of parties playing cards, and swearing awfully. Our friend was at breakfast. When he saw us he came outside, and, taking a look around at the rough sight, he cried out, " Will anyone tell me what I have done that I have been transported to a place like this?"

We decided to go into the drift, Sunday as it was, and have a look at the work. The strata lay so near the surface that each two men had to have two places—one for dry weather and the other for wet where the covering was thicker, because in the former case when the rain came it soon found its way through the crevices. The coal when hewed in those places was just the colour of newly made bricks. When we came out after the inspection Pearson said to me, " Now, what does tha think of it? Will she suit?" And right off I replied I would not stop here if he would give me five dollars a day for doing nothing. "That's right enough, but how will tha get away?" I said, "Just wait till to-morrow, when we go down for our traps, and watch me, and you will soon see how I'll manage."

On the Monday we went down the hill to the station, accompanied by the boss and a heavy sleigh, in which were two horses for the purpose of bringing our belongings up. Every man went in and claimed his own, and placed them in the vehicle, except myself, and I stood quite unconcerned to one side. When all was out but mine the boss said, "Wilson, where is yours?" "In the luggage room," was the reply. "Bring them out, and let us be going." "I will when the train comes." "You don't mean to say you are going away?" "Yes," I said, "but I will not wait for the train; I'll walk down to the next station." And I entered the station house, got my bags, which I slung over my shoulder, and taking the track I cried out, "Good-day, boss; I am off for Lockhaven, and on to Pittsburg." With that Peter Allan and a Cockney shouted, "Are you going, Wilson?" "Certainly. Can you not see I am?" "Wait a minute, and we will go with you," and snatching up their bags they ran after me, and we walked some five miles to the next station on the track, and caught the first train for Lockhaven, where we parted. I had decided to go to Pittsburg and try the River again, and I therefore took the Tyrone Valley Railway, changing at Tyrone, on the Pennsylvania Central for Pittsburg.

CHAPTER XXIII.—IN SEARCH OF WORK.

I managed to get work at Oceola, on the Youghogheny river, and immediately sent for Mrs Wilson. We got ourselves nicely placed in a nice house just across the river from the mine. It was surrounded by a beautiful garden, and had a porch (or verandah) running the whole length of the house, upon which we used to have tea, and after it sit and see the little humming birds as they went through their swinging flights back and forward, the baby amusing herself with a rude sort of cart which I had made for her, and the good wife busy with her sewing, and myself with a book, and now and then a few words of conversation. As the darkness came on, then the fireflies in their thousands came on the scene, with their flashings and crossings and sportings. With those and plenty of work I was like the " Miller of the Dee "— I cared for nobody. Kings or Presidents, Republics, limited monarchies, or autocracies mattered not. I would not have changed places with any of them. In their kingdoms there were strifes and intrigues, and those who wore crowns or wielded power lay down at night with uneasy heads. Not so in our little and pleasantly situated cottage. There was a kingdom very small, but in it all was happiness. There " none was for a Party, but all were for the State." " Kings might be blest (there is always an uncertainty about that), but we were glorious, O'er a' the ills o' life victorious."

But the shadows fall upon all earthly joys.

"The web of our life is of mingled yarn, good and evil together are." Our lot at Oceola was no exception. After a few months of happy and brisk time the depression set in, and I knew not where to turn for work. I tried everything. If ever a man hawked his labour about I did; but, like the labourers in the parable who stood in the market, I was bound to say "no man did hire me." I knew the feeling of the unemployed whose prospects were getting darker day by day. There was stress and strain outside, but inside the cottage there were cheer and encouragement. I could at all times apply to myself the lines of Burns in his "Cotter's Saturday Night," when speaking of his cotter returning home :—

"His clean hearth-stane, his thriftie wifie s
        smile,
His lisping infant prattling on his knee,
    Does a' his weary kiaugh an' care beguile,
An' makes him quite forget his labour an' his
        toil."

But the end of all things arrives, and it did not require a very powerful telescope to see the end of our material resources. So it was decided that I should leave the two dearest to me again, and see what a wider field of search might have in store for me. There were three of us took the road together—two Scotsmen (Tam Sheilds and Gibbie McLean) and myself. Our intention was to make for the eastern portion of Pennsylvania. If we took the railway all the way we should have to go down to Pittsburg, some twenty miles, and then on to Harrisburg by the "Central." Instead of doing that we resolved to walk across country about eight miles to Irwin Station, and save about fifty miles of the train journey, and, of course, the expense, which was with all of us a great consideration. And so we set off over the hill to Irwin.

We slung our bundles over our shoulders, and bid the wives good-bye in the belief that we should not see each other for some weeks, if not months. But as the old song has it :—

"There is many a dull and cloudy morning
    Turns out to be a sunshiny day."

And oftimes we find brightness where least we expect it, but the pessimism of our nature induces us to brood over and complain about the dark spots, and to forget the many cheery and gladdening surprises which meet us in life.

There was to us all a great difference between the start from Oceola in the morning and the finish of the day. Speaking for my own home, it was as near the poverty line as anyone ever was not to be over it; but no man ever went out from the midst of such circumstances with more encouraging words behind him and a more hope-giving picture to look on than I did when I left that morning. The inspiring words were from her who never in the whole course of a long acquaintance and married life said a single complaining word to increase the burden, but who lived continuously on the plane of optimism, and the picture I saw was the mother and baby standing on the verandah waving a cheery good-bye.

We were a trio. Our natures were diversified, and yet both at that time and for a year and a half afterwards we were close friends. My own nature was, as it is now, somewhat eccentric, varied in its shades and defying accurate description. Tam Sheilds was a jolly chap. He had a musical voice, and could sing a good song well. He had a very light heart, and could dance splendidly, and was ready at all times for it. Gibbie McLean was a philosopher, if there ever was one. He was of the Diogenes type. I have seen somewhere in print that true philosophy may be described as follows :—"Never fret for that you have not got, and make the best of that you have, for of what use is it to complain and be miserable about that which is out of your reach, and there can be no use complaining about that which is already yours." That was Gibbie's principle. As an example the following may be taken : For some time after this he and I worked together, and the contrast in our natures was marked and obvious. If we were not getting plenty of waggons (or tubs) I could be heard for my much speaking. Gibbie was the reverse. He might be seen, but was seldom heard. In those circumstances he would say to me, "Ah, weel, Jock, tak' it easy; if we haven't it in the pocket we have it in the bones." A very useful lesson.

As I have said, the first stage in our journey was cross country to Irwin Station, our intention being to take the cars eastward. Now, Irwin Station was the centre of a coalfield. The coals were sent away by rail, and as a consequence there was regular work, and wages were very good. It was a place to be desired if employment could be got. The boss was a small man physically, but in his own estimation he was the apex of humanity. If he had been as tall and stout as his temper was hot and his own estimation of himself was great, Goliath would have been a pigmy to him. In addition to his ideas of his own importance, he had another strong trait in his character. He either had a strong hatred for or fear of the miners who came from the Monongahela or Youghogheny rivers, where we were from. He would almost as soon have put a copperhead snake in his breast in its most poisonous season as have employed one of them. That, of course, stood in our way if he got to know where we hailed from, but we were determined not to let him know.

It was agreed that I should make the first attempt. As we passed his office door I turned in. He was sitting at his table writing. I, in as polite a manner as I could, asked him if he was setting any men on. Without ever looking up he hurled at me in his loudest and sharpest tones the fatal "No." Off I went and joined my companions in the tavern just below. When I reported progress it was a cold douche, but we agreed to wait a few minutes. Then Gibbie went to the office. The boss looked up when he asked for work and said, "Where are you from?" Being forewarned he was forearmed, and putting truth for a moment behind his back, and bringing into service the best and most useful lie he could call up, he said, "I have come all the way from Schulkill county" (about 300 miles—and he had only come eight). Then replied the squire—thinking, no doubt, that so direct and obvious a lie would not come out of the mouth of such a sedate Scotsman as he saw before him, "Yes, you can start any day you like." Then Gibbie traded a little on the good temper and said, "I have a cousin who is with me from the same county. Can you give him a start, too?" The reply was in the affirmative. He, being afraid to ruffle the old man's feelings by too much asking, did

not mention my case, but made his way down, and told us of his success. I immediately went to the office again, feeling confident he would not know me, as he had never looked at me when I spoke to him before. As I entered he raised his head, and with authority inquired what I wanted. I replied that I had come to seek work as a coal miner. Then came the all important and fatal question (if truthfully answered), "Where did you work last?" "In Schulkill, in the anthracite region." "Are you with that man, McLean, that was here just now? I think he got work for you." "No," I replied, "that was his cousin" (they were nothing related). "Yes," he said, "you can start up the Hollow." "It was a lie you told," some may say. I admit it, but those who condemn me must think of two things. First, the circumstances, which I confess should never condone a lie told for the purposes of deception, and bringing evil upon a person, which this was not. He got three good, regular workmen. Second, as a matter of ethics our action was on as high a plane as his was. Because of the evil repute the rivermen were held in, what right had he to brand them all as bad? He was fought with his own weapons. "Can any good thing come out of Galilee?" said the Pharisees, and they were wrong. Squire Carruthers held the same doctrine, and he found he was wrong. If it had been to-day, and any time during the last forty years, I should have answered differently, even to my boss, but the deviation from the strict line on that occasion may be excused in the words of Charles Dickens when speaking of Tom Pinch: "There are some falsehoods on which men mount as on bright wings towards heaven. There are some truths, cold, bitter, taunting truths, wherein your wordly scholars are very apt and punctual which bind men down to earth with leaden chains. Who would not rather have to fan him in his dying moments the lightest feather of a falsehood such as thine than all the quills that have been plucked from the sharp porcupine, reproachful truth since time began?"

CHAPTER XXIV.—BACK TO THE OLD COUNTRY.

We went and sought lodgings, and then made our way back to Oceola, where we arrived late at night after all were in bed. It was to them a pleasant awakening. We started at Irwin in a day or two, but for a few weeks we lodged with a man named Collins, going home on the Saturday afternoon and returning on Sunday evening for work on Monday. I found two Haswell families living there—one that of John Percy, who was at one time the leading singer in the Primitive Chapel there, and the other Mr and Mrs Noble, with whom we went to America. This made the locality somewhat home-like in its surroundings. We were not long in removing over next to them, and very pleasant and helpful neighbours they were, and a right happy time we spent in their company.

The work, locality, and people were all we could desire. There were a number of Durham people, and some from other parts of the old country. In fact, no matter in what part one might be some English dialect fell on your ears. We were there a year and a half, and when we arrived we were near a lee shore. My chancellor of exchequer managed to save as much in the time as brought us home and paid the man from whom we got our furniture when we set up again at Haswell. She would have done better if the Prime Minister of the Wilson Republic had been as careful as she was, but the turning point had not been reached, and she many a time had great reasons to find her careful soul grieved. On no other ground had she reason, I am glad to say, and the thought of that is to me (now I have lost her) some consolation in my loss.

When we had been at Irwin a year our daughter Elizabeth was born, and when Mrs Wilson and I were over in 1904 we went to Irwin to see the old place. It was greatly altered from what it was at the time of which I write, but still we saw the old house. We had not been long there before the home attraction seized hold of me, and I was strongly imbued with the desire to return home again. Why I had the feeling so strong I know not. I could not account for it then, neither can I now. Mrs

Wilson was quite content, and did her best to dissuade me. Her words and urgings were something like the following: " What do you want to leave for? We are very happy. Our home is very comfortable. You are getting plenty of money. We are saving, and would save more if you would listen to me. What

(From a photograph of Mr. and Mrs. Wilson and daughter taken at the period referred to in this column.)

better would we be situated if we were back to-day? You would not make any more money. The pit rows are not so pleasant as this, and you would not be any better, for you would get among your old companions."

That lecture was given to me repeatedly, but was of no effect. There was always the impression that I must get back again, and so she yielded, and we prepared for it. We might

5

have left sooner, but there was a strike of seven weeks' duration which interfered with our providing. There were other three men who were making ready to start with us. These were J. Luke and Owen Williams, who were coming back to Haswell with us, and a young Welshman named Phil Roberts. He started three days before the rest of us. The date of our departure from Irwin was the 16th of July, 1867, after a very happy residence there.

An incident illustrative of the sharpers of New York arose out of Phil's early leaving. After he left Philadelphia on his way to New York he made the acquaintance of a young man about his own age, who was got up in English garb, and who told a plausible story. He was a grocer, belonging to Liverpool, and had come over to see if he could better his fortune, although his relations were well off at home. Phil was a somewhat innocent, credulous young man, and being alone was pleased to join in companionship with this gentleman. who, after he learned the name of the ship Roberts was going in, said it was the one he was going with. That was fortunate, and as they had a few days in hand they decided to see some of the sights of New York. This they did, to Phil's cost.

When we arrived in New Jersey Phil and his friend were there to meet us, and went on to the ferry boat with us. I called him to one side and said, "Phil, who is that man, and where did you pick him up? I don't like his look. Be careful." He then related the circumstances of their meeting, and told me they had spent the night in what turned out to be a gambling saloon, and had lost £40 each. I then repeated my warning, but he gave no heed to it, and they went off together, and again lost the same amount each.

The next morning (which was the day of sailing) Phil told us of their bad luck. After breakfast his friend came, and he was in a terrible plight according to his story. He had lost all his money, and his passage was not paid. He had a splendid gold watch, which he would leave on deposit until Liverpool was reached with any gentleman who would lend him the money. He had got all out of Phil he could (for the rest of his money had been sent on through a bank), and he was trying us. He showed me the watch. It looked well, but I have learned a few maxims in life, one of which is "All that

glitters is not gold." So I said to him, "It is a pity to see a man stranded if one can help him, but I am no judge of gold or watches. I am prepared to do this: If you will go with me to a jeweller's, and he places a good value on your watch, I will assist you." It was agreed, and we all went in a body, my good guardian keeping close to me, and urging me to be careful. The tavern we were staying at was near the wharf, and consequently there were a few queer streets to pass through before Broadway was reached. There are in New York a number of "dives" or gambling places. They are ostensibly jewellers' shops, but they are dens where the unwary are robbed, if not worse. We came to one of these. The gentleman stopped, and with an air of innocence he said, "Here is a place; let us try this." In a moment I connected him with the concern, but was determined to see it through. "All right," I replied; "go ahead." He preceded us, and I therefore could not see his face, but I fixed my eyes on the man behind the counter. The signs of recognition were clear. "Well, gentlemen, what can I do for you?" "We want you to value this watch," said our friend. "That is a strange request, and I fear I may offend some person." "No fear of that," I assured him. "Well, I assure you in my opinion it is worth a hundred and five dollars." "Now," said the watch seller, "are you willing to advance the money?" "Let us go into the street, and we will talk the matter over," I said, for, having some idea of the character of the place, it was safest to lead him to believe he had hooked us until we were up the steps and safely into the street. When we got out, in eager tones he said, "Come on, and I will show you a shipping office where we can get a ticket." "Listen to me for a moment," I said. "That man in there is one of your gang, as the man at the bogus shipping office will be if we are foolish enough to go with you. You must understand you are not playing with Phil Roberts now. Come up into Broadway to a respectable jeweller's, and we will abide by his decision. If you won't come, good-day to ye." He would not, but turned down the street, swearing loudly. His oaths fell on heedless ears, and we saw him no more, as Christian says of Apollyon when he fled away defeated.

Our passage home was booked in the steamship Queen, one of the National Line. We were twelve days on the voyage, and it was all we could desire. For ten days the weather was beautiful, and the ship as steady as a house, not the slightest heaving or rocking motion—so steady that the elder of our girls (two and a half years) could run around the deck at all times, and without the slightest stumble. The boat was quite new (her first return trip, I believe), and yet she was fitted up in the same crowded and disgraceful manner for the steerage passengers. On the eleventh day we struck some nasty weather off the Irish coast, which remained with us until we reached the Mersey. We remained one night in Liverpool, and reached Sherburn Station at 6 p.m. A rather humorous incident finished our railway journey. The wife of Mr J. Luke, who was with us, was on the platform waiting for her husband. I was the first man to get out. In her eagerness she made a rush at me, and, throwing her arms around my neck, commenced to kiss me. There was no harm in that to me, but there was to her, and to put her right I cried out, "Hold on, my lass; you have got hold of the wrong man. There is the man you want."

After being back for a week or two I commenced to hew at Haswell, and the house allotted to us was in the Long Row, near the one we left when we started for America. Not only did I gravitate to the same pit and the same work, but to the same old habits. This continued for some time, but there was a change coming. Whatever points of difference men may have on what we Methodists call conversion, to me and in my case it was needful if I were to be of use to myself, my family, or my kind. As I was my life was not without purpose, but I fear what influence there might emanate from it was in the wrong direction, not merely in a negative but in a positive sense. Of what use is life if its influence is bad?

My conversion was sudden to my neighbours

when it came, but not to my wife, nor more so to myself. She could see from material reasons that there was a change. After being at home a few months the public-house in part lost its attraction and alcoholic liquors their pleasant taste. I was as fond of them as any man ought to be. The desire for gambling (and I have great pity for the man who feels it stronger than I did) was shaken off in a moment. I cannot say by an act of will alone (although I feel I have my share), but by some peculiar and accountable impulse, which came to me in unique and most unlikely circumstances for an impulse like that to arise. No one who saw Saul set out on his way to Damascus, "breathing out threatenings and slaughterings," would have thought that he would be stopped in the manner he was. Since that day, although differing in manner, many a man whom people looked upon as being hopeless has been checked, not by a great light, as in his case, but still suddenly. He has seen a sight they could not see, and heard a voice which was inaudible to them, but clear and convincing to his own soul, and truths which were sown by some good old man, in nervousness it may be, have forced themselves upon his attention. and the words of the Methodist hymn have been applicable to his case:

" In evil long I took delight,
  Unawed by shame or fear,
Till a new object struck my sight,
  And stopped my wild career."

If I could have dealt with this stage of my life without fuller mention of it I would, but I cannot see how. Wickedness is not a thing to boast of; it is to some more a matter of shame. I have never been much enamoured of converted convicts, or other names of the same kind, if they be used as advertisements for a sensational preacher to detail the sin and shame of his past life. What I say on this subject will be brief, and only mentioned because it is necessary.

CHAPTER XXV.—CONVERSION.

It is necessary that I should go back a little in this life's history. When we were leaving Irwin Station to come home there was living near to, at Larrimer's Station, a man (Mr T. Hepple) who had left Haswell before we did.

He asked me if I would bring home a family Bible for his father. I gladly accepted the commission. When I arrived I handed over the book, thinking that would be an end of the transaction. In that I am glad I was mistaken

It was, so far as I am concerned, one of the most profitable pieces of work I ever took in hand.

The name of the old gentleman was "Willie" Hepple, and he was a saintly, well-meaning man. The bringing and handing over the Bible made us acquainted, and he availed himself of every opportunity to call and see me. He had a twofold purpose in view: he loved to talk about his son, and he had a very great desire to give me good counsel and to induce me to lead a better life. By and by the conversation had effect, and I began to reason with myself and question whether I was not wasting my life, and whether it were not possible for me to make a better use of my time and powers.

As I have indicated, there were two things of which I was enamoured; very few more so. I mention these to show how they were shaken off. The gambling went first, and in this way I say no more than that it was with me an infatuation, and as a consequence it took a strong effort, but it was done. A party of us, some six or eight, were playing cards on the "duff heap" at Haswell. Four were playing, and the others betting. At a certain stage in the proceedings a curious wave of sensation came over me. I stood quiet. The cards were dealt out. The man with whom I had been betting looked up and said, "What is tha gannen te bet this time?" "Nothing," I replied. "And another thing I will tell you, I will never bet more as long as I live." He gave a loud laugh and said, "Thoo canna give ower betting; it is impossible." In reply I said, "You will see. Good-day." And I turned away and walked home, and I am glad that from that day until this moment I have never felt the slightest inclination to bet. I went into the house. It was a long time prior to my usual time to return, and Mrs Wilson looked at me with surprise, but made no remark. I sat down and commenced to play with the children, which was another cause for surprise on a Pay Saturday. To relieve her mind I said to her, "I have given up gambling, my lass." She came over to where I was sitting, and placing her arms around my neck she said, "I am glad, hinney, and I hope you will keep the decision." Her hope was well founded. She had reason to be glad, but she never had any cause to fear that I was going back.

There was yet the other force from which I had to break. It held me fast for some time longer, but the freedom from it came in the following manner. I have said that old Mr Hepple used to call as he was passing our house. On his way to Sunday-school one Sunday morning in the early part of February, 1868, he came with an old friend, Mr T. Dagg. They both came in. I had taken too much the night before, and was sitting holding my head, and trying to coax an appetite, but everything (presented to me by a wife too kind for me under those circumstances) was nauseous. In his cheery voice my old adviser cried out, "What's the matter this morning?" "Oh," she said, "he was drunk last night, and cannot take his breakfast." As if moved by inspiration the old man said (inconsequently, no doubt), "Be a Sunday-school teacher." My answer was readily given, "Yes, I will." Without another word they turned and went out as quickly as they could, and did not give me time to recall my word. After they had left I said, "Do you see what I have done? I have promised them to be a teacher in the Sunday-school, and I don't like to break my word. I never thought what I was saying at the time."

It was their monthly teachers' meeting, and when that part of the business was reached Mr Hepple proposed, and his friend, Mr Dagg, seconded, that I should be accepted as a teacher. There was a general surprise. "Which Wilson is it?" The answer was, "He lives in the Long Row." "What! Jack Wilson! Why, he never comes to chapel." "Never mind," said the confident old men. "Take his name, give him the month's trial, and we are sure he'll be here, now he has promised." All beside themselves doubted, and thought it was a mere matter of form, and would please the old men, but the end of the month would show how far wrong they were, for I was sure to go wrong before the time of probation was up.

It proved they were wrong, although there were reasons for their doubts. It would have been easy to form a syllogism having its major premise in my past life. The old men called on their way home, and told me what they had done and pledged in my name, and I assured them (after thinking carefully over the question) that I would keep my word, and be at school when the month was up. Whatever might be their fear when they came, they had none when they went away. At the end of the probation I was ready for them when they called. As we went up to the chapel, one on either side of me, they were as proud as if they had found a diamond of the first water, and with tears in their kind old eyes and joy in their hearts they presented me to the school. I was placed to one of the infant classes, which was most suitable for me—not on account of the letter of learning, but because I was commencing a second childhood, and it was necessary I should learn the elementary truths of the spiritual life. I never lost my great regard for the two Christians, for such they were in the truest sense of the term, and I have to-day the highest respect for their memory. It would be a blessing if there were more like them. Simple minded they were, "Christ's men," going about doing good. I have always felt thankful to them. To me and mine they were God-sent on that Sunday morning, and by their trust they called forth the best that was in me. If they had stopped to lecture me on the evils of drink and my bad conduct they might have created a different feeling. Instead of that, having got my word they accepted it in good faith, and threw themselves on my manhood, and their faith had its reward.

From that Sunday morning I gave up drink. I write this after forty years, and I have no regret for doing so, but I have for not doing it sooner. Oh, those precious years in the spring time of life, wasted and worse. For a man to be a negative force in life, like a field lying fallow, is bad, but to live a life whose influences are positive for evil is immeasureably worse. I was like many before me, and since, who would like to bring back the yesterdays of life, with their golden opportunities, but that being impossible I set myself towards the future and possible improvement.

From that day drink has had no attraction for me. It was as if I had never known its dreadful appetite. I felt that there was more required; I had only made a start, and must go further. I felt that to be a teacher in the Sunday-school in the proper sense I must be fitted for it. There was in me a craving and a desire for something which nothing I knew of could satisfy. I took to reading with avidity;

still the want was there. I was working "stone work," and had with me a young man who was a Primitive Methodist. Without informing him of my object I took every opportunity of turning our conversation to the work of their society and its procedure. He told me of the class meeting, and the happy hours. Finally I decided to go, and in March, 1869 (somewhere about the middle) I went to the class meeting under the leadership of Mr A. Cummings, in the Butcher's Row, Haswell Colliery. It was held in his own house, and the company was large. I took my seat, and when he came to where I was sitting and asked me to tell him how I was getting on (meaning in a spiritual sense) I was speechless. The others, in response to his query, had replied readily, but my eloquence was in my tears, which I am not ashamed to say flowed freely. At the sight good "Abey's" "halleujah" (and he could shout "hallelujah") was loud and startling. It was to me a happy cry. I must let the cynic and sneerer explain it, but he must not do it on the ground that I could be easily made to cry. That statement would be falsified by my life. I had seen too many of life's stern battles to cry, except it was at the sight of other people's distress. In this class meeting there was no distress. All was joy, and not the least joyous was myself, even while the tears were chasing each other down my cheeks. It could truly be said that as I left the class meeting I went on my way rejoicing.

I went home and told my partner where I had been and what I had done. Again the step I had taken found full appreciation with her It was more than a mere gladness at the change which it would bring into her married life economically. That was too selfish for her kind heart. No, she went further. In her opinion I should be safer if we walked together in this, as in other matters, and a very short time elapsed before we travelled the spiritual road side by side, and until she was taken. For near forty years we kept the same helpful co-partnership, and I have no doubt but that on yon side, as on this, we shall re-unite in the same companionship. To alter a verse from Burns:—

"When soon or late I reach that coast,
    O'er life's rough ocean driv'n,
I shall rejoice with her now lost,
    A family in Heav'n."

This change made, I began seriously to consider how I could be useful in life. And I felt how foolish I had been to waste the chances of youth, and to find myself unfit to take a proper part in the public affairs of the nation. I could read fairly well, and could string a few words together in a fashion without regard to grammar or logic, while my writing was of a very poor order (not much to boast of now).

" How soon had time, the subtle thief of youth,
Stolen on his wing my one-and-thirtieth year.
My hasting days fly on with full career,
But my late Spring no bud or blossom show'th."

That verse from Milton, with the alteration of the age, exactly fitted my case; but regrets were useless. In fact, there was neither time nor place for them. They were only useful as incitants to greater energy. I therefore took as much part as I possibly could in the various phases of social and national life which were prominent at the time, and I sketched out an educational programme, to which as far as possible I adhered, more or less, every day.

The main subjects were grammar, logic, history, shorthand, and the dictionary, which I read regularly, marking the words I was not conversant with for future reference. The dictionary I used was an etymological one, and to these when I was placed on the local preachers' list I added theology. These subjects I took for an hour a day in consecutive order. In respect to grammar, I had an old one (rather small) which I occasionally took to the mine with me, and if there were a few minutes to spare I availed myself of the opportunity to commit a portion of it to memory. Or when just going out to work I did the same thing, and more especially a rule in syntax, which I considered one of the (if not the) most important parts of grammar. In history I had an old copy of Rollins in six volumes, which was kept close to the table end, and was oft brought into use when at my meals. In addition to these, which I looked upon as studies, I read poetry— Homer, Shakespeare, Milton, Pollock, and Cowper.

CHAPTER XXVI.—HOW I BECAME A PREACHER.

I would not desire that anyone who does me the honour to read this record should think I became proficient in any of the subjects that occupied my attention in my efforts at self-education already mentioned. Far from that, because I had my work, laborious in the extreme, and the growing cares of a family pressing in upon me. In that part I was blessed with a helpmate. Then I had books to buy, but in that I was very fortunate. Just at the time when I joined the church a local preacher died, and his son and daughter decided to give up joint housekeeping. He had a very good library, which they asked me to buy. The price asked was so small that I asked them to take some of the books for themselves. They refused, and I found myself not only with a large number of books, but with a useful library.

The time I had to spare from education I gave to the social and political movements then before the public mind. These I will mention later. One useful result accrued from that action. I acquired some slight power of ex-

pression on various platforms, especially temperance and co-operation. In connection with our chapel there was an Improvement Society, which further assisted me in that direction, and the necessary research for information which lay at my hand in the library I bought added to my general knowledge of the Bible (especially its historical portions), and helped me to hold my own. I had then learnt and practised Lord Bacon's teaching, " Reading makes a full man, writing an exact man, and speaking a ready man."

In all this the leaders of our church had kept me in observation for some time, with a view to placing me on the " plan " of preachers; but they wanted to see whether I was established, and whether my abilities warranted my appointment. The deciding point came in the following manner. It was the custom at the Improvement Society to have a sermon from one of the members, and then a general discussion on the subject. There was an old bed-ridden local preacher, who at one time was held in good report in that work. It was a favourite resort for the younger members on the Sunday evening after the day's services were over. His name was T. Bones. For myself I used to spend as much time as I could at his bedside during the week, and really I sat at the old man's feet and learnt much useful religious information. He would give me a text and ask me to think it over, and then show him an outline of it when next we met. One Sunday evening we were gathered in his house, when the question of a preacher for the next meeting came up. It was found there was no one fixed. At this the old man from his bed said, "There is Wilson. He will preach for you, and I will give him the text." It was no use demurring. My objections fell on deaf ears; I must take the place. I would have refused absolutely, for I felt preaching was too great a subject for me. I was but a novice in these things. I had not the ability, and my time had only been short in the church; but I did not want to hurt my old friend by a refusal, and so I consented.

The text he gave me was the following:— "In whom we have redemption through his blood, the forgiveness of sins, according to the riches of his grace." Ephesians, 1st chap., 7th verse.

I made the most of my time in preparing for the ordeal, and received the congratulations of those assembled and a warm commendation from my old friend, who had inquired very anxiously about my endeavour. The matter did not end there, for my name was sent on by the leaders to the next Circuit Quarter Day with a request that it should appear on the plan and I should be allowed to accompany some other preacher. I chose my friend, Mr T. Taylor, of Haswell.

In order that I might be certain as to the date of this (to me at least) most important occurrence, I wrote to my old friend, the Rev. W. Gelly, at present (July, 1909), superintendent of the Thornley Circuit, to ask if he could supply me with the exact date. I give his letter below, and desire to thank him for this and other past kindnesses that I received from him when I first joined the Primitive Methodists. He will remember (as I gratefully do) that he was a colliery missionary at that time, and our natures being in harmony we had many happy times in our house, and how he gave me such good advice both in relation to religion and tem-

perance, and how many times he used Mrs Wilson's blacking brush to print his bills, one of which he invariably pasted on our window shutter. "Those were happy times, friend Gelly, and your words and presence were encouraging and very helpful." The letter is as under:—

"Thornley,
"January 14, 1909.
"Dear Wilson,—I find the following minute in the book:—

"September 11, 1869.—Minute 6: 'That Brothers Wilson, Frater, and Berriman come on to the plan in the form of exhorters.'

"March 12, 1870.—Minute 7: 'That Bros. Wilson, Frater, and Berriman be raised on the plan to preach a trial sermon.'

"June 11, 1870.—'That Bros. Wilson and Frater be raised on to the plan as approved preachers.'—Yours,

"W. GELLY."

Since then I have remained on the plan, and I have occupied the pulpit in many parts of the United Kingdom and America. Very few lay preachers have done more, except it be some revival preachers, a position I never attained to. It is not for me to say whether my preaching has been of a very high order. Some of my friends have thought so, for they have not been willing to allow me much leisure since the year 1874, when I first tried my hand at special services and lecturing. I am confident of this one thing, I have tried to do what good I could in that direction, and I have been cheered in a few instances where men have told me that they received the impressions which changed the current of their lives from words I had said. And I am cheered, too, by the idea of the Great Teacher that we need not do great things to merit the Divine commendation. The smallest service based on pure intention "In my name" receives its reward. I have made mistakes in the pulpit, for I have never taken any work upon myself of the speaking kind which has pressed so heavily upon me. I have no praise for the work of the man who goes to it with a careless indifference; neither have I any faith at all in the useful effect of his efforts. It is a serious but most important part of the moral teaching of the nation, and the greatest instrument that can be used to establish righteousness on the earth. It is not a place where men should parade their rhetoric, and show off their skill in debate. I have fallen far short of the standard of the human preacher that I set before my mind when I first attempted to preach. He was Mr J. Featonby, of Haswell, from whom I received many useful lessons, and at whose feet I was pleased to sit. I had read Cowper's description of the real preacher, and I decided that it was not fitting to play brilliant parts before the people's eyes when they were hungry for the bread of life, for there was needed:

A divine simplicity in him
Who handles things divine.   And all besides,
Though learned with labour, and though much admired
By curious eyes and judgments ill informed,
To me is odious.
He that negotiates between God and man,
As God's ambassador, the grand concerns
Of judgment and mercy, should beware
Of lightness in his speech. 'Tis pitiful
To court a grin when you should woo a soul,
To break a jest when pity would inspire
Pathetic exhortation, and to address
The skittish fancy with facetious tales
When sent with God's commission to the heart.

That was the idea by which I tried to shape my preaching. No one knows better than myself how far I have fallen short of it. That did not arise from any negligence or indifference in preparing for the work of the Sabbath, because in the first few years I gave all the time I could to it. If there is any weariness in the work now, it does not arise from the lack of desire, or because I am not as much convinced of the importance of the work as ever, but because of the gathering weight of years.   If I were inclined to give it up I feel behind me the imperative "I must" of the Saviour. If it were necessary for Him to say "I must work the works of Him that sent me," is it not as incumbent upon us on a lower level and in a smaller way? If not, what is our life for? I have been trying to carry out that idea and answer that question in a way in harmony with His life and His desire and example; and now, after forty years of the work and at 72 years of age, I feel the desire within me to let the remaining years be a prolonging of the good work in which I have been engaged, and which was the means of fitting me for other spheres of labour. For it has been an apt illustration of the exhortation, "Seek ye first the Kingdom of God and its righteousness, and all things else will be added thereto." With that outline and that resolve I will, so far as this memoir is concerned, leave my life's preaching with Him whose approval should be our first consideration, and who will overlook all defects if sincerity lies at the base of our efforts.

CHAPTER XXVII.—POLITICAL MOVEMENTS OF THE PERIOD.

When I returned from America the country was in an agitation. There were four aspects of it: a desire for an extended suffrage, and a greater share in the political life of the country by the working classes; greater opportunities for education; the rise and spread of the co-operative movement, and the growth of trades unionism. So far as the facilities for education and the spread of co-operation are concerned, a bare mention will suffice. My wife and I were both inclined to it. The first goods we required were bought from the Haswell Co-operative Society. It was then in its early stages, and was struggling for an existence. So weak was it that at the first quarterly meeting after I joined it there were just as many people in attendance as would form the committee, and I being one (although I had no money in its funds) was placed on that committee, and remained on it after I removed from the colliery. The society was in a very low state. I took upon myself a share of its debts contracted before my time, amounting to 13s 3d per member; and I entered into its struggles, and did all I could, with a few more determined men, to keep it going.   Just at that juncture the manager was dispensed with summarily. My good friend, Mr T. Edwards, was taken out of the mine and put in the position of manager, and I, being the youngest of the committee, was sent for a few weeks to help him. There never were two men more proficient in bungling than we were. If there had been a prize given for it we should have been an easy first. Neither of us knew how to put up a pound of sugar, but we used as much string as ever was used in a grocery with the same output. The parcel of groceries would sometimes break before we could give it to the customer. Then a joke was very handy. Something like the following :— " Tak a haud of it, hinney; thoo knaas whe's put it up." For a few weeks we went in at six and put up the parcels, and stayed in after six to the same end, with the shutters up lest anybody should see us. My colleague would have thrown up his place and gone back to the pit, but I urged him on, telling him perfection would come to him by practice; and it did, for he became one of the best managers and commercial travellers in the North of England, known everywhere, and as highly respected as he was widely known; a perfect gentleman, upright in conduct, courteous in manner, a man whom to know was an honour, a privilege, and an inspiration.

The other two matters, however, require a much longer notice, and the desire for reform comes first in order. Both political parties— the Liberal, under the leadership of Mr Gladstone, and the Tory, led by Mr Disraeli— recognised this as the foremost question of the day, although not actuated by the same feelings. The former was motived by principle, the latter by expediency. With one party the primary question was, "Is it right?" The other looked upon an extension of the franchise as a means of prolonging their term of office, or of attaining thereto. To properly understand the position it is necessary to go back a year or two. At the election in 1865 the Liberal party were returned, with Mr Gladstone as Prime Minister. On the 12th of March, 1866, he introduced a Reform Bill. It was not very heroic. The substance of the Government scheme may be explained in a sentence. The Bill proposed to reduce the county franchise from £50 to £14, and the borough franchise from £10 to £7. There was a savings bank franchise and a lodger franchise.

Still, with all its moderation, it met with great opposition, not merely from the Tory party, but from the disaffected Liberals. It was at this period, and in opposition to this measure, the cave of Adullam was formed, out of which issued those who attacked the Gladstonian policy, and were eventually the means of defeating Gladstone by a majority of five, and this in spite of the great efforts by the reformers, led by Mr Gladstone and Mr Bright. In order that our young men may have an idea of those efforts I insert a portion of the marvellous speech by which Mr Gladstone introduced the Bill :—

" We cannot look upon this large addition considerable as it may be, to the political power of the working classes of this country, as if it was an addition fraught with mischief and with danger. We cannot look, and we hope no man will look, upon it as some Trojan horse approaching the walls of the sacred city, and filled with armed men bent on ruin, plunder, and conflagration. I believe that those persons whom we ask you to enfranchise ought rather to be welcomed, as you would welcome recruits to your army or children to your family. We ask you to give within what you consider to be the just limits of prudence and circumspection; but, having once determined those limits, to give with an ungrudging hand. Do not, I beseech you, perform this act as if you were compounding with danger and misfortune. Give to those persons new interests in the Constitution, new interests which, by the beneficent processes of the law of nature and of Providence, shall beget in them new attachments; for the attachment of the people to the throne, the institutions, and the laws under which they live is, after all, more than gold and silver, or more than fleets and armies, at once the strength, the glory, and the safety of the land."

His speech at the finish of the debate had the following peroration :—" We stand or fall with it. If we do so fall, we or others in our places shall rise with it hereafter. I shall not attempt to measure with precision the forces that are against us in the coming issue. Perhaps the great division of to-night is not the last that must take place in the struggle. At some point of the contest you may possibly succeed. You may drive us from our seats. You may bury the Bill, but you cannot fight against the future. Time is on our side. The great social forces which move onwards in their might and majesty, and which the tumult of our debates does not for a moment impede or disturb—those great social forces are against you; they are marshalled on our side, and the banner which we now carry in this fight, though perhaps at some moment it may droop over our sinking heads, yet it soon again will float in the eye of heaven, and it will be borne by the firm hands of the united people of the three kingdoms, perhaps not to an easy, but to a certain and to a not far distant victory."

In spite of this powerful appeal the Bill was defeated, but his optimism was realised. At the election following the defeat the Tories were returned, and Disraeli was the leader. He lost no time in entering upon the same task, for on the 5th of February, 1867, he made a statement to the House, in which he sketched out the manner in which they as a party proposed to deal with the question. The subject which they opposed in 1866, and by the help of the Adullamites were able to defeat the Liberal party upon, had in the space of a few months become so imperative in its necessity that they were prepared to give it the chief place in their programme. Knowing the fate of their predecessors, he laid it down as their opinion " that Parliamentary reform should no longer be a question which ought to decide the fate of Ministers." The principles of the measure were :—A reduction of the occupation in boroughs to a £6 rating; in counties the qualification was £15 rating, any person having £50 in the funds or £30 in savings bank for a year; the payment of 20s in direct taxes. Then there was an educational qualification " conferred on all graduates or associates in Arts of any University of the United Kingdom; on any male person who had passed at any senior middle-class examination of any University of the United Kingdom; on any ordained priest or deacon of the Church of England, or minister of any other denomination; and on barristers, pleaders, attorneys, medical men, and certificated schoolmasters."

Mr Gladstone called a meeting of his followers, and placed before them ten amendments which he proposed to make in committee. All of these were carried, and so completely was the Bill changed that " Punch " of that day said the only original word left in it was the first one, the word " whereas." The change was so great that it drew from the late Marquis of Salisbury (then Lord Cranborne) a strong protest. I quote from G. E. Russell's Life of Gladstone :—

" In committee the Bill underwent such extensive alterations at the hands of the Liberals and Radicals that when it was read a third time Lord Cranborne expressed his astonishment at hearing the Bill described as a Conservative triumph. It was right that its real parentage should be established. The Bill had been modified at the dictation of Mr Gladstone, who demanded (1) the lodger franchise; (2) the abolition of the distinctions between compounders and non-compounders; (3) provision to prevent traffic in votes; (4) the omission of the taxing franchise; (5) omission of the dual vote; (6) enlargement of the distribution of seats; (7) the reduction of the county franchise; (8) omission of voting papers; (9 and 10) the omission of the education and saving bank franchises. All these had been conceded. If the adoption of the principle of Mr Bright could be described as a triumph, then indeed the Conservative party in the whole history of its previous career had won no triumph so signal as this. I desire to protest in the most earnest language I am capable of using against this political morality on which the manœuvres of this have been based. If you borrow your political ethics from the ethics of the political adventurer (Disraeli) you may depend upon it the whole of your representative institutions will crumble beneath your feet."

CHAPTER XXVIII.—DURHAM MINERS' ASSOCIATION.

We will leave the Reform agitation with the necessary outline previously given, as I shall have to deal with other two stages in the march to political equality, and turn to the formation of the Miners' Association as being the third of the questions upon which the public mind in Durham was being stirred. It may be that some of our young men may think (as they have been born in trades union times, and as there is little if any interference with those who believe in the need for associated effort and the right to unite), that this state of things has always existed. Let me assure them that they are in error. There was a time when trade unionism was feared, its initiation opposed by all means possible, and the man who sought to establish it was regarded as a messenger of evil, to be driven out of the locality.

At the risk of being thought a little egotistical, I will give my own experience as illustrative of that position. There were many more who were subjected to cruel treatment, differing from that imposed upon me in variety of application—still cruel nevertheless. If any of those who read this life's outline desire to trace the rise of our association and its progress up till now, they can do so at length by reference to " The History of the Durham Miners' Association."

As I related above, in 1863-4 attempts were made to establish a union. Those, however, were abortive. Still the spirit was not dead. There were a few scattered here and there in the county who felt the throbbings of manhood and the love of equality. They refused to bow the knee to Baal, and were only waiting to embrace every opportunity to assert the right. They were continually sowing the seeds of associated effort—secretly, it may be, and in danger of being driven from their friends; yet in the spirit of perseverance and hope they struggled on. Their opportunity came in 1869, when the strike took place at Monkwearmouth. Thence came the impetus, which has never died out, but which to-day has a firmer hold on the workmen of the county than ever it had. It was small and feeble, not only when it first began, but for a few years after; but the men who were in the van were of the right mettle. They were not dismayed by apparent failure. The opposition of the employer or the lethargy of the workmen (in whose cause they were labouring) did not stop them. We have reason to rejoice, for this generation is reaping where they sowed in tribulation and hardship, but they were cheered by the occasional formation of a lodge at some colliery by the resolve of a few men to give in their adhesion to the movement, and thus lessen the area of indifference.

Haswell was very indifferent, in spite of efforts both from without and within. The influence from without consisted of meetings addressed by Mr Crawford (who had been appointed agent) and others. From within everything was done to arouse the men. There was no colliery in the county where the opposition to the union was more fierce and subtle than at Haswell. Terror and strategy were alike used in full measure, and for a while it appeared as if those influences would succeed; but in the end the patient effort of those who were in opposition to the management bore fruit.

The following may be taken as a sample of the effort. Mysterious notes began to appear on the pulley frames and waggons and other conspicuous places. They were written on pieces of paper about three inches square. As near as memory will assure the following may be taken as one of them:—

" Men of Haswell, how long will you bear tyranny and oppression? How long will you submit to dictation as to the price of your labour? Have you not a right to a voice in fixing the conditions in which you work and the amount you should be paid? Look around you; see how men are uniting everywhere. Why do you hesitate? Arise and assert your manhood. Be not like dumb-driven cattle, but be heroes in the strife."

Those were the sentiments, with variation in phraseology. Strong efforts were made to find the writer. In one or two cases the piece was cut out of the waggon with the notice on and taken up to the colliery office, with a view to discovery by the writing. As I am giving a record of my life, I need not hesitate to say that the writing was mine; but the papers as to size were prepared and gummed by my wifely colleague, for she was a trade unionist of the first water. The papers being ready, on a dark night, or when I was in the foreshift, they were secretly placed where they could be seen.

In the end the efforts resulted in a small lodge being formed, but I am proud to say it was soon equal to any in numbers and strength. Our difficulties did not end with the formation. The most important to us was a meeting place, or at least a room to take the contributions. This could not be got. We tried every public-house in the village, but without avail. There was a great fear, and we were compelled to have recourse to a field, and many a time the payments have been made and the business done in it. As a last resort we turned to the Co-operative Store for the use of the long room. We were successful for a time, but in the end we were put out, and by the following means: A sudden determination took hold of the colliery official mind to institute means to educate the workmen by means of a reading-room and library. A public meeting was called, ostensibly for that purpose. The manager was in the chair. It was obvious that the business was cut and dried. The necessity for such a step (never seen until then) was affirmed. Then a librarian was wanted. There was no one so well qualified as John Wilson, and consequently he was moved, but, believing the whole thing was a dodge, he refused. Another was found, and then came the question of the place in which the library could be held. There was no place so well adapted as the store long room, and the meeting resolved to hire it.

A deputation, consisting of three of the leading officials on the colliery, were sent as a deputation to meet the store committee, with an agreement ready drawn up. I was on the committee, but all the others were men in positions on the colliery. The deputation attended. They produced the agreement. I remember one clause (the vital clause). As near as I can remember it ran as follows:—"The owners of the colliery would take the room at a yearly rental for a reading-room and library. The store committee could have the use of it on two nights per week for any purpose they chose, trade union purposes excepted." With regret I say it, in spite of the opposition myself and another could offer, the agreement was signed, and the union lodge was turned into the street; but fortunately one publican had got past the fear, and we found accommodation there.

During the year I came into collision with the under-manager. It was not serious in itself, but it afforded an illustration of the ideas that were held then, and indicated what was in store for me when the opportunity came. It arose as follows: There were occasions when the press of business was great at the Co-operative Store, and, being the youngest, I was invariably chosen to assist in the flour department. In those circumstances I made a practice of asking for leave to go for a month or six weeks, the time varying in harmony with the press of business. On one occasion I had got leave for a month, but I overran it by two weeks. At the end of the time Mr Crawford came to give an address, and I went to hear him. After the meeting was over the question of lodgings for him arose. No one was inclined to offer the

hospitality. We only had a two-roomed cottage, and I hesitated because of the accommodation. However, rather than see him beaten I asked him to go with me. He did, and left early in the morning. I went to the store at eight. The manager of the store had been out for a walk, and had seen the colliery manager. They were very friendly. When he came in at eight he said, "You have had Crawford staying at your house." "How do you know?" I inquired. "Oh, I have just seen the manager, and he has told me. Someone came from the meeting last night and told him." "They have been sharp about it," I said. "I have run over my time about two weeks, and it will be best to ask him for another extension." We agreed that would be the proper course to adopt, and it was acted on. When I got to the door he came out. I stated my object, but without regarding my request he in angry tones said, "What were you at Crawford's meeting for?" My reply was, "I go to any meeting I have a mind to go to." "He would do you no good." "I am confident he did me no harm," I replied. "You took him to lodge, too. Why did you do that?" In a voice as loud as his own I said, "I know not, neither do I care, who is the mean creature who has told you. The house I am in is paid for by my labour, and it is therefore mine while I am working on the colliery. I will take whom I like to lodge, and I will neither ask you for leave to do so, nor tell you why I do it."

He was a rough but kindly old man. The finish of our interview was the extension of time I needed, for I believed he was only shooting the bullets made by others who were harsher in their nature than him. The year rolled on, and the union was gaining strength, for on the 3rd of December, 1870, the first annual meeting was held, and the first council meeting on the 25th of March, 1871. This was within a week or so of the bindings of that year, which proved to be the last of the yearly engagements. As the year progressed I found myself growing more in favour with the people, who were eager to show their appreciation of my changed life in a substantial manner. There were three checkweighmen, and I was appointed assistant to them all. They were all well advanced in years, and as a consequence I was often called upon to take their place. In addition I was appointed secretary of the Co-operative Store.

These, with the preparation for public speaking in the pulpit, and on political questions, co-operation, temperance, and trade unionism, kept me busy. I soon found myself in demand on these platforms, and took a pleasure in preparing for and acquitting myself on them in the best manner I could.

The Binding of 1871.

A crisis came when the binding day arrived. The manager of the store had a friend who was an overman on the colliery, and he told Mr Edwards to inform me that I had not to be bound. His words were, "I don't like to see a good man insulted, and therefore you had better tell Mr Wilson he will be refused and insulted." That message was given me, but I was determined to test it. On the morning of the binding I was sitting on the grass near the office, waiting until the throng was over. Mr A. Cummings, back-overman, was one of the group. As I rose from the grass I said, "I will go and see what they intend to do, for I am given to understand I have to be refused." "Oh, that cannot be true, for what can there be against you?" said Mr Cummings. "Wait a moment; I will soon test it," and I went into the office. There were five officials and clerks sitting at the table, and each in turn made some insulting remark and reference to my being refused, as if he had some personal gratification arising from it. "All right, gentlemen," I said. "Where is the manager? I would like to see him." As I turned, I met him coming in, and I stopped him, saying "I would like a word with you. I have been told that you refuse to bind me. I am not going to ask you to withdraw it. My object is to get to know the reason why you have ordered it to be done." He gave as the reason that there had been certain times during the year when I had not worked regularly. In reply I said: "You know that I am assistant checkweighman to the three aged checkweighmen, whose age compels them to be off work. You know, too, that you have given me leave to go and assist at the store when they were short handed. You are aware, too, that you give 1s per score bonus to any man who earns two pounds ten per fortnight. Will you get your bills, and you will find, as you are well aware, that I am one of the men who has got your bonus with the exceptions I have men-

tioned." And, placing my hand on his arm, I said, "You know that is not the reason, and you and I should always speak the truth. Good-day," and I walked out.

My friends were waiting anxiously outside, and when I informed them they assured me of their great regret; but with faith in the future I expressed my firm belief that it would all work out for the best, for I had confidence in the Scripture, "That all things work together for good." I made my way home and told Mrs Wilson, and from her received the encouragement she was ever ready to give. "It will all come right, hinney. You have done your duty. We have been in dark places before, and a way has been opened. It will be the same now. You know in whom you have believed. These are the times to try our faith."

I was at the time secretary of the Co-operative Society. In a few days I was made so permanently. That is, to devote the whole of my time to the work. I secured a house right opposite the store, and set myself down to do all I could to spread the co-operative idea amongst the people. That, however, was not in keeping with the intention of those who had refused me leave to toil. It was not enough to deprive me of work. From their point of view the peace of the village could only be guaranteed by my removal and that sentence was pronounced.

It so happened that the members of the store committee were all men who were in official positions on the colliery. These men were threatened with the loss of their places if they did not give me orders to leave. That, of course, lay with the members in the quarterly meeting. I was in ignorance of the gathering storm, and was made cognisant of it in the following manner: I was deputed to attend, I think it was the first meeting to establish the Wholesale Co-operative Society. It was held in Chester-le-Street. I was walking to Durham, and on the road was joined by one of the committee (a deputy). He asked if I had heard the report of what was intended. I asked to what he referred. "We have all been informed we must leave unless we give you notice." My reply was, "You know where I am going to, and that I may not be able to get back before the committee finishes. If I do not, tell our colleagues that I resign my office, as I have no desire to hurt any of you." He did so, but I managed to get in just before the business was ended. The chairman, my old and esteemed friend, Mr Featonby, said, "Mr Clough has told us you are going to resign." "Yes," I replied, "that is so. I understand there is a threat hanging over you all if I remain, and therefore the only just course to my mind is the one taken. I am young, and can work." They objected, but when they were assured that my mind was made up they accepted, but added "Take your own time in seeking work. We will pay you as usual until you get suited."

It took me three weeks to get a start. At one or two places it struck me that my name was a disqualification, because, as soon as mentioned, the manager did not want any men. At the end of the time named I got a chance at Wheatley Hill, and commenced there about the 21st of May. The colliery was just opening out. The putters were putting on to the flatsheets except on the side in the direction of Thornley, in which part there had been an inundation, partly giving it a bad repute. It may be that, so far as my case was concerned, it was an illustration of the old proverb, "It is an ill wind which blows nobody good."

There was no union at Wheatley Hill, but we were not long before we were placed on the roll of lodges, and soon were considered one of the foremost in the county. My time was given to assisting in that establishing and strengthening, and fitting myself for Sunday's preaching and other cognate subjects. No effort was made to get beyond local duties, but to those I gave all the time and ability I could command. The energies of the young association were called into requisition with special reference to four subjects, one of those being general and the others peculiar to our own county. The general question was the Mines Regulation Act, 1872. The county gave it all the support it could, Mr Crawford being sent as a deputation to Lobby members in favour of the Bill. On the home side there were the formation of the Joint Committee (August, 1872); the abolition of the yearly bond; the fixing of 4 a.m. as the hour for the fore-shift hewers to go in, with the hours of boys to commence at 6 a.m., and repeated settlement of wages arising out of the great boom in trade, consequent upon the Franco-Prussian war.

The Election Riot at Hetton, 1874.

This reference to the formation of our union will suffice, and if there be any who desire a fuller knowledge they are referred to the History of the Miners' Association. There were two events in 1874 to which fuller reference may be made. In the spring of that year the first general election under the new Ballot Act took place. The county at that time was divided into North and South, each of them returning two members to Parliament. In the '74 election the candidates for the North were Isaac Lowthian Bell, C. M. Palmer, G. Elliott, and R. L. Pemberton. There were very riotous proceedings in many parts of the division, Durham city and Hetton-le-Hole being especially riotous. With a few other helpers in the Liberal cause I was asked to assist at Hetton. My work was to stand at the polling booth door and tick off the voters, and at various times address meetings. From early morning it was obvious that there was mischief meant, for about ten o'clock a band of men numbering about twenty, and all dressed up in red ribbons, were brought into the village. They were mainly belonging to Haswell, where there were a few men who for some years had sold themselves, and were used for political and other purposes where unmanly acts were required, their pay being threefold—a smile from the manager, a good place in the pit, and beer ad libitum. Give them those things and their bodies and such souls as beings like them have were at the service of their paymaster for any vile purpose. There was no depth in the slough of iniquity to which they would not willingly sink.

These persons were marched into Hetton, and, fully decorated, were paraded from one end of the open square, or Market Place, uttering insulting remarks and challenges to fight, and were repeatedly taken into the colliery inn and primed. This roused the young miners who were of the Liberal school. Mr C. M. Palmer came into the village, making his round of the polling stations, when the rowdy element came out of the inn and rushed up to the horses. That was the deciding point. The Liberals surrounded them, the consequence being the liberation of Mr Palmer and the stripping of the red

colours from the breasts of the mischief pro-
vokers. From that time onward the turbulence
increased in violence, which manifested itself
in various ways. Stones were thrown, one of
the policemen (of whom there was a large force)
being struck in the eye. Extra police were
brought in from Houghton. The police became
exasperated, and used their truncheons without
much regard to persons. I was on a waggon
speaking when two of them knocked a man
named R. Sugget down against the wheel of the
vehicle, and then, bleeding as he was, they
dragged him and two others to the lockup. A
resolve was made by the crowd to release the
prisoners. The road through the Market
Square had been laid with whin stones of a size
handy for throwing, and a number of men had
filled their pockets with them. A few of us
were doing our best to get order. At the highest point of the disturbance I stood on the
waggon speaking, when two young men got up
beside me and took up a position one on either
side. They drew out of their pockets small Tom
and Jerries and commenced to play. In surprise I turned and said " What is the meaning
of this?" One of them replied, " Tak nee notis,
hinny, she'll gan off directly. Just watch and
ye'll see some fun." He was right. The game
begun, or, as he put it, " She went off." The
police were returning from the lockup after
securing their prisoners, when they were met
by a shower of the whin stones. They were a
dangerous missile, having very sharp edges, and
when they struck would cut deep. The officers
were taken at a disadvantage, for the attack
was well concerted, and the stones were de-
livered with precision. The officers retreated,
and were chased to the lockup. Their stay was
short, for the crowd broke the windows, doors,
all the woodwork, and the furniture of the resident officer, the estimated damage being about
£100. The three prisoners were released. A
visit was then paid to the houses of some of the
leading Conservatives resident in the place, and
the colliery inn, where in every case considerable damage was done. As a consequence of
the disturbance twenty-three men were charged
before the Houghton magistrates, when fourteen of them were committed for trial, and the
rest bound over to keep the peace. At the
Assizes, held on Friday, July 10th, 1874, those

committed pleaded guilty, and were sentenced
to four months in each case.

It will not be considered unfitting if I give in
this connection a letter written the day after
the riot, and which by the kindness of the
Editor of the " Durham Chronicle " I have been
permitted to copy.

The Polling Day at Hetton.

" Dear sir,—The exciting scenes which
generally accompany elections are nearly over.
At some places the greatest order and decorum
have been maintained, at others, I am sorry to
say, damage has been done to body and property, and at the polling booth might has been
acknowledged right, or at least used as such.
An undue influence has been brought to bear
upon the more peaceable portion of the electors,
licence has become liberty, and terrorism has
become law. We are told the working classes
are to blame. That is not a fair statement of
the case, for while we must confess (and we are
sorry it is so) that men of our class were the
active movers in the case, yet we must look
higher for the source of a major part, if not all
of those sorrowful scenes. Yes, sir, to that
part of the community who while they are
separated from us by the term masters are, by
the ties of a common brotherhood closely related to us, and who for that alone ought to
have taught us by their moderation to be
moderate, but who, forgetting all affinity, would
to help the party they bowed down to, use some
of us as instruments to promote that party interest, and after their purpose is effected will
with a sneer say ' Are these fit for the franchise?
Do they know how to use it? They are more
fit for a lunatic asylum.' Sir, I speak from experience, and take the polling day at Hetton as
proof, and the scenes that transpired as data,
and I say without fear of contradiction that
those who ought to have known and taught
others better were the real cause of all those
riotous proceedings—of all that danger to life
and limb, of all that destruction to property,
and of all the sorrow caused to parents and
families through the consequences which will fall
upon those who were led in their infuriation to
break the law. If we look at the commencement of the day we have sufficient evidence to

convince us that a party of men known only by their want of principle and their inveterate love for strong drink, were sent forth from the inn primed with drink, and flaunting the red colours, bragging and boasting through the streets for the purpose of irritating those who had the manhood to take the side of right. This conduct was repeated, but repetition of the act brought its condign punishment. Not serious, it is true, but enough to show those men they were on the wrong side, which they manifested by doffing the red and trying to skulk away or assimilating with the popular party. But it will be asked how was it, then, that the storm did not subside? The reason was those who set the men out at first had called into operation a power they could not allay, and which in spite of the praiseworthy efforts of the Liberal committee continued to manifest itself in acts of mischief until half past three. The police, who had paraded the streets throughout the whole of the day, drew their truncheons and made a furious onslaught upon the crowd, that onslaught being indiscriminate in its character, not confined to the offenders (if there were any), but fell upon all, irrespective of age and sex. They are the sworn preservers of the peace, and the protectors of peace-loving citizens, and the least they could do would be to reason with the men, and from manhood alone, if not from national positions, they ought to have protected defenceless women, to have helped the weak and infirm, and to have been a shield to the quiet and inoffensive. This they did not do, but charged like a body of Nana Sahibs, venting their extravagant rage upon all who came in their way. That raised the passion of the men to the highest pitch, and rendered it impossible for order to be restored. I do not wish to say that the men were legally right in their conduct. I know they broke the law and are amenable to it, but this I do say, that while they are guilty by law and will have to suffer for their conduct, those who, pandering to the passions of the men, took advantage of their appetite for strong drink, are morally guilty, but they will remain guiltless before the law. You will agree with me when I say such proceedings ought to be stopped. If there are per-

sons so morally depraved that they will stoop to lead their fellow creatures into crime to further their ends, and will take advantage of any means, however low, to do so, they ought not to have access to those means. I have sufficient confidence in human nature generally, and in my own class particularly, to affirm that if all public-houses were closed on polling days those fearful scenes would never take place, and I hope the time will come when this anomaly will be banished from our midst. I mean giving drink to men to madden them and keeping a body of policemen to look after them and lock them up when the law in their madness is broken. I could lay down three modes of precedure which, if carried out, would produce order and harmony. Close all places where drink is sold on that day; take away the large body of police who are usually seen parading the streets on the polling day, and organise a committee of the most influential amongst the working men to look after the proceedings. I think, as at Hetton, so at other places, all the evils and disorder may be traced to those who falsely are called our superiors. This will clear us from the imputations, 'Not fit for the franchise;' for if the thief and receiver are alike culpable in the sight of the law which was manifested at the late execution at Gloucester, where the inducer and the perpetrator of the crime were both hung, so I think in this case the same rule should apply. If those who commit are not worthy of the franchise, then those who can so far forget themselves as to incite to committal are as much unworthy. But I hope that my fellow workmen will learn a lesson from this, and see in this corruption the last struggle in a dying cause, like the last flicker of a burnt out taper, and that they will resolve to show themselves men in the next struggle—men who are not only worthy of, but are determined to have this inequality removed from our midst, men who in future are not to be bought as slaves or tools with liquor, but who in sobriety can lay aside brute force as a useless weapon and fight with one more peaceable, but no less sure—the ballot box.

" JOHN WILSON.
" Wheatley Hill, February 10, 1874."

CHAPTER XXIX.—MINERS' POLITICAL REFORM ASSOCIATION.

In the year 1872 an association was formed with the object of assimilating the county to the borough household franchise. There was a difference which bore hardly upon the miners in the county, and excluded them from voting at a Parliamentary election. In the borough household suffrage was the qualification, while in the county it was a certain rental. By a system of compounding the rates the miners were kept below the line. This was felt to be (and was) a great grievance, and the outcome was the formation of the association named. In the spring of 1875 I was appointed the secretary, which position I held until 1885, when the assimilation took place, and I was returned to Parliament for the Houghton-le-Spring Division, and until its dissolution in 1894.

The primary work of the association was the extension of the suffrage, yet at the council meetings questions of a cognate character were discussed. If I state the agenda of business for one year it will give some idea of the aims of the association:—The necessity for returning working men to Parliament; the devotion of the land and properties left for charitable purposes to such ends, such charities to be placed in the hands of the School Boards where they were educational, and under the control of local Boards where left for other purposes; the land question in its varied aspects, including royalty rents; the disestablishing and disendowment of the Established Church; and the removal of the control of the sale of intoxicating liquor from the magistrates to the people or their representatives.

With the view to place on record the manner in which the committee did their work and the arguments they used, it will be well to give a portion of a circular they issued in 1878 on the defeat of Sir G. Trevelyan's Bill:—

" Fellow Workmen,

" We think this a very favourable opportunity to say a few words on the present position of our work, and its future as it presents itself to us. You are all aware that the Bill, upon which depends our hopes, has been by a majority of the members present in the House at the time of the debate thrown out. We say by a majority of the members, but not by a majority of the electors sending those members to Parliament. According to the statement of Sir C. Dilke (the able seconder of Mr Trevelyan's motion), the minority in last Sessions' voting had 132,000 more votes than the majority. This is a specimen of England's equal representation. A minority of 222, with 1,125,151 electors, are out-voted by 275 members, with 1,083,758 electors.

" The Bill has certainly been thrown out, but who can call it a defeat? It is an obstruction. But over all this right must prevail. Its onward march may for a time be retarded, but that only increases its force. The boys, as they throw their tiny dams across the water channels, may think they stay the progress of the water; but the fluid tending to its level, although opposed for a while, at last bears down all obstructions. So the tendency of mankind being to a political equality, it may be obstructed, but not ultimately. It will in the end, as it gathers strength in the repetition of agitation, thrust aside all artificial obstacles. As a class, all we ask for are the privileges held and retained by other classes. We say, ' remove your force-made restrictions. You brand us with class-failings. This is mere assertion. We have failings, we admit, but to us they are not peculiar.'

" There is no class in England peculiarly faultless. There are some, and these not thinly scattered in the homes of poverty, where the tendency of the battle for bread is to destroy the safeguards of honesty, who retain their integrity. But there are some (and the records of a daily press shows a dark abundance), although living with every want met and every desire realised, are far from the paths of virtue. We have yet to be told of the whereabouts of the class who, on the point of class purity, can cast the first stone. All we ask is a fair field of competition; and, if once within that field, we as a class are still willing to remain behind, then let the shame and loss be ours. We say we have not been defeated. The ranks of our friends are unbroken.

"More than that, when the muster roll of the House was called it was found that ranked on the side of right were the same good men and true, with the addition of the Leader of the Liberal party. His words alone are expressive of the position. They show that it is but a mere argument of numbers which is against us. We insert, for your consideration, his words: 'There is one answer which might be given to us, and which would, if it were given and if it could be maintained, be a conclusive answer. If the gentlemen opposite would say, and would maintain and prove, that the classes which are excluded now are different from those which have been admitted, or less qualified for the possession of the vote, that would be an intelligible ground why we should stop at the point to which they have led us. But that is precisely the argument we don't hear.'

"Brothers, you would do well to read not this extract from this single speech, but the whole of the speeches for and against the Bill. You will find that the only one who has been able to say anything against us is R. Lowe, the Adullamite of 1867. He has made himself the medium through which the Tory imputations might be cast upon us. He, in one part of his speech, has said that all we want as a class is to know the power of cohesion (in English, meaning union), and then this matter would be settled—and that he objected to the extension of the Franchise, because it will make one class (meaning us) the ruling class.

"We might give you a volume of statements like these, but these two will direct your attention to our future work. Is there a want of cohesion (union) in us? In both this and our labour department, has a bitter past and a bitter present not taught us this lesson which R. Lowe would bring before us? The able pen of our secretary, Mr Crawford, has forcibly enforced this point. In your lodge meetings, from the lips of your speakers, you have heard the same axiom. At your galas the eloquence of the trained representatives of Labour has enforced it upon you. The petty tyranny of those for whom you work in the battle for your bread, the Pharoahs who are aiming at making the county an Egypt, who are seeking to increase the tale of bricks, is now—even now teaching you a lesson in cohesion (union). And now we ask you to learn it from the strongest opponent you have against the Franchise, R. Lowe.

"The lesson is simply this: our strength lieth in a united effort; during the year we must seek to consolidate ourselves; we must gather ourselves closer together, and let the spirit that actuates Durham spread into other counties, until as if by a sudden impulse the whole body of England's labourers demand in a manner that will admit of no gainsay. Again, we would draw your attention to the expression that we, as a class, would dominate all others. This, Mr Lowe assumes, because the class now in power did so. You would say Mr Lowe is making bad use of his logic. He may reason suppositiously, and say that because a certain class has done so another may do; but there is certainly not sufficient in that to form a correct syllogism. His reasoning you can pass, but not the lesson in it. Mr Lowe, whose experience of the workings of the House clothes him with authority as a guide in this matter—and, we may safely say, one who would not say it unless there were grounds for it—says the party in power now mis-use their power. They did so in the struggle for the maintenance of the Corn Law monopoly, when, to make themselves rich, they would starve a whole nation; when, to get a good price for their grain, they would place a heavy import duty on foreign corn.

"Will you rest satisfied after this admission on Mr Lowe's part that the party in power will act wrongly, and make their interest the interest of the nation? Can you allow your interests to remain in the hands of this party? If you do, then with the spirit of apathy put on a spirit of wrong-bearing, for as long as ever the interest of the class in power and yours collide yours must subserve to theirs. The time has come when you must seriously ask yourselves, 'What are we in this nation?' The nation may 'drift into war,' you are compelled to drift helplessly with it. The fearful National Debt, which, incubus like, weights the wheels of industry, may be increased by a present vote of £6,000,000, and the prospect of an additional weight by a prospective war.

"And by whose vote is this to be done? The votes of a majority of 658 men. Who sent them there? Supposing this 658 to be an unanimous body, do they give expression to the will of the nation? What part have you had in sending them there? You might toil—the food to feed your families and the clothing to clothe them would be heavily taxed as the result of this war, but you are not fit to take part in the saying whether war shall be or not. This is a subject which affects the nation. You are part of the nation, therefore it affects you. There is a work before you. No slackness must you manifest. This state of things must have an end. You must tell this power mis-using class that you consider not only a mere price for your labour, but that there is in you a spirit which will not rest short of equal political rights."

CHAPTER XXX.—CORRESPONDENCE WITH MR. GLADSTONE.

It is not an unjustifiable claim that the Durham Miners' Franchise Association took a very (if not the most) prominent part in inducing Mr Gladstone to introduce the Bill for the extension of the suffrage to the householders in the counties. With a view to consecutiveness one or two instances may be given. In October, 1881, the committee sent a long letter to Mr Gladstone urging upon him the necessity of dealing with the subject at an early period. The importance of the subject will justify the length of the quotation from that letter. After recognising his great work in the direction of reform and thanking him in the name of the miners the committee proceeded as follows:—

"Sir,—We admire the impartial character of your measures. You have had a regard for the welfare of the lower classes without unduly interfering with the legitimate rights of others. You have raised statesmanship above the low level which some before, and even contemporary with you, have placed it upon. Some have thought that for the weal of the nation it was expedient that one class should be political and commercial martyrs—that a class should live in the land without a single tie to bind them to it; homeless except at the will of others; rightless except those doled out to them by others as a boon; and hopeless because every avenue of advancement was shut. You, however, have shown that true statesmanship is to place hope within the reach of all, to declare that land is not a luxury, but a trust, and to demonstrate that there is no class that can claim peculiar privileges above others. You have shown that the true basis of national greatness is not the elevation of one class by the debasement of others, but by an equality, and by making the national privileges a national heritage.

"Whatever may be in the minds and mouths of those who stand politically opposed to you, and who oft allow political difference to degenerate into private ill-will, we can assure you that there is now in the North, as we believe that there is in the entire Kingdom, among the working classes, a grateful remembrance of your disinterested endeavours to remove the injurious burdens from the people, to clear the commercial atmosphere of all protective tariffs, and to make party interests subserve national progress. These have been your guiding stars. Not honours such as men confer with a breath, and which are taken away with as much ease, but an inward consciousness of right doing, a recognition that your actions were in conformity to the will of that Being whose purpose it is that we should be here, and a realisation that He is best worshipped by a life spent in the elevation of men. Your political life has been concurrent with England's greatest political period. Ushered into senatorial life at an early age and when England had first awoke to the glaringly anomalous state of our electoral machinery, your name has been associated nobly with all the greatest measures that have made our history glorious. You sought not for vain popularity, but the establishment of true principles —you sought not to win a name, but to do noble deeds, to win bloodless but beneficent victories, and to make Britain a home for Britons— sympathising with all, and not a class, realising that not by war, but by peace with the nations of the earth is true national greatness attained. You have in your acts embodied the idea stated in one of your speeches, 'I do not care for military greatness and military renown. I care for the condition of the people among whom I live—crowns, coronets, mitres, military display, the pomp of war, wide colonies and a huge Empire, are in my view all trifles light as air and not worth considering, unless with them you can have a fair share of comforts, contentment, and happiness among the people.' And for this, sir, the people rightly praise you, truly honour you, and implicitly trust you.

"The political point to which we refer is the extension of the franchise. To the nation at large this is becoming a very important question. But a simple mention of the situation of our residences will inform you of the peculiar interest it has for us, and will be sufficient extenuation for our mentioning it to you at this time. The association of which we are the committee is composed of the working population who labour in and about the mines of the county of Durham. The geographical situation of our homes, not our inability to understand and decide upon the general questions of the day, is the bar to our introduction within the pale of the franchise. A number of us live in close contiguity to the boroughs of Shields, Gateshead, and Sunderland, and to the city of Durham. In some cases we are simply separated from the privileged ones by an imaginary line. We mingle with these people in the social affairs of life, and in that contact we observe no superiority in them sufficient to warrant this artificial distinction. This is not said in order that we may raise ourselves by debasing them, but to show that no conventional lines, which may serve very well for corporate and parochial purposes, can separate classes of men.

"In asking you to make this one of the measures of next session, we are sure that you do not share in those dark, unfounded forebodings that have filled the minds of others. Some have seen in the future the working classes misusing the freedom given them, and rolling like a mighty human avalanche, filled with the vilest passions, overturning and destroying the institutions of the nation. Cassandra-like, they have seen nothing but woe as a deadly consequence to the extension of political power to the people; but you, sir, have an opinion of the people more creditable to them, and more in keeping with your superior knowledge of the nation. You 'cannot consent,' as you said in 1866, 'to look upon the large addi-

tion to the political power of the working classes of this country as if it were an addition fraught with mischief and with a danger. We cannot look, and we hope no man will look upon it as some Trojan horse approaching the walls of the Sacred City, and filled with armed men bent upon ruin, plunder, and conflagration. I believe those persons whom we ask you to enfranchise ought rather to be welcomed as you would welcome recruits to your army, or children to your family.'

"The justice of our claim you have as fully admitted. With you the extension of the franchise is no yielding to what may be termed the brute force of the nation, but a recognition of right. Your love of justice leads you to abstain from inflicting injustice upon others, and hence you, as head of the Government, have pledged yourself and colleagues to bring in a measure which shall have for its object the removal of the political inequality manifested at our elections by the exclusion of those who contribute to the purposes of the nation, and therefore have a right to share in its powers. You, expressing these ideas, can realise our position and feelings in the late election in North Durham. We believe that the hope of the working classes lies in the Liberal party. Our desire is to keep that party in power, and to make it stronger for good; and yet we have been compelled to stand aside and see a candidate returned whose speeches in the main (consistent with his Parliamentary conduct) have been denunciatory of the Liberal, laudatory of the Conservative cause, and an avowal of his belief in and determination to support Protection."

To that letter Mr Gladstone, by his secretary, sent the following reply:—

"10, Downing Street, Whitehall, 4th October, 1881.

"Sir,—Mr Gladstone is much obliged to you for forwarding to him the letter which the committee of the Durham County Franchise Association have done him the honour to address to him. The receipt of it has afforded him much gratification, and he begs that the committee will accept his best thanks for the kind terms in which they refer to his past services. He ventures to think that the manner in which they have given expression to their feelings so far from requiring the apologies tended reflects credit upon their intelligence.

" As regards the request of the committee for an early extension of the franchise in the counties, I am directed by Mr Gladstone to assure them of his desire to further the fulfilment of their wishes. As, however, the time has not yet arrived for considering what measures her Majesty's Government should first choose for submission to Parliament, he is afraid that he can give no promise as to next session.

" I am, sir, your obedient servant,
" Mr J. Wilson.   E. W. HAMILTON."

The next step taken to secure the extension of the suffrage was to send a resolution to the Trades Union Congress, held in Nottingham, in September, 1883. The following is the text of it as moved by myself :—

" That without accepting an equalisation of the county with the borough franchise as a final solution of the great question of Parliamentary reform, this Congress is of opinion that the Government should lose no time in introducing this promised measure, and calls upon the organised trades of the country to assist by every means in their power to promote the popular movement in support of this long expected reform, and authorises the Parliamentary Committee to join with the Durham Franchise Association and other kindred associations in the proposed deputation to the Prime Minister."

On January 31st, 1884, the deputation met Mr Gladstone in the Foreign Office. The preliminary list of delegates contained 230 names, but the very large room was filled to excess. The deputation was introduced by Mr H. Broadhurst, M.P., secretary to the Trades Union Congress, and Mr T. Burt, M.P. There were three speakers, Mr J. Arch, as representing the agricultural labourer, Mr A. Wilkie, representing the shipwrights and other trades, and myself, representing the miners. The order of speaking was Wilson, Arch, Wilkie, the premier position being assigned as a compliment to the Franchise Association. As this is my life I am writing it will not be unduly egotistical if I quote a sentence or two from the remarks 1 made.

" Mr Wilson said that he had been chosen from the miners who formed part of the deputation to address the Prime Minister on behalf of the mining population. He was the secretary of an association which comprised about 60,000 men who were working in and about the mines of Durham. Till within a few years he had been a miner, and yet he had never had the opportunity of recording his vote, inasmuch as he had always lived outside the limits of a borough, and there were large numbers of men in the county of Durham who were in the same position. These men claimed through him that they should be received as component parts of the electoral body of the Kingdom. They had received large benefits at the hands of the Prime Minister and his party in short hours and educational facilities, but now their desire was to be put on an equality with the residents of the boroughs. They honoured Mr Gladstone because he trusted them, and had no fear that they would bring a deluge of destruction on the institutions of the country, and they were confident he would give them the justice they were seeking."

If space would permit it would have been a pleasure to insert the other speeches and the grand reply of Mr Gladstone. It will be sufficient to record that the promise given by Mr Gladstone was soon carried out. On February 29, 1884, he explained the principles of the Bill. The opposition to it was not direct, but because the complete scheme, including redistribution, had not been explained. The Bill, however, passed the Commons, and was sent to the Lords on June 26. There it suffered defeat by 205 votes to 146. An autumn session was called on October 23rd. As announced in the Queen's speech, it was " to give further consideration to the great subject of the representation of the people in Parliament." It passed the third reading on November 11th without a division, and the Franchise Bill was read a third time in the Lords on December 5th, but did not become law until June, 1885.

CHAPTER XXXI.—SECOND LETTER TO MR. GLADSTONE.

Before parting with the work of the Franchise Association it may be of some historical interest to place on record a letter which was written to Mr Gladstone on his retirement from public life. With the attainment of the household suffrage for the counties it was felt that the raison d etre for its existence was ended. The last notable thing it did was to address the letter referred to. It commenced in the following terms:—

" To the Right Hon. W. E. Gladstone, Esq., M.P.

" Honoured sir,

" You will have had many expressions of regret at your resignation, and many thanks for the life's work you have finished, but, as the committee of the Durham Miners' Political Association, we hope these we tender to you in this manner may not be considered in any way less heartfelt than any you have received personally or by letter. Our members (about 60,000) to which we might add the whole body of workmen in and about the mines of this county, prevent us from expressing our regrets and thanks in person, although we feel confident there is not a man who would not have liked the opportunity of doing so, and have felt himself cheered and elevated by contact and intercourse with yourself. We are prevented by many causes—such as locality and circumstances —but not by will or inclination—from that pleasure and honour; and we hope that this letter (which like all written expressions of thanks must at its best be cold), will be accepted by you as conveying the tenour, but not the warmth of our feelings. The voice, let alone the pen, would fail to express adequately the depth of our gratitude as the representatives of a class and the height of our pride as citizens; knowing that we belong to a nation which has been guided by the counsels, and is now blessed by the presence of the greatest living statesman.

" Our action springs from two causes. We recognise your services as a statesman. You have during a long life in the political arena, and in the occupation of many of the onerous offices of the State, kept before you the just and equitable relations between the various classes which compose this great nation. You have added to the dignity and glory of our widely extended Empire by declaring that might should at all times give place to right; and that true wisdom and nobility lie in the passing of impartial measures; and in yielding even to a weaker people, when they had right on their side. None of the Acts initiated by you were class-biased. They were promoted because you have realised that the basis of national greatness is not the elevation of one class by the depression or deprivation of another. There is no nation that can say that you have forced terms upon them because you were at the head of a powerful and well armed people. You have acted upon this plan—the deepest degradation consists of the misuse of power; and while you have done more than any of your contemporaries to consolidate the Empire, you have sought at all times and amongst all peoples to disassociate the name of Great Britain from that of tyrant and oppressor. Abroad you have brought respect for us as a people. At home you have shed light and hope upon the homes and in the hearts of thousands who, before your desires became embodied in Acts of Parliament were in mental darkness and labouring under cruel and hopeless conditions.

" We honour you as our great national ' guide, counsellor, and friend.' You began your political life at an early age, when the country was awaking to the glaringly anomalous state of the electorate. Your political life has been concurrent with England's greatest political progress; and your name actively associated with the great measures which have made our history glorious. You have not sought for honours conferred by monarchs, but the higher honour—that inward consciousness which results from right doing, and your most pleasing reward is the knowledge that a grateful people will hold you in kind and lasting remembrance.

" We put on record here (and we desire you to accept) our thanks for your efforts to benefit our class. We are miners; many of us commencing work at an early age; and we were reared in a rough school. Our lot in life has been brightened and made safer by the measures you and your successive Governments have enacted. As a section of the great body of labour we have special inducements to thank you; but we are sharers in the general benefits which you have conferred upon us as a class, and through us upon the nation."

The various measures referred to were then described in detail, and the letter concluded as follows:—

" We join our sorrow with all those who regret that you are compelled by physical infirmity to resign the position you are so well qualified to fill. There has never been as great a vacuum caused by the retirement of any Statesman prior to your day. In all your aims you have had your country's good before you, and now the nation's sorrow indicates its appreciation of your work. You have been misconstrued, because the selfish could not enter into the purity and generosity of your feelings. You have presented to the world a happy combination. The accomplished scholar—the able financier—the practical statesman—the master in debate—and the father and friend at home. These traits of character have brought you respect abroad, and honour in your own country. At an age when men seek for, and long after rest, we have seen you with mental energies unimpaired. You were not weary in well-doing, and up to the last you have been foremost in one of the severest political struggles, and shown that those who have to guide the affairs of a great nation, should be lovers of justice more than of party welfare; and should realise that every class is helpful to the true interest of the whole community.

" In conclusion, while we feel that our letter is long, we realise that we are prevented by want of space from fully expressing to you the depth of feeling in the minds of the workmen of this county in relation to yourself. We are but the medium (and an inadequate medium) of conveying to you their thanks. We hope that amongst the many cheering recollections of duty done which will give you strength and joy during the rest of your life, none will be brighter than these which come from this great mining centre, as we are sure there is no part of the nation where your memory will be held in more vivid and lasting remembrance. There is not a boy who has had the benefit of the Education Act, and whose opportunities for mental improvement have been enlarged by that Act and the Mines Regulation Act. There is not a man who was deprived of these privileges, because he commenced to work at an early age, but who rejoices in the prospect opened out for the youth of his class, and the greater care thrown around his own life while following his occupation. There is not a single lover of justice who has seen your efforts to finish your great work by extending justice to and meeting the aspirations of the Irish people but will join us in our regrets and our thanks, as set forth in this letter we have ventured to address to you."

The letter was signed by T. H. Cann, P. Franey, N. Hoy, S. Hill, J. Kavanagh, S. Armes, H. Jemison, S. Galbraith, and John Wilson, secretary.

In connection with the agitation for the extension of the suffrage it may be well to mention an incident in which Mr J. Chamberlain played a prominent part. He was at that time looked upon as the hope of the Radical and more advanced section of the Liberal party, as he was the Jack Cade of the Tories. In January, 1884, he was announced to address a meeting in the Percy Street Circus, Newcastle. The admiration for him was so strong amongst the Liberals and the miners of the North that it was arranged to present him with three illuminated addresses; one from the Newcastle Liberal Association, and one each from the Northumberland and Durham Miners' Associations. Mr Crawford, as secretary, was appointed to read ours. He feared an appearance on platforms, and about half an hour before the time he asked the Executive Committee to let me read it instead of him. His request was granted. The circus was packed. We were the last in the order of reading. When the chairman called on me Mr Chamberlain rose with me. After I had read the address, and while handing it to him, I said " I want you to take a good look at me." He in surprise stared through his monocle, and the audience were silent, wondering what was coming. " Do you see anything in me which would lead you to think I am not an Englishman?" Still the look of wonder, and still the silence. "Because," I said, " there are times in our history when I am not. I have never had a vote yet." Then the idea was caught. A roar of cheers broke out which nearly raised the roof. It supplied him with a text, and gave him inspiration for one of his great speeches.

CHAPTER XXXII.—MY CONNECTION WITH THE UNION.

My First General Office in the Union.

For the first few years of the Union I was content to only take office locally, and although pressed by my friends to allow myself to be nominated for the Executive Committee I always refused. It was not because my love for trade union was growing cold, or because I had not a firm belief in its principles or its utility as a means for the betterment of our condition as a class. My objection was based upon my desire to fit myself for preaching, and to take my place intelligently in the affairs of the day and the social and political movements. Proficiency in the former of these was my chief aim. With it there came proficiency for the others, and the co-operative, temperance, and political platforms found me very often as an occupant and a speaker, if not an orator.

At the annual Council of the Durham Miners in December, 1875, I was selected to take office. When our delegate returned home (his house being next to ours) he said, "You have been appointed on every committee there is in the Association." And I am proud to say that I have never been off them from that day until now. I should have taken my place on the Executive Committee in January, 1876, but for the following reason: I, with other two new men (W. Gordon and C. Simpson), were prevented. There was an arbitration proceeding, and it was deemed advisable to allow the old committee who had commenced the case to hold office until they finished it. This was a proper course, and the result was beneficial in the end. Had it been otherwise my official days might have been few, for the result of the arbitration case was the dismissal of the committee by the vote of the county. The hearing of the case was held in London. The committee as a whole decided to attend. For that attendance the treasurer refused to pay. The consequence was a collision between them, and when the matter came before the Council the treasurer was supported in his action by the lodges, and those of the Executive who had been in the case were dismissed. Until new men could be appointed

in their places the two men named and myself, with the agents, had charge of the business, the period covered being about three months.

I continued my work at Wheatley Hill when not engaged on one of the committees or arbitration cases until February, 1877, when the owners of the colliery were declared bankrupt. In their failure they not only failed to meet the creditors, but they withheld the wages of the workmen. The wages were paid in part, but there is £600 still owing, and to this day that dark "Pay Friday" is known as the first "Put Pay," the second one being in 1884.

A Poor Rate Case.

As a consequence of the bankruptcy, the withholding of the wages, and the stoppage of the colliery for some considerable time there was great poverty amongst the people. It would have been worse, but the newly formed Relief Fund (which had been arranged to meet cases of stoppages for depression of trade) met in part the necessities of the people. The payment was 8s per week. For myself, I had no need to have recourse to that fund. I was fully occupied in the affairs of the Association, but the general distress was very great. In the midst of it we were served with notices to pay poor rates. We protested. It was the first instance on record in the county where miners occupying houses on the same terms as ours had been called upon to pay poor rates. After some delay, myself and other seven were cited to appear before the Castle Eden magistrates. We determined not to employ a solicitor, and by resolution of our meeting I was requested to take upon myself the office of pleader.

The court day arrived, and we were placed in the dock, my position being at the end nearest the Bench. I asked if they would take my case as a test. My words were, "Will your worships take Wilson's case as a test?" From the chairman there came the inquiry, "Which is Wilson?" "That is him speaking to you." Consent was given, and the trial commenced. The Bench were told what they knew, that we were not lawyers, and we therefore claimed their indulgence for any mistake we might make, and we assured them that if we could put before them extenuating circumstances they would treat such with generosity. This prepared the way for a statement of the condition of the people from whom rates were claimed. First, they would remember there had been a bankruptcy, and a very large portion of the wages were still unpaid. That in itself was a very grievous matter, but the colliery had been standing ever since, and the opportunity to earn a maintenance for themselves and families was cut off. It might be said the men could get work elsewhere, but the state of the county precluded that possibility, for everywhere there was depression of trade, and large batches of men were being discharged, and had it not been for the provision the miners in the county had made by their Relief Fund, whereby 8s per week was paid per man, the people at Wheatley Hill, with many hundreds more, would have been on the rates instead of being called upon to pay them. Then a suggestion was made. The chairman was a near neighbour; it would be a good thing to adjourn the case for a fortnight, and then ask the chairman to visit the village, see the families, and report when the hearing was resumed. That course was adopted. A day was fixed for the visit, and a deputation appointed to meet him. He went into two houses. They belonged to widows. He was not long in. When the prisoners again appeared before the court his speech was short, but to the point. Its brevity was its greatest virtue. It was to the following effect: " I have been to Wheatley Hill, and have seen some of the homes, and I agree with the statement made that the people are not in a position to pay rates." Either the eloquence of the advocate or the pathos of the report were convincing, or a combination of both. Let that be as it may, the result was a dismissal of the case. This may be said, the general verdict was that the advocate should have been a lawyer. He had missed his vocation. That might be on the principle that to the victor belong the spoils of praise or profit.

Second Time Refused Work.

After standing for a considerable time the colliery re-started. Arrangements had to be made for it, and a deputation was sent to meet the manager, amongst whom was myself. He produced a list of names (about thirty in all) of men who were not to be employed. My name was in the list. Then arose the question of the money which was in the hands of the company as a result of the bankruptcy. When I, as spokesman, put the question, " How about our money which you are withholding if you refuse us work?" " Do you speak as a representative," he said, " or on personal grounds?" I replied, " Let us take the two aspects. Suppose I ask on personal grounds?" " I will pay your money out of my own pocket if you will leave the place." " As I have no intention of leaving the place, suppose I speak as a representative?" " In that case every man whom I am not going to employ will find his money at the office, and you can get yours as soon as you leave the house." The whole batch were engaged except myself. The Executive Committee moved to put me on the "sacrificed" fund. Being a member of the committee I objected to it. My reasons were: if I were put on the fund the rule would require I should seek work elsewhere, which I had no desire to do; because the manager had resolved to drive me from the place, and I was as determined he should not do so.

Then commenced a struggle between his desire and my determination, and in the end I conquered. Although there were four John Wilsons at Wheatley Hill at the time, the distinctive name " Wilson, of Wheatley Hill," attached solely to myself. My first need was a house. At that time the number of rented houses was small, and there was only one empty. It was a shop belonging to Mr R. Wilson, schoolmaster at Thornley. He at the time occupied a colliery house in Thornley. I knew it was a case where decision was essential if I had to win. From the deputation mentioned above I went straight to Mr Wilson, and put the whole facts before him. I pointed out that if I could not get the house there was no other, and I should be compelled to leave the locality. He was a lover of the right and hated tyranny, and without hesitation rented me the house from that day. I was none too quick in my action, for as soon as the manager got to his office at Thornley he sent for Mr Wilson (who told me of the proceedings afterwards) and said: " We are short of houses for our Thornley workmen. You are living in a large colliery house, which would be useful to us for a family. Can you not give it up and go and live in the one you have at Wheatley Hill? It would only be about a mile from your school." The reply was manly and direct: "No. I understand your motive. You do not want my house because of your need at Thornley, but because you want to drive John Wilson from the village; and

(From a photograph of Mr Wilson taken at the period referred to in this column.)

you are well aware that my house is the only one he can get, and if I act on your suggestion he will be shut out. Let me tell you as straight as I can that I have let my house to him, and whatever may be the consequences to myself I am not going back on the bargain." When he told me that, and how surprised the manager was when he found I had beat him, I thanked him more with my heart than I could with my tongue.

I lived in the colliery house for a month before I removed into the shop, paying Mr Wilson the rent as from the beginning. A month or so after I removed I went down to the office to

ask for my money. The manager asked why I had not gone sooner to get it. I replied, with just a shade of conceit in my words: "I was not in need of it, and I believed in your words that it would be here when I left the house. That I have done. You did not stipulate I should leave the locality. If you had I would have made you a present of the money, for I am not the man to be driven away. It would be quite sufficient recompense to know I had beat you, which you are bound to acknowledge I have done, by the manly help of Mr Wilson, the schoolmaster."

When I took the shop I was sure that with the many opportunities on committees and arbitrations and what we could make in the business from a monetary point of view we would be all right. I had confidence in my fellow trade unionists, and I was not disappointed. The business was largely stationery (which, being somewhat bookish, was in harmony with my inclinations), and a sort of general dealing. The whole of the concern in my absence was managed by Mrs Wilson and our two daughters. They were not old, but willingly they did what they could at any time and in all weathers, as the papers were to carry around the village. If ever man was blest in his family I have been, and am to the present, and in that somewhat trying time, as in others, they have been a help.

A Trades Union Missionary.

In 1878, at the Miners' National Conference held in Manchester, the question of organisation in the Midland districts was under consideration, and it was resolved to appoint two organisers. Three names were put forward. These were W. Brown, of North Staffordshire, Wildman, of Lancashire, and J. Wilson, of Durham. The first and second were selected. Wildman only remained for a few months, and I was chosen to succeed him. There were three districts to which special attention had to be given—North Stafford, Warwickshire, and Leicestershire. My commencement was in the first of these, in which Mr Brown was agent. I made my centre at Alsager, in which place Brown lived. We used to attend some colliery, and do a little visiting in the afternoon, and then have a meeting at night, returning about 10 or 11. It was in this manner I first made the acquaintance of Mr E. Edwards, who is at present the President of the Miners' Federation.

To a Primitive Methodist the commencement of my work was interesting. The first meetings were held on very historic ground, Harrisehead, where the first Primitive Methodist Chapel was built, and in it we held our initial gathering. It was announced by bill, and was preceded by a public tea, after which we had the assistance of the chapel choir. The second meeting was held on the Mecca of Primitive Methodism, Mow Cop, and in their school there. There was a peculiar fitness between Mr Brown's meetings and a religious place of worship while I was with him. His ordinary meetings were generally opened by singing a moral song, and prayer, and for that purpose he had a collection of those songs he had gathered and put into a small book, similar to those used by revival preachers, or like a collection of Sankey's hymns. The following lines form the first verse of one he sang often :—

"Who can judge a man by manners,
  Who can tell him by his dress?
Paupers may be fit for princes,
  Princes fit for something less;
But He who counts by souls, not dresses,
  Loves and prospers you and me,
And will sink all base distinctions,
  E'en as pebbles in the sea."

I was with Brown three weeks in all, and had a good (if a little varied) time. The meetings were not all in chapels, nor among altogether pleasant circumstances. Neither did the audience manifest the eagerness to attend, nor the tidy appearance so striking around Harrisehead or Mow Cop. Brown was as good a man as one could desire to be with. A splendid singer, an eloquent platform speaker, but somewhat of a practical joker. He knew the locality and the people, and on more than one occasion he used his knowledge. I remember we went to a place where, speaking from a trade union point of view, there were large numbers of unconverted, and only little if any enthusiasm. We reached an open space, in which stood a tree or two. There were a few men standing at the usual rendezvous, but none came near us. Brown quietly said to me, " Thee get the meeting started while I go and get a shave." Seeing a butcher's shop close by I went in and said to the man, " Will you lend me your cradle?"

The man stared at me, thinking I wanted the cradle in which his wife rocked the baby, and asked what I meant. " That is what I want," said I, pointing to the stand upon which he killed the sheep. " What are you going to do with it?" " I am going to hold a meeting out here, and I want it for a platform." With a smile he consented. I dragged it out and across the street, placing it under a tree. I mounted and shouted to the men who were standing around to come nearer, as I wanted to speak to them about a very important matter. Finally, after some persuasion I got around me a very fair crowd, and when Brown got through the ordeal of shaving I had been talking some half-hour. I said to him, " That is either the slowest barber in the world, or you have a very stubborn beard, for you have certainly been a very long time." The cream of the joke was he had been enjoying himself watching and listening to me through the barber's window.

I remained in North Stafford for three weeks, and then went to Warwickshire, making my headquarters at Bedworth. There was very little unionism in Warwick at the time, and I adopted a rather unique method of drawing attention to my visit. We had a good friend in the editor and proprietor of a Nuneaton paper, and with his connivance I carried on a correspondence with myself in the columns of his papers for some weeks before I went. It was after the following fashion: The first letter was signed by " A Workman," who inquired why I was coming to hold meetings. Was there any need for such visit? Were the miners not well treated? If so, why have this agitator in their midst? I then wrote a reply in my own name. I thanked him for his inquiry, and for giving me the opportunity of stating the object of my visit. I agreed with him that if the conditions of labour were good, if the workmen were treated as men ought to be, and if they were paid a just wage for their labour there was no necessity for either myself or any person to hold meetings or attempt to form a union; but from the reports I had heard there was much room for improvement. However, these things would be well known, and when I held a meeting or two it would be competent for either the writer or any other person to ask questions, or make a statement to elicit facts, or confirm his view of the situation. The correspondence went on for a few weeks, the result being to arouse the attention of the people and prepare the way for the missionary and the strengthening of the association.

Leaving Bedworth I went into Leicestershire, and got lodgings at Coalville. There was no union at all, or very little. I was a complete stranger to the locality, but I had the help of our good friend the Nuneaton editor and Mr I. College, the miners' agent in Warwickshire. I was in the district three weeks. It was stiff uphill work, but in the end successful. On one occasion I had to obey the injunction, "When they persecute you in one city, flee ye to another." In one place there was not a single person turned up for the meeting. There were a number of men outside, and I went to them, and with all the zeal of a religious missionary I urged upon them to come to the meeting, and spoke to them about the benefits of trade unions, and even took a hold of their jacket collar. But it was unavailing. Their fear or indifference, or both combined, were too great. Not one came to the meeting, and I rested satisfied with the desultory talk in the street.

I fared worse in another village. Its name is Hugglescote. I was passing up the street when a band of women, who had been informed of my coming, made an attack upon me, and threw various kinds of missiles at me. It is a blessing that in the order of Providence a woman cannot throw straight. The risk of being hit arises from running about. If, however, they could not throw a stone accurately, they could say queer things. They were not choice, but they were emphatic. The sum of their epithets was that they did not want any agitator there stirring up the minds of their men folk and inducing them to strike. However, I cleared out

quickly, and did not stop to shake off the dust of my feet; but I had an opportunity of telling them, or some of them, about it. A few years after the Primitive Methodists there invited me to preach and lecture, in the course of which I playfully reminded them of their former treatment, and told them that, like another personage, I was not so black as I was painted. In good nature they accepted the playful reminder.

In the same neighbourhood (Ellistown, to be precise), I had a rather unique experience. I had a meeting arranged for the pay night. It was in a long room in connection with a public-house, yet detached from the main building. There was a very good attendance. I counted sixty men, who were black on their way from work. My chairman was one of them. He and his mate were drinking their pay night beer, and on the tables were a number of quarts and pint jugs, which were frequently replenished during my speech. The talk in the taproom could be heard, and the usual songster was adding to the noise. I could hear distinctly the song he was shouting out—it would not be correct to say singing. I have forgotten all of it except the last line of the chorus, which was, "I will be a Member of Parliament when the pigs begin to fly."

The meeting was a success. There was no need to adopt the words of the prophet, "Who hath believed our report?" In a very few minutes 63 names were taken, and before we left a lodge was formed and the officers chosen. The result of my three weeks' work was the calling of a delegate meeting, with 23 delegates in attendance. It was held in Coalville. After arranging for district officials I left for home, where I arrived near to Sunday morning, and so finished my round of missionary labours.

CHAPTER XXXIII.—THE STRIKE OF 1879.

There are points in the history of nations, communities, and individuals which stand out as milestones or prominent landmarks, and this year is so to myself and our organisation. It is a point to which the miners of Durham can look back without regret, for if ever a body of workmen had right on their side, and acted in a reasonable manner with a view to settling the dispute, they did. I have no desire to enter into a detailed description of the strike, or the

causes which led up to it. These are given in the "History of the Miners' Association," and can be read there by anyone who desires to form a closer acquaintance with our rise and progress. I feel (at the lapse of thirty years) no small pride that I had some share in the negotiations which led up to it; that I bore my share of the abuse that met the Executive Committee in all parts of the county; and that I was privileged to see, with the others who were abused, the confidence of the membership placed in us without the slightest reservation at the finish. So it always is. Clouds and darkness may surround those who do right and fear not, and evil-speaking may be their only recompense at the time, but sooner or later they will find themselves justified in their action. "Truth struck to earth to-day will rise again to-morrow." If it were otherwise there would be gross and great injustice in the universe. "Be just and fear not" is the safest course, and so it proved in 1879.

There was some ground for the feeling of irritation amongst the rank and file of the members of the unions in the county, but there was none for the treatment meted out to the committee by men who use these times of danger to rise to position. The employers had made a demand for a large reduction. This had come as a result of a long period of trade depression. The workmen offered arbitration, which was refused bluntly by the owners. The alternatives were absolute surrender or a lock-out. The Executive Committee, with a full knowledge of the situation—the depressed state of trade, the number of pits that were stopped, with the consequent large number of men out of employment —urged their members to make two alternative offers as a means of settling the dispute and keeping the pits at work. That was the opportune moment for a few men who would wreck all if they could ride on the wreckage. These have ever been an evil, and it will be a blessing when the breed is extinct, for they have been at all time a clog in the wheels of progress.

I take the liberty of quoting a few words from the history referred to which are descriptive of the feeling created:—"Immediately these offers were made known there arose a fierce agitation in the county, and on every hand mass meetings were held protesting against the terms. As is the case in matters of this kind, orators, vehement if not polished, sprang up from every quarter, whose stock-in-trade consisted of foul epithets, which they hurled at the committee and Federation Board. So desperate was the situation that certain of the committee were in fear, and came into public view as little as possible. A personal incident may be excused here. A mass meeting was held on the Sands in Durham. The writer, as chairman of the Wheatley Hill Lodge, marched to it. The first words heard were, 'There's one of the ——.

Let us put him in the river.' The crowd surged and rocked. What the consequence might have been it is hard to tell, but just when the feeling was highest and he was most in danger a man was knocked over on to a drum which stood end up. It went off with a loud report, and the cry was, 'They are firing guns.' In a moment a panic seized the people, and, as is recorded of the battle of Stanhope over the moor hen, 'those who ran fastest got soonest out of town.' There was a low wall (low on one side, high on the other), over which hundreds fell head foremost, and a good, kind lady, who had come from Wheatley Hill to take care of her husband (the man whose presence was the cause of all the hubbub), was carried away by the crowd, and was so rushed along by the panic-stricken stream of humanity that she was, with twenty others, landed in a stable, the door of which stood invitingly open like a city of refuge. The only inmate of the stable to dispute their entry was a very large, fat pig. The result was the meeting was disturbed, and the culprit, one of the malodorous committee, was left unhurt— Providence in the shape of a drum being the means of saving him."

If that special intervention had not taken place this simple annal of a wandering and strenuous life might never have been written, for that might have ended it. As it was, my wife was able to take me back with her unharmed. It did not end the agitation. Apart from the ludicrous incident of the bursting drum, the feeling manifested towards the committee there was only on a par with that found everywhere throughout the county. If one of those at the head of affairs appeared in the street and passed a group of men, insult was rampant.—slander, being cowardly, feels safe in a crowd. Still the committee were not to be driven from their task. They regretted the action of the employers in refusing open arbitration—and who, knowing the condition of the Union, were determined to force their full demand—and they were sorry for the opposition of their members, but they knew they were moved by sheer desperation and played upon by designing men, who cared more for popularity, even if it were fleeting, than the welfare of the Union, and who would not hesitate to bring ruin if perchance small gain would come to them from it.

At the time of writing this portion of my life's

story I received a letter from a friend, which by a curious coincidence fits in to it, and while it gives prominence to the circumstances of that period, it gives emphasis to the personal aspect. His letter was to thank me for a photo which had been sent to their church. Along with it they had received others, and the writer said: "Each picture opens out sweet memories. Yours takes me back to 1879, and to a miners' meeting on Pittington Hill. That was the first of my seeing and liking you for the courage you there displayed, whilst the meeting seemed to be against you, and when that man, who went by the name of 'General Jackson,' said all he could about the agents and committee. He went with the stream, but you went against it. I have been much interested in your work and life ever since. Your photo will recall many other memories, and I trust it will be an inspiration to our young people to every good work."

Whether any inspiration be derived from the photo by any of our young people or not, I can assure my friend his letter has inspired and buoyed me up. It is pleasing to think that the doing of one's duty in unpopular circumstances has left impressions which thirty years of subsequent life has not diminished, and I am hopeful that there are many more who have received and who cherish like impressions.

Death of Alexander Macdonald.

On October 31st, 1881, the miners of the United Kingdom suffered a serious loss in the death of Alexander Macdonald, M.P. He died at Wellhall, near Hamilton, Scotland. The following in reference to his death is taken from the "History of the Durham Miners' Association":—"He was the ablest leader the miners of Scotland ever had, and one of the first Labour representatives in the House of Commons, being elected with our good friend, Mr Burt, in 1874. He was often called the 'Miner's Friend.' Although not a Durham man, he was so intimately and closely connected with our early history and progress up to his death that there would be a great hiatus if no mention were made of him. The first council meeting after his death passed a resolution expressing deep sorrow at his death, and regarding it as an irreparable loss and national calamity to the mining population of England, Scotland, and

Wales. His self-sacrificing efforts for a number of years on their behalf cannot be fully known, but his memory will ever be held dear by a grateful people. A movement was immediately started to commemorate his work, the result of which was the statue which is in front of the hall in Durham. As Mr Crawford said, 'It is the last tribute of respect we can pay to one who, through good and evil report, kept steadily in view the one object of his life, viz., to reduce the misery and alleviate the sorrows of the mining population while following their hazardous occupation.'

"He was born in 1821, and began work at eight years of age. At that time the condition of the mining population was dreadful. There was no law to protect the miner, and there was little regard for health or life. The hours were fearfully long. Women worked in the mines under the most debasing conditions. In the midst of this he set himself the uphill task of self-education—uphill now, but how much more so then. In early life he left the mines and became a teacher. The knowledge he acquired he determined to devote to bettering the condition of the miners. Between 1850 and 1855 he was assiduous in procuring amended Mines Acts, and those of 1855 and 1860 were mainly due to his efforts. From that time until his death he was earnestly working to ameliorate the conditions of the life he knew so well, and at his death was busily engaged in further amending the Mines Act. He was a sample of men who have been endowed with splendid powers, and who might have made large fortunes if they had followed commercial pursuits as eagerly as they followed after reform and better temporal conditions for others; but who, when there was nothing to gain, counted it their highest good if they could in any way assist their class on to a higher plane and into a brighter life. They choose rather to suffer with the people in their affliction, and help those who needed it, than to make for themselves monetary positions. When he died a truly great man was taken from the ranks of reformers, and to the honour of Englishmen be it said, they honoured him in death as they appreciated him in life, as witness the splendid statue which was unveiled on November 17th, 1883, by his worthy and highly respected colleague in Union and Labour representation in Parliament, Mr T. Burt."

CHAPTER XXXIV.—ELECTED A MEMBER OF PARLIAMENT.

Treasurer of the Association.

I have no hesitation in using the definite article when speaking of the Durham Miners' Association. To me it is the organisation par excellence, and it was to me a proud day when at the council meeting held on the 6th of May, 1882, I was appointed its general treasurer. My predecessor in office was Mr N. Wilkinson, a man who was very influential in founding and building up the association. My colleagues were:—J. Forman, president: W. Crawford, corresponding secretary; and W. H. Patterson, financial secretary. It would be a great pleasure to speak of the ability of these worthy men, but that has already been done in the History of the Durham Miners, and I must deny myself the pleasure of repeating it here. This much I will say: no trades union or institution of any kind ever had three better men for the positions they held. They were whole-hearted in their endeavour to secure the greatest good for their people. Their hatred of wrong and tyranny was only equalled by their desire to secure the right. To fall into the colleagueship of these men was congenial to my inclination, and helpful in my new sphere, which I occupied until the death of Mr Crawford, in 1890, when I became financial secretary; and at the death of Mr Patterson, in 1895, I was appointed general secretary, which post it is my pride now to fill.

The only special notice I desire to make of my work as treasurer refers to an event which happened in 1884. The second "Put Pay" took place at the Thornley, Ludworth, and Wheatley Hill Collieries in May of that year. The company went into bankruptcy, and no intimation was given to the workmen until they went for their wages on the Pay Friday, when they were calmly told there were none. As may be supposed, great consternation seized the people, and at once word was sent to the agents in Durham. In response to their urgent request I went out, and found a terrible uproar. The air was full of threatenings and slaughterings. The manager, who was no more to blame than any other workman or servant of the company, was in a state of fear. His sympathies were entirely with the defrauded workmen and their families, and in order to procure part of the wages he sold the branch engine to the N.E.R. One of that company's engines was sent to take it away, but the angry crowd refused to let it go, and as a means of preventing its departure they tore the railway up, and by that process kept both engines impounded. It was felt that the action of the manager was deserving the approval of the people, and the proceeds of the sale should have been accepted by them as part payment. They were, however, obstinate, and it was deemed advisable to adjourn the matter until the next day, which should have been Pay Saturday. A large mass meeting was held in a field close to the village. The following description is taken from the "History" mentioned above:—"The day was fine, there was a large crowd, and the treasurer was in his most eloquent mood, when a very laughable incident occurred. There was a pigeon flying match from Newcastle. It was about the time when the birds were expected. Some of the men were thinking more of the match than of their pay, and were watching the heavens more closely than they were listening to the speaker. Their all absorbing topic was, when would the birds arrive? Just when the orator was in the midst of one of his best sentences and highest flights of oratory a voice was heard (which was the descent from the sublime to the ridiculous), 'Haud thee hand till the slate cock comes in.' In a moment speaker and occasion were lost, and the gathering generally watched the bird, the hero of the hour, as like an arrow shot from some great bow he came right on to his 'ducket.' Then in deliberate manner the same voice was heard exclaiming, 'There, he's landed. Thoo can gan on wi' the speech.' But rhetoric and reason were both ineffective after the 'slate cock' had landed."

The Miners' Executive, however, were not slow in the proceedings, and put in a workman at each colliery as bailiff to prevent anything being taken away. The law moves slowly in these matters, and it took a year and an outlay of £1,000 to secure the wages of the workmen of the three collieries. The total amount was £4,724, which sum, with the pay sheets, was handed over to me as treasurer. There were union and non-union men, and the payment took place at Thornley, and took three days to do it. Many of the latter wanted their wages without paying anything towards the cost of procuring them. The committee resolved to make them pay some share of the expense, and adopted the following method:—When a non-unionist came up to the table he was told that he must sign a receipt authorising me to keep 7s off his money. Some in picturesque, but not in the least proper, language refused. Then they were told we were willing to give the union men theirs because already their money had been spent to procure the wages. We were determined to make all who received share in the outlay. That was just. They could refuse to pay, as they had refused to pay their contributions to the union, but if they did their wages would be returned to the liquidator, and they might fight it out with him, when it would cost them more. That statement invariably brought them to a reasonable state of mind. There were a strong force of policemen under Superintendent Scott, who kept their actions, if not their language, in order. The money eventually was paid out as per the pay sheets. A man made a claim five years after the bankruptcy, and in June, 1909, an old woman from the Sunderland Workhouse sent notes for £3. The man's marrow had drawn his.

Elected Member of Parliament.

I have described my connection with the Franchise Association, and the part it took in securing the extension of Household Suffrage to the counties. The fight for it was bitter in both the Commons and Lords, but the consequence of it was a political education of the miners in Durham, as was seen by their readiness to take hold of the opportunity in a manner not equalled in any county. The measure was no sooner carried than action was taken, for i January, 1885, a political council was held of all the sections comprising the Federation Board. At that council it was decided to select three candidates to run in conjunction with the Liberals. They were to be what eventually became known as the Liberal-Labour. The choice fell on Mr Crawford, Mr L. Trotter, and myself, and we were allotted to Mid-Durham, Bishop Auckland, and Houghton. In the case of Mr Trotter there were two matters which resulted in his withdrawal. These were the opposition which arose on the part of electors, and the other was a financial difficulty. The electors objected to a candidate being sent to the Division in whose selection they had neither part nor lot, and the members of the Mechanics' Association refused to be responsible for the returning officers' fees in Mr Trotter's case. He was therefore withdrawn, and Mr Paulton was adopted as the Liberal candidate.

In respect to Mr Crawford and myself no such complication arose. We were both elected by large majorities. The contests were not easy ones. In the neighbouring county there had been Labour representation for eleven years, but in Durham it was an innovation, and must be opposed. The opposition was not at all times choice in its methods, and was seen in its grossest form in Houghton. Things were said which, if they were half true, would have been sufficient to exclude me from Parliament and every other place of public trust. Personally I was a bad man morally, and in general politics I was a dangerous Radical and a destroyer of institutions. In the mind of one vicar the fate of the Established Church depended upon my election, for he was confident there would be an end to all order and established institutions. That was an argument he used very frequently, and with much emphasis, in his canvassing amongst the miners. He came across a man on one of his expeditions who climaxed his folly. He urged the destructive idea with his usual force. Finally the voter, who was a particular friend of mine, said, " De ye mean to tell me that if Wilson is elected he will destroy the church?" " Yes," was the reply. " Man, that will be a bad job; but, see here, if he does will ye gie me the stone which is ower the door to mak a pigeon trough of? It'll just come in handy." It was a humorous demolition of a foolish statement.

The result of the election of 1885 was to return Mr Gladstone at the head of a large majority, amongst which were twelve direct representatives of Labour. These were T. Burt, H. Broadhurst, W. Abraham, J. Arch, W. Crawford, W. R. Cremer, C. Fenwick, G.

Howell, B. Pickard, J. Rowland, J. Leicester, and J. Wilson. There was great curiosity as to what these men would be like, although two of them had been in before, and were a guarantee. It was arranged that the group should march down to the House together. There was a crowd outside Palace Yard, whether there to see us or not I have never been able to decide. In " Punch " there were two pictures in the " look on this and on that " style. One of them had the words after the following order: " The Labour members, as we think they are," and we were set forth in our working clothes. Arch had his delver's dress, with trousers tied at the knee with string, and spade in his hand; while the miners had short breeches and picks over their shoulders. In the other picture we were set forth well dressed, while a number of the aristocracy stood anxiously looking at us, and the words they were uttering were, " Why, these people are just like ourselves."

My life in the first Parliament was of very short duration. When I speak of it I fall back upon my sailor vocabulary and call it the " dog watch Parliament." That is the name of the two short watches (or shifts) when at sea, and are between the hours of four and eight in the afternoon. I use that designation because the Parliament was so short. It was terminated on June 13th, 1886, by the great Liberal defeat on Home Rule, which was brought about by the party now known as Liberal Unionists, led by J. Chamberlain. The defeat necessitated an appeal to the country, which resulted in the demoralisation of the Gladstonians, and myself amongst them. The majority against me was a large one.

I remained out of Parliament until 1890. Mr Crawford, who had represented the Mid-Durham Division from 1888, died on the 1st of July that year. The Federation Board selected me as the candidate. The Tory candidate was Mr Vane-Tempest. We were able to hold the seat by a large majority, and I have been honoured by the confidence of the electors ever since, and in the election of 1906 I was returned unopposed.

It will not be of service for me to dwell upon the personal side of my Parliamentary life. That would be too much of the egotist. This much I may say, there are points in it which I might mention with legitimate pride. I went into the House as a thorough believer in and a

supporter of Mr Gladstone and the Liberal party in general politics. From that I have never swerved. That is my political creed now (1909), and without a shadow of a boast it will remain. The Liberals in the division were told that in 1890, but with it they were told that the first plank in my platform was the welfare of my class, and to that I hold as tenaciously now. And although not so active physically as I was when I first received the appellation of the Member for Mid-Durham, yet in spirit my desire is still towards that goal, and my hope is still strong in the possibilities of progress in that direction, providing we, knowing our duty to ourselves, do it.

One matter in my Parliamentary life should not be left unnoticed—not because of any personal connection, but because of its relation to a question within the purview of practical politics, and because it gives prominence to the real motive which actuates the representatives of Labour in their agitation for the payment of Members. There are people in these days who claim, among other matters, that it is the outcome of their presence in the political arena. In none of the questions to which peculiar and special claim is made is that true, and in the payment of Members least of all. Prior to 1893, the time to which I am referring, it had been brought forward. The justice of the claim was admitted, and the bulk of the Liberal party, Mr Gladstone included, were in favour of the measure if the opportunity could be found. Some of them—kindly disposed, no doubt—were desirous of meeting our situation, and a proposal was made to us of the following kind: We and others regardless of party, should each receive a yearly payment as Members of Parliament until the subject was dealt with by Statute. Without any collusion or consultation there was a universal refusal from eleven of the Labour representatives. Mr Burt was at that time Under-Secretary for the Board of Trade. The group not merely refused, but requested to meet Mr Gladstone on the question. In response to that request a meeting was arranged in his residence in Downing Street. He asked whether we were willing to receive payment in that way. We explained our position to him, and laid emphasis on the fact that we were poor men, and to live in London during the

Session incurred great expense. We were fully aware that the offer made, looking at it from a purely monetary point of view, would be of great service to us, but we had never discussed the question on personal grounds. We claimed it as a national right, believing that a Member of Parliament was the servant of the State, and as such he ought to be paid for his services.

Mr Gladstone accepted that position, and said it was the only real grounds upon which the claim could be made, and he would not suggest any course which would depreciate the representatives of Labour in the House, for they were a body of men for whom he had the highest respect. He was in complete sympathy with our aim.

CHAPTER XXXV.—PEACE DEPUTATION TO AMERICA.

In October, 1887, a memorable deputation left England for America. It was composed of thirteen persons. Nine were members of the House of Commons, one a member of the House of Lords (Lord Kinnaird), and three trades unionists—J. Inglis, for Scotland; C. Freak, for London, and myself, for the provinces. Those three went out with the sanction and approval of the Trades Union Congress held that year in Swansea, and they were empowered to speak in the name of the trades unionists of Great Britain.

The deputation was the outcome of the labours of Mr (afterwards Sir) W. R. Cremer, M.P. He was the founder and the secretary of the Workmen's Peace Association from 1870 until his death in 1908. He devoted the whole of his energies to the promotion of peace and international arbitration as a means of settling all differences between nation and nation. Amongst the first steps he took was to visit America on two occasions, to prepare the way for a deputation from Great Britain to President Cleveland and the Congress of the United States. Having prepared the way he then arranged the following address, which was signed by 234 members of both Houses of Parliament :—

"To the President and Congress of the United States of America.—The undersigned members of the British Parliament learn with the utmost satisfaction that various proposals have been introduced into Congress urging the Government of the United States to take the necessary steps for concluding with the Government of Great Britain a Treaty which shall stipulate that any differences or disputes arising between the two Governments which cannot be adjusted by diplomatic agency shall be referred to arbitration. Should such a proposal happily emanate from the Congress of the United States, our best influence shall be used to ensure its acceptance by the Government of Great Britain. The conclusion of such a Treaty would be a splendid example to those nations who are wasting their resources in war-provoking institutions, and might induce other Governments to join the peaceful compact."

The party did not travel in a body. The time fixed for the meeting with President Cleveland and the presentation of the address was Monday, the 31st of October, 1887, and each person was left to travel as he deemed best, it being understood that we should meet in the Arlington Hotel, Washington, on the night of the 30th at 9 p.m. My colleagues and I, with Mr Cremer and Mr B. Pickard, sailed in the Cunard liner, the Umbria, on October 15th, and were landed on the 22nd. We stayed in New York four days, at the Broadway Central Hotel. There were five of us, and Mr Cremer and I went in to negotiate for rooms. We walked up to the counter. "Have you any rooms?" said Cremer. "Yes, we have plenty of rooms; this is no small hotel." He was right, for my number was 720, and was on the fifth floor, which did not matter, as the elevator made the getting upstairs easy. "What is your charge per day?" "Two dollars and a half" (ten shillings). "What does it include?" "Well, it includes a good bedroom and four square meals a day." Again he was right. The rooms were good, and the meals square and abundant. The waiters were all African princes—splendid in physique, black as ebony, in full evening dress, and very masterful in manner. One of them (the boss of the group) stood at the door, and, preceding us with a dignified wave of his hand, he took us to the seat he thought we should sit on; not what we thought. It was no use pointing to any other. It was Hobson's choice. Take that or leave it, for he was the Autocrat of the dining-room, and from his fiat there was no appeal.

After a stay of four days in New York all the members of the deputation, with the exception of Sir Lyon Playfair, left in a special train provided by Mr A. Carnegie for Washington. On the 30th of October we met at 9 p.m. in the Arlington Hotel to make arrangements for the interview the next day. There was a general understanding that there should be only two speakers—Mr Carnegie as introducer, and Mr Cremer to make a speech on behalf of the British and present the address. When Sir Lyon arrived he upset the arrangements by demanding to speak in the name of the House of Commons. As soon as he stated his request Mr Carnegie said, " Then one of the working men will have to speak in the name of the trades unionists." It mattered not, he was determined; and eventually it was decided, and my colleagues told me I must prepare the speech. It was then near ten at night, and Mr Carnegie made the task the heavier by informing us that the President wanted a copy of the speeches by ten in the morning. The time was short, for it necessitated two copies, one for the President and one to use. Pickard kindly came to my assistance and said, " You write out with pencil on sheets for yourself, and I will make a copy of it for the President." With that assistance I prepared the speech.

We met at 9.30 a.m., when the speeches were read and criticised, and then Mr Carnegie took them to President Cleveland. At three we met again, when he told us Mr Cleveland had read the speeches. He considered them all good, but (I must be allowed this little conceit) he sent his special compliments to the working man. In a body we went to the White House, and were introduced to the President and his Cabinet. The order of speaking was as follows:—Introduction by Mr Carnegie. He was followed by Sir Lyon Playfair. Then Mr Cremer, who presented the address. After him I was introduced as representing the Trades Union Congress, and the following is the speech as reported in the " Arbitrator:"—

Sir,—I concur most heartily with the recognition of the deep obligation we are placed under by being permitted to address you as the head of this great nation, and in the realisation of the difficulties which meet us in the initiation of this momentous change. Personally, I feel honoured in being thus privileged to place before you the views of those who have deputed my colleagues and myself to form a part of this deputation. The memorial and the gentlemen who have preceded me have set forth the object we have in view. They have addressed you as Members of Parliament, and as representing an association formed for the abolition of war. We come direct from and speak in the name of the working classes of Great Britain and Ireland. In order that you may clearly understand the feelings they entertain on this question it will be necessary to explain the composition of the assembly which delegated us. In England it is known as the Trades Union Congress, and it meets each year in one of the great centres of industry. It has been in existence about 20 years. There are a large number of delegates from all parts of the United Kingdom. The authority with which we come is not formed of vague expressions of opinion, but by the following resolution: ' That this Congress heartily thanks those members of the United States Congress who have taken the initial steps to secure the adoption of an Anglo-American Treaty of Arbitration; and records its satisfaction at the warm encouragement which has been given to the project by 233 members of the House of Commons. This Congress further expresses an earnest hope that the deputation of Labour and other members of Parliament who are about to visit America will be successful in their peaceful mission, and we hereby give to any member of this Congress who may accompany the deputation authority to speak in its name within the limits of the memorial.' This question is not new to the working classes. For a number of years they have felt the evils of war, and manifested their desire for the substitution of reason, for its dread arbitrament; hence their readiness to join this delegation. Now, more fully than at any other period, do they realise the necessity for a change. The reasons assigned are not peculiar to their class, nor can they be charged with a lack of patriotism. They desire the prosperity of the nation, but are convinced that it will only be found in the paths of peace. While they recognise the general evils of war, they feel that as the wage-earning class lies at the base of the national structure, so upon it falls the greatest pressure and the keenest incidence. Every war means an increase in taxation, and therefore lessens the means of living to them and their families. In their opinion war is not only inhuman, but it is foolish and inconsistent with the spirit of the period in which we live. They believe that the resources of civilisation and the progress of science are not to sacrifice but to save life; not to spread desolation and death, but to do battle with and subdue the social evils and foul conditions of life that are found in every nation. The true object of a nation's strength is the elevation of its citizens physically, mentally, and morally. Large standing armies and expensive navies cannot safely co-exist with a truly prosperous, industrious State. Every war, even though it may be victorious, is a national misfortune—leaves behind it a legacy of hate, and is a confession of the failure of our civilisation, and a disregard of the principles of our religious professions. In conclusion, allow us to express a hope that you will take upon yourself the great task which to-day has been placed before you. Greater work could not devolve upon you, or this great nation, but it is fraught with blessings, and its results will be glorious. It could not have fallen into better hands. We are not coming to a nation which, while it professes peace, increases its warlike forces. You have shown the world that it is possible for a nation to advance in commercial prosperity with but a nominal standing army. From you, nations of the whole world (and none more than Great Britain) can learn important lessons. You have pointed, and are now pointing, to many new paths, and to-day, in the name of the great mass of British labour, we appeal, through you, to the people of America; and hope that we, who are kinsmen in speech and religion, may, as the result of this meeting, be bound in a lasting and blessed bond of amity, and that the other nations, following the bright example, may join in the compact of reason, concord, and peace."

At the conclusion of the speech the President came across the circle in which we stood, and took me by the hand, and, addressing me in most eulogistic terms, expressed his great delight in meeting me; and since has twice sent over his compliments and good wishes. The re-

port of the speech and interview was circulated throughout the States, with the consequence that wherever we went there was a great reception waiting for us. We went from Washington to Pittsburg, and at some of the points in the mining centres crowds of the workmen came on the cars (many of whom I knew) to shake hands with me. At Pittsburg there was a great gathering in the Monongahela Hotel. The deputation were placed in a row, and about five hundred of the leading citizens followed in procession, shaking hands, until as a result there was a terrible pain in the shoulder by the process.

From Pittsburg we went to Philadelphia, and about twenty miles from that city the cars were boarded by a crowd of Pressmen, and I was called upon to make a speech, with the train rushing and roaring along. The platform was one of the seats, and the long open car the meeting room. Of the speech I know nothing. I have some recollection of the difficulty I felt owing to the swaying of the car and the noise, which was sufficient to drown the voice of a Demosthenes, and therefore I stood poor chance of being heard.

In Philadelphia we found the same reception. A great meeting to address, and a presentation to the Governor of the State and his Council. There was an interchange of speeches between the members of the Council and the deputation. One of them was unique. One of the Council was General Louis Wagner. He was one of the officers in the Civil War. When called upon by the Governor to speak he made one of the shortest speeches on record. "Well, gentlemen, we mean to have peace, suppose we fight for it." And then, stepping to where Cremer, Pickard (my two colleagues), and myself stood, he said, "I want to shake hands with you, men. You come from the people, and are the real lords for me."

Another incident which happened in the city will illustrate the desire there was in the American mind to see a "live lord," and will show a humorous practical joke Jock Inglis played on our driver and myself. Each open carriage contained four, and in these we were driven for three days around the city and neighbourhood. Pickard, Freak, Inglis, and I occupied one. The driver knew there was a lord in the party, but as we were so much alike the puzzle was which was the identical man. I was sitting in a corner of the carriage reading a paper on the first morning, when the driver spoke quietly to Inglis, asking which was Lord Kinnaird. Taking the man to one side he said, "You see that man reading in your carriage? That is Lord Kinnaird." This was unknown to me, and there is no doubt but the man pointed me out to many people, and conceited himself upon the honour he had received in driving such a lordly-looking personage. When we were leaving, the joker enlightened us. The result was a good laugh, the driver remarking, "Well, if he is not the real lord, he is as good-looking as the man who is."

From Philadelphia we were taken to Boston. The same kindness was shown us, and we were shown all the places of note. While in the State House, Governor Ames placed me in his chair, saying "Come, and I will make you a Governor of Massachusetts." There was a reception and a banquet in the Hotel Vendome. The gathering was composed of the elite of the city and State. At the table where I sat was Oliver Wendell Holmes, "The Autocrat of the Breakfast Table," and I sat between Dr. Irving (the successor of Dr. Channing) and General Walker, the political economist, whose book I had just finished. In conversation with Dr. Irving I mentioned the fact, when he informed me that the writer was on my right. That pleased me, and I had a conversation with the General on his book, which at that time was new. In the midst of it I received a rude awakening by being called on to speak. My feelings may be imagined. Here was I called up without notice to face 175 of the leading men of the State. I remembered the "Autocrat," however. I have an outline of the speech. The opening words are: "Mr Wilson referred pleasantly to the presence of Dr. Holmes, and said he had felt some fear in being at the same table with the 'Autocrat of the Breakfast Table.' Once he had come in contact, however, with the genial personality of the 'Autocrat' that fear had vanished, and he felt fully the warmth of the welcome given."

That public function ended my part of the mission, although I was pressed to stay and address meetings of the members of Congress. My time was limited, and I was compelled to return home. The meeting was a successful one. A resolution was carried in the American Senate and House of Representatives affirming the desirability of establishing such an arrangement as our Memorial proposed, as follows:—

"That the President be and is hereby requested to invite from time to time, as fit occasions may arise, negotiations with any Government with which the United States has or may have diplomatic relations, to the end that any differences or disputes arising between the two Governments which cannot be justified by diplomatic agency may be referred to arbitration, and be peacefully adjusted by such means."

That was forwarded to the British Government, and on June 16th, 1893, a resolution was moved in the House of Commons by Mr Cremer. After some considerable discussion it was amended and agreed to as follows, receiving the eloquent support of Mr Gladstone:—

"Resolved, that this House has learnt with satisfaction that both Houses of the United States Congress have, by resolution, requested the President to invite from time to time, as fit occasions may arise, negotiations with any Government with which the United States have or may have diplomatic relations, to the end that any differences or disputes arising between the two Governments, which cannot be adjusted by diplomatic agency, may be referred to arbitration, and peaceably adjusted by such means; and that this House, cordially sympathising with the purpose in view, expresses the hope that Her Majesty's Government will lend their ready co-operation to the Government of the United States upon the basis of the foregoing resolution."

My subsequent relations to that Mission lie in two incidents. About a year after returning home I received a note from Mr A. Carnegie. It was sent by messenger to my office from the County Hotel, Durham, and contained a request that I should go to the hotel to see the writer. He and his party were on a driving tour from London to the North of Scotland. There were twelve persons in all, and amongst them was James Blaine, one of the United State Secretaries of State. I spent some hours with them showing them around the city. Mr Carnegie told me he had asked me to meet him for two reasons: first to renew the acquaintance we had formed when on the Mission, and the other was to convey to me Mr Cleveland's special compliments and to give me a message, which Mr Carnegie afterwards used in one of his speeches, and which, as I am human, was pleasing to me, but which I am not conceited enough to insert here. I believe in the proverb, "Let another man praise thee, and not thine own mouth; a stranger, and not thine own lips."

The second incident took place shortly after Mr Carnegie's visit. I was in the office one morning, when I heard in the purest American, "Is John Wilson in here?" One of the clerks pointed to the door. In walked two gentlemen, General Howard (whom I knew, and who was with us on the Mission) and another. As soon as the General got within the door he said, "How is John Wilson? I would not have been in your shoes for a hundred dollars when you were called upon to speak in Boston before the great men of the State."

CHAPTER XXXVI.—AGED MINERS' HOMES.

Before bringing this life's story to a close I would like to place on record mention of the inception and progress up to 1908 of the movement for the provision of free homes for our aged miners. I am proud that I have had a small part in it from the first. The definite point of commencement is difficult to fix. Like many others of our great movements, it is hazy and uncertain. If we were to take the year 1895 we should not be a long way out. The first mention came from the late J. Hopper, who acted as secretary until his death. He made the suggestion the subject of a letter in the Press. This was repeated until some small attention was drawn towards it, the result being that the following gentlemen met informally:—Canon Moore Ede (now Dean of Worcester), Mr H. Wallace (Lord Ravensworth's land steward), J. Hopper, J. Johnson (M.P. for Gateshead), and myself. The outcome of their first meeting was the preparation of plans by Mr Wallace, who from the first was a very generous helper of the scheme. The plans submitted by Mr Wallace were on a community principle—individual sleeping apartments and a common meeting and dining-room. This was not in harmony with the general view of the promoters, as they were in favour of specific homes of cottage shape. The first step was the securing of a large hall and two acres of ground, situated near Boldon Colliery. The building lent itself to a tenement dwelling, with the ground for gardens. This was got from the Ecclesiastical Commissioners at a very easy rent. At the request of the Boldon workmen the building and surroundings were given to them for the use of their old people on their promise to be responsible for the repairs and rent. Then the committee applied again to the Ecclesiastical Commissioners, with the result that they secured nine acres of land in three separate portions in different parts of the county. On two of these, Middlestone Moor and Wrekenton, nice little colonies have been formed. The third, near Ebchester, is not settled as yet. The rental is £3 per annum. The lease is for 999 years. Just at this juncture there was an opportunity to purchase the colliery village known as Haswell Moor, consisting of 112 houses, all of them, with few exceptions, having gardens. The whole of it was freehold, the entire cost of purchase being £840. The houses, through being unoccupied, were in a more or less dilapidated condition, with the exception of 20, which were occupied. After all repairs were completed the cost per house was £25.

That fortunate bargain inspired the committee. They resolved to place the whole movement upon a voluntary basis. The sum asked from each workman was 1s per year, which would realise £3,000. Their trust in the people was reciprocated. With a view to getting the scheme placed before the members of the union the county was arranged into districts, and meetings were held of representatives from each lodge within the district. The scheme and proposals were placed before the delegates, with full liberty to ask any questions, and in every case the most favourable reception was given to the movement.

The reception was encouraging not only from the workmen, for whose direct benefit the scheme was set on foot, but from other classes. The first to give help was our good friend, Coroner Graham, and the example he set was most generously and largely followed. To the effort great assistance was given by Bishop Westcott ("the pitmen's Bishop"), who when the district meetings were being held willingly opened the castle at Auckland, allowed the use of the splendid drawing-room, and presided over the meeting. His presence and counsel did a great deal towards establishing and asssuring the progress of the movement.

The first group of houses, those at Haswell Moor, were opened on 28th of October, 1899. As chairman of the movement, the honour of opening was conferred upon me. The inaugural address was given by Bishop Westcott in a large marquee. The following is an outline of the splendid speech :—

The Bishop said they would all rightly believe that that day was a very memorable and very happy one in his life and in his work. He thanked them most heartily for the honour they had conferred upon him in asking him to take part in that most memorable ceremony. It marked an enterprise that would, he ventured to say, be epoch-making, and marked a work in which, as on other occasions, it seemed to him Durham had shown the right way to England (hear, hear). He valued the honour and privilege for two distinct reasons—for a personal reason and for a social reason. For a personal reason because they clearly showed to him that they believed that while he had worked among them now for nearly ten years he had had a great and deep desire to serve them as he might be enabled (applause). He had a social reason, too. From the character of this enterprise it seemed to him to represent two great principles —the principle of self-help and the principle of co-operative sympathy. These two were very often set in opposition one to the other, but yet they were, they would all feel, truly complementary. The one by itself was really most imperfect and most ineffective. They had contributed most generously to this work of their own resources, and they had welcomed the spontaneous contributions of others; and in this work they were not each of them building a home for themselves, but they were building a home for the common good (applause). These two principles, self-help and co-operation, were most important. Self-help guarded and developed personal independence; co-operative sympathy developed fellowship, and these two together

formed a sure and solid foundation of human happiness (hear, hear). . . . Durham played a conspicuous part in industrial questions, and he was proud of what they had been enabled to do. Some at least on the platform would know what were the conditions in Durham fifty years ago. ("We do"). Well, that had been the results of self-help and co-operation. Let them think what they had been enabled to accomplish —of the Conciliation Board, of the Permanent Relief Fund, and of this last venture of faith, their homes for aged miners. These movements were all continuous; they all expressed the same thought, the same conviction, and witnessed to the power of faith. And as it had been in the past, so it would be in the future. He did not think that in this movement all the common sympathy in them was exhausted. He was sanguine enough to believe that their Permanent Relief Fund would before very long become a sure and sufficient old age pension fund, the development springing again out of these two principles—self-help and co-operation (applause). There was one thing which always gave him deep cause for thankfulness when he thought of the condition of the Durham miners, and that was the help given by children to their parents (applause). It was a sign which filled him with great hope. It moved them to further develop family life among them in spite of the difficulties of the conditions under which they laboured. He asked those present when they looked back upon what had been done for them as opportunity was given them to develop family life— to make every home a school of noble purpose, a temple in which the spiritual should be duly shown (applause). As the family was so would the nation be. There was their work; there was the return which they could make to those who had fashioned their present conditions of labour. These seemed to be some of the thoughts which this memorable occasion suggested, and he himself could not but look forward to that day's ceremony as an example which would bear much fruit. Here, in peaceful rest, he trusted those who had finished their labour would find a quiet haven. Here their work, done in one sense, would continue. The old generation would help the generation that followed by wise counsels, help them by the memorable records of their own experience, and help them by that clearer vision of the duties of life in the unseen order which came through the light, that as familiar words told them "enters our earthly tenement through the chinks which time has made." In all these ways age would help and inspire youth. And what should he say to his younger friends? They had received a splendid inheritance—splendid with noble achievements and noble traditions—and they as men who had mastered themselves and realised their obligations, they would use it well, guard it well, and hand it down to those who came after enriched by the fulfilment of hopes cherished long ago and illuminated by the brightness of hopes which those who came after them would perhaps be allowed to fulfil (loud applause).

There was one pleasing incident which deserves a special notice. It was a matter of great pride to me that I was honoured with the intimacy of the grand old Christian and scholar. As the day drew near for the opening at Haswell Moor he wrote and asked me how and when I was going, as he would be pleased to go with me. I told him in a cab, and at twelve. He came at 11 a.m., when I remarked he was rather before time. "Yes," he replied, "but if you will let me sit down I shall feel obliged." "We are going to have a cup of tea. Will you join us, your lordship?" "I would rather sit quiet for a short time." At twelve we started off in a cab. When we reached the homes he said, "I have some sandwiches with me. Can you find me a place where I can sit down?" "I can do better than that, your lordship. Just below here is an old lady who has a nice clean table set out for tea, come along and have some." He was willing. I got other five or six gentlemen to go with us. When the old lady knew the Bishop was to be her guest she was fearful, and she brought in two of her neighbours to assist her. They dressed themselves in their best black, with clean white aprons. In trepidation they waited upon this (to them) gathering of great men. When the Bishop and his companions were coming out of the front room through the kitchen the three ladies stood before the fire. One of them—the smallest in stature—could restrain herself no longer, but with a full heart she rushed to the Bishop, and seizing his hand with both hers, she gave it a hearty shake and cried out, "Good-day, hinny;

Aa's glad ta see tha." He was delighted, and said to me when we got into the street, "Mr Wilson, that is the best compliment I ever had paid to me in my life."

At the time when I finish this outline (September, 1909) the grand encouraging words of the Bishop have borne much fruit. It would have cheered his great saintly heart to see the many groups of houses scattered about the county; two or three of them within touch of the castle in which he lived. These monuments of mercy indicate the large generosity of and the noble example set by the Durham miners. These are in the following order and number:—Haswell Moor, 112; Shincliffe, 64; Houghall, 32; Wallace Village, 30; Middlestone Moor, 18; West Pelton, 12; Boyne, 6; Crook, 4; St. Helens, 6, making a total of 284. To these must be added the "nursing homes" for single old men. Of these there are three, situated at Haswell Moor, Middlestone Moor, and Houghall. Affording accommodation for 30 men, they are attended to by a matron, who in her work is assisted by a charwoman.

If there be one piece of useful work in the whole of my life in which I have been a co-worker and which gives me most pleasure it is this provision of homes for our aged people. I know something of the limitations of age, but I am thankful nothing of the sorrow which comes from penury, and no prospect on this side the last bodily resting place. But I can enter into the feeling of sadness of the old heart in such circumstances, and I am cheered and strengthened myself by the thought that to my credit there is recorded some little (as a colleague of a body of disinterested men) done to meet the necessities of the aged and worn out workmen.

Bishop Westcott.

Another thing which gives me pleasure in connection with the movement is that by it I was brought into contact with and formed the acquaintance of such disinterested gentlemen as those who initiated and have carried on the movement, and especially that by it I had the honour and privilege of being counted a friend of that grand old saint, Bishop Westcott. It is true the movement did not make us first acquainted, but it did bring us closer together. When he first came to the diocese he adopted a course somewhat peculiar to himself as a Bishop. His custom was at certain intervals to invite a number of gentlemen to his castle. It was a mixed gathering; leading employers, literary men, clergymen, economists, and trades union leaders. As one of the last class I was always invited. His idea was to discuss social and economic questions. The mode of procedure was to give some one connected with the two Northern counties a subject which he was expected to introduce at the next meeting, or the Bishop invited some gentleman who was well known as a promoter of reform of a subject within the two main ideas I have mentioned. In that case the gentleman invited was the introducer. The meetings were generally held on Thursday night and Friday. Whoever was invited was expected to be at the castle about 5 p.m. in time for tea. Between that time and dinner it was Liberty Hall. After dinner for an hour or two all assembled in the drawing-room, when an informal conversation took place, the topic being the question of next day. Then at ten all the guests, family, and servants gathered in the chapel for prayers. On Friday morning at ten the conference opened, with the Bishop in the chair. The speaker was called upon to introduce the subject, after which the order was to speak as he called upon you, and as far as possible the classes or ideas were called in turn. These meetings were of immense benefit to all who took part in them. Speaking for myself, I say that with confidence, and I have many a time thought it would be well if all church dignitaries would use their influence in the same direction.

Well do I remember a conversation I had with him in his drawing-room. He was showing me an overman's leather cap which was given to him when he went down Auckland Park pit to see how the hewers worked, and persisted in walking in as the ordinary workmen did. The cap was kept brightened on a sideboard. It was amongst many souvenirs of great monetary value, but it held a chief place. In the conversation, with the cap in his hand, and with his beaming face—a reflex of his generous heart—he said, "Mr Wilson, I do not want to be merely a preacher of the Gospel in our churches. I want to know the people and their circumstances and social surroundings. My desire is to be a Bishop in the best and most compre-

hensive manner, to come in helpful contact with them, and take a sympathetic part in all their endeavours after better conditions, and a higher life."

There were many manifestations of that desire (for we oft saw it in a concrete shape), but nothing more striking than in the strike of 1892. I have many letters he wrote to Mr Patterson, who at that time was the corresponding secretary of the Durham Miners' Association. All of them show his sympathetic spirit and desire to see the regrettable affair settled. They would all repay insertion, but I will rest satisfied with what he wrote Mr Guthrie in reply to a joint vote of thanks sent to him by the Owners' Association and the Federation Board (representing the workmen).

"My dear sir,—Allow me to acknowledge the safe receipt of the copy of the resolution of June 1st. May I ask you to convey to the Owners' Association and to the Miners' Federation Board my heartiest thanks for this most beautiful memorial of the most anxious, I think I may say, and the happiest day of my life? I confidently trust that the memorable meeting may have lasting fruit. No Bishop of Durham, I am sure, ever rejoiced with greater thankfulness for the privilege of his office than I did when I was allowed to bring together in equal conference the representatives of our most important industry.—Yours faithfully,

B.F. DUNELM.

His life amongst us procured for him the title of the "Pitmen's Bishop," which was a designation he well deserved. By his death, in 1901, we suffered a loss which has not been compensated for yet. His death was a unique circumstance. He was the speaker in the Cathedral at the gathering which is held in connection with the gala. The address was masterly and sadly prophetic in the closing words. He informed the large gathering that it would be the last time he would address them. Whether this was a presentiment of the approach of the last messenger we cannot tell, but it is certain that the kindly heart and eloquent tongue were stilled by death, and the miners were in sorrow for their friend within a short week after he had thrilled their hearts, and a great sorrow had fallen upon the county without regard to class, creed, or social status. He was one of England's greatest scholars, but his learning did not blunt his sympathies nor check his desires to help the people in their struggles. He was highly religious, but it was not the religion of the visionary. It found expression in actions. He proved his faith by his works, and demonstrated it by the true exponent of a man's creed, his active participation in every movement which tended to purify the conditions of working and home life.

As a conclusion to this reference to a truly good man I will insert a resolution passed by the Durham Miners' Executive Committee a few days after his death. The terms of the resolution show the appreciation of his worth by them.

" That we, the Executive Committee of the Durham Miners' Association, in the name of our members, express our universal sorrow at the death of our respected Bishop and friend, the late Bishop Westcott. We recognise that we have lost a sympathiser, counsellor, and helper in all our efforts for the better conditions, both in our home surroundings and our working life. From the first day of his residence amongst us we felt that it was his desire to be a Bishop of the diocese in the truest and best sense of the term; and as the years have passed that feeling has been strengthened by the words of kindly counsel he has given us, and by his generous and helpful actions. While, therefore, we share in the loss that has fallen upon the whole community, we join in the expression of regret and sorrow which will be felt in every portion of the sphere in which he moved, and we tender our sympathy to the relations of the truly great and kindly Christian who has been taken from a life in which he lived usefully and well to a reward which awaits all who try to correct the wrongs and brighten the darkness of this life."

CHAPTER XXXVII.—AU REVOIR.

The County Council.

In 1888 a complete revolution was made in the management of our local affairs by the passing of the Local Government Act, by which the power was taken out of the hands of the clergymen, squires, and county magnates, and placed in those of the whole body of the people, if they chose to use it. In Durham full advantage was taken of the opportunity. In the discussion which took place in Parliament and the country the Marquis of Salisbury had said that the people were more desirous for a circus than for the use of the power the Bill sought to confer. That was intended as a jibe by the master of them. Wherever it might find application, it did not in Durham. It must be admitted that in some counties the same class of people were left in control, so that the Act was of no real use, but in Durham a different state of things resulted.

The effect of the teaching of the Franchise Association was seen in the readiness of the working classes generally to adopt the Act in the most active manner. They had been not merely urged to use their power as it applied to Parliament, but to their local affairs as well.

At the first election about one-third of the members of the Council were direct representatives of the workmen of the county. That number has not decreased, but has kept steadily on the increase.

The same may be said in respect to the Parish and District Councils as provided by the Act of 1894. As a result of the same teaching the county was waiting, and eagerly entered into the elections. At the conclusion it was found that at least sixty per cent. of the seats on these Councils were held by working men, and to their credit it should be said that improvements have been made in every direction, and no class has legitimate reason to complain that their interests have been neglected or the rights of property in the least unjustly dealt with.

From the first, I am thankful to say I have been honoured with a seat on the County Council. For the first term of three years I was elected for the New Herrington Division. At the conclusion of that term I was placed on the roll of Aldermen, where it has been my proud privilege to remain until this year, 1909. During that long term, and at the earnest request of my supporters, I had the further honour of being chairman for three years of the Council, and simultaneously with that appointment I was placed on the roll of county magistrates as an addition to the long list of honours which have been (far beyond any personal merit) bestowed upon me. This much I may say, that whatever may be the lack of merit it has been my aim to fill the offices I have been called upon to fill, not merely with credit to myself, but to those who placed me there.

The Struggle of My Life.

The only other matter which I record, and with which I close this outline of a somewhat strenuous life, is the blow which fell upon me in the month of May, 1908, by the death of my beloved wife, life long companion, and consistent helpmate. That appears to me to be the proper ending except a few words by way of au revoir to those who have followed me in the devious road along which I have travelled. Her death came suddenly, for the doctor had but a few days before spoken in glowing terms of her splendid physical condition, and gave her many years of life, and therefore, while she had lived to the age of 68, yet under the circumstances the blow was severe. It would have been sad at any time, even if she had been lingering, and with death in immediate prospect, for we had faced the storms of life together, and the web of our married life had been of mingled yarn, but at all times she had a smile which illumined the darkness, and a cheery word which imparted strength and inspiration in the hour of weakness.

I have spoken of her on a few occasions, but not as long as I should desire, for while I was the seen and ostensible in the actions recorded, she supplied the motive power. I am not proud enough to say anything else. It would be doing her memory an injustice if I did not say that much. My desire is to say more. It has been said " The finest thing that God has made is a beautiful old woman." She was all that in mind as well as face, and the aroma of her presence and influence is with me now. I miss her. I long for the touch of a vanished hand, and the sound of a voice that is still. To me the stately ship has gone to the haven under the hill, but by hope and faith we are in close touch. That is the assurance which enlightens the gloom and which inspires to active service in what would otherwise be despair's dark and desolate hour.

Au Revoir.

I part company here with those who have done me the honour to read the account of what was, at the start of life, rough and stormy, and has been all along spent in stress and strain. I have faithfully recorded all that has been set down. There has been no embellishment, nor the smallest item written for glory's sake. As I said in my introductory remarks, I am human, and there have been many events in my life which are best forgot, and with that view before me I have left them out. They would have been neither creditable nor profitable, and therefore of no service, which should be the aim of all either in living our life or in describing it. The great questions before us all are : How much have I benefited the world by living in it? Have I raised or depressed its moral tone? Has my life been inspired in the direction of a noble and higher aim?

I need not point out that testing my life by that standard, it divides itself into two portions. That prior to 1868, when there was no principle to guide or goal to aim at, and when "drifting" was the proper description to apply to the course. And that portion since the year named, when, I hope, there has been something attempted something done to influence for good. It may be much or little, that is not for me to decide. This much I may say: I have tried, and the intention has been sincere. None knows better than myself what failures there have been. I have regrets for the wasted spring and early manhood; regrets which I would like my young readers to avoid. It will make their lives more useful, and save them from sorrow, for where is there a man who can look back upon neglected years with any satisfaction. The neglected yesterdays of youth form a terrible indictment for old age.

Speaking for the second period, I find no room for regret at having lived it as I have, and for the purpose to which it has been devoted. My work has been in harmony with my feelings. Ofttimes perplexing and anxious, but never irksome and unpalatable, and now after over forty years I am glad to say, and have pride in saying, that I am not waiting like an hireling for the shadow of the day. The wages received in money I am thankful have not been the only payment I have earned. This world would have been a long way from the point it has reached if men of mercenary minds had been the moving spirits in the upward movements. Such men are only found seeking for front places when positions are made and tyranny conquered. They have hands wide open for money, and are crying "Give, give," but they have not the spirits required to prepare the way. In the background when men are wanted, but loud in declamation when the times of ease and safety are secured.

I have seen dark days and been called upon to face the contentions and conflicts of life, but I am thankful I have helped progress in many ways. In the commencement of my official life in the Miners' Union I was thrown into colleagueship with men of the right stamp, who filled the offices con amore. Their economic ideas were in accord and harmony with my own, and there was, therefore, no difficulty in working together, and as a result the community for whom we laboured was benefited. It would have been a pleasure to give each one a large place in this life history, as it would those of my present colleagues, but I am deterred by the thought that I am not writing a general book of reminiscences. The object before me was to outline in a matter of fact way my own life. I have given a fuller account of them elsewhere. This much I will say, speaking of those who are gone, there never was a better set of officials at the head of a trade union than they were; and in regard to those who are with me now their places will be difficult to fill. The welfare of the Association is their first concern, and no amount of work nor length of hours is counted excessive if the communal interests can be conserved and promoted.

The writing of this life's story has necessitated the use of the first person more than is at all palatable to me, but it is impossible to write it in any other form. Not only is it obnoxious to me, but there has been one man at least who has expressed disapproval of it, and in a somewhat peculiar manner. One of my grandsons is under the Durham County Council. Like all grandsons who think their grandfather is the best man alive, he was eager to read the instal-

ments as they made their weekly appearance in the "Durham Chronicle," and as soon as possible on the night of printing he procured a copy at the printing office; the people in the country not being able to get them until the day after. Some six or seven weeks after the first appearance of the life he procured the "Chronicle," as usual. He was on the station platform on his way home. While waiting for the train he was reading that portion nearest to his heart. Two miners were standing near. One of them, seeing the name of the paper, said "Aa see thou 'es the 'Durham Chronicle' there. Aa cannot get it till Friday." "Yes," was the reply. "I go to the office for it." Then the querist said, "Aa see thou's reading that antibiography. Aa like that thing; but Aa wad like it better if that chep wadn't taak see much about hissell." I hope my friend, and others like minded, may have found out that it is (to say the least) difficult to write one's own life without using the first person. I can assure him, while it has been necessary, it has been at the same time irksome.

When I yielded to the solicitations of my friends to write this record, self-praise or popularity was the farthest remove from my mind. I tried to make that clear at the commencement. There was one thing upon which I conceited myself, and that was my hope of exciting some small influence upon those who might read it. Influence in three directions—the formation of character, the proper use of the advantages procured, and the devotion of the powers of mind and body to the betterment and progress of the people. These have I desired, and now, as

"The wan moon is setting behind the white
    wave,
And time is setting with me,"

the desire is stronger than ever, and looking around upon the class amongst whom I have lived, and with whom with pleasure I have laboured, and knowing the large wealth of mental capital there is in it, I shall feel that my life and the labour spent in writing has not been in vain if I can inspire some right and useful living.

The first consideration should be the formation of a character. "It plays a larger part than intellect in the happiness of life, and the cultivation of the unselfish part of our nature is not only one of the first lessons of morals, but also of wisdom. Every one can in some measure learn the lesson of self-sacrifice, practice what is right and correct, or at least mitigate his dominant faults. What fine examples of self-sacrifice, quiet courage, resignation in misfortune, patient performance of painful duty, and magnanimity, may be often found among those who are intellectually the most commonplace. Youth is pre-eminently the period when habits and tastes are formed, and the yoke which is then lightly, willingly, wantonly assumed will in after years acquire a crushing weight. Few things are more striking than the levity of the motives, the feebleness of the impulses under which in youth fatal steps are taken, which bring with them a weakened life and an early grave.''

So says Professor Lecky in his " Map of Life." In a less eloquent manner and a cruder form of language, I have tried to teach the same truth. And in concluding my life's story, and believing I have done some little in that direction, and in the hope that some may receive an upward impetus I again appeal to my young brothers. I rejoice that I have been privileged to be a co-worker with large-hearted men who have passed to their reward, and with those who are still bearing the heat and burden of the day, and who feel the luxury of doing good, but who will join me in my final appeal to our young men.

Appreciate fully the conditions you live in, but don't let the benefits you have blind you to your responsibilities. You are debtors in a three-fold sense to the past and the great hearts who laboured for you. To the present, as you are bound to wisely use the opportunities they left as a legacy to you. To the future, because you are in duty bound to hand that legacy on in increased volume. I would like to give a clear conception of that important truth, and to say something to stir you up to good and profitable use of the time and facilities you have. It has been truthfully said that " the lack of thought is an evil, but the lack of forethought is a greater.'' To omit the duty you (my young brothers) owe to yourselves; to neglect the opportunities which are open to you, to think all of pleasure and sport, and nothing of mental culture, to leave the institutes which are opening out to you with their libraries, and with

their stores of knowledge, bringing you into living, thoughtful contact with the mental giants of the race, to live only for present enjoyment, with no preparation for the to-morrow, which will need you, and make demands upon you, is surely a lack of forethought, which is condemnable for two things, because it stunts your own nature (for no uneducated man is complete), and hinders your usefulness when matured manhood demands you should take your place in the affairs of your class and nation, to assist in the progress of the former, and the rectification of the national evils.

I speak thus warmly and feelingly to you, because I know the large mental calibre there is amongst you; because I see it in many cases wasted or devoted to the low, vicious, and destructive; and because the cause we have at heart, and upon which our future largely depends, rests with you. You are the hope of the older men. Our places will be to fill, and I for one would like to see them filled more ably than they are now. As much more ably as your opportunities for acquiring fitness are greater. There is no blame attaching to us for being unable to do all with perfectness. You have not the same extenuation. If any one feels inclined to carp or find fault, we can with justification point to our start in life, to the early age at which we were called upon to start at laborious and dismal work, for long hours, and to the meagre education we received, and the obstacles which met us in our endeavours after self-education in the shape of weariness at the conclusion of a long day in the mine, and the dearness of the requisite books. What justification can you offer? None. In these days there is no excuse for ignorance. There is the opportunity of going to school until you have a store of knowledge as a whole which forty or fifty years ago was the rare exception, only falling to the lot of the favoured individual whose family circumstances enabled him to remain under tuition until he reached the advanced age of twelve or thirteen. Now all are kept out of labour and at school until that age is reached; then it was only in isolated cases. In our youth to be ignorant was a misfortune. In yours it is not merely neglectful, it is a crime.

You must not be satisfied with being our equals, and remain there. That plea would condemn you. There must be advance placed to your credit. A limpet sticking on a rock may be satisfied with its stationary position, but not a man. Neither must you be money seekers for love of it alone. Prudence dictates that; but it is better far to increase in knowledge. Wisdom crieth out to you in every direction. Be ye not regardless of the call. Let me conclude by asking you to ponder these words of Joseph Mazzini:—

"Your liberty, your rights, your emancipation from every injustice in your social position, the task each of you is bound to fulfil on earth; all these depend upon the degree of education that you are able to attain.

"Without education you are incapable of rightly choosing between good and evil; you cannot acquire a true knowledge of your rights; you cannot attain that participation in political life, without which your complete social emancipation is impossible; you cannot arrive at a correct definition and comprehension of your own mission.

"Education is the bread of your soul. Without it your facilities lie dormant and unfruitful, even as the vital power lies sterile in the seed cast into untilled soil, and deprived of the benefits of irrigation and the watchful labour of the agriculturist."

Life is too short to waste, and the years too precious to be treated lightly, and I therefore urge you in the words of Mr Gladstone, to "Be inspired with the belief that life is a great and noble calling, not a mean and grovelling thing, that we are to shuffle through as we can, but an elevated destiny."

"Is true freedom but to break
Fetters for our own dear sake,
And with leathern hearts forget
That we owe mankind a debt?
No; true freedom is to share
All the chains our brothers wear,
And with heart and hand to be
Earnest to make others free."

[THE END.]

THE MINERS' PAPER.

The Durham Chronicle.

Miners should read "The Durham Chronicle"

for the following reasons:

The Chronicle has always been recognised throughout the County of Durham as the paper which caters most completely for the mining community.

The Chronicle has invariably supported the cause of the miner, and may justly claim to have assisted in improving his working conditions and in securing for him a healthier home and more attractive surroundings.

The Chronicle devotes a large amount of space to mining news. Full and careful reports are given of mining topics, local councils, public and social gatherings, etc., etc., the events of every colliery village being faithfully recorded week by week.

The Chronicle correspondence columns are the favoured medium for the discussion of all questions affecting the welfare of the miner.

The Chronicle also contains other bright and attractive features which make it a welcome visitor to the miner's home.

The Chronicle has by far the largest circulation of any weekly paper published in the County of Durham, and the number of readers among the miners is steadily increasing.

72 Columns for One Penny.

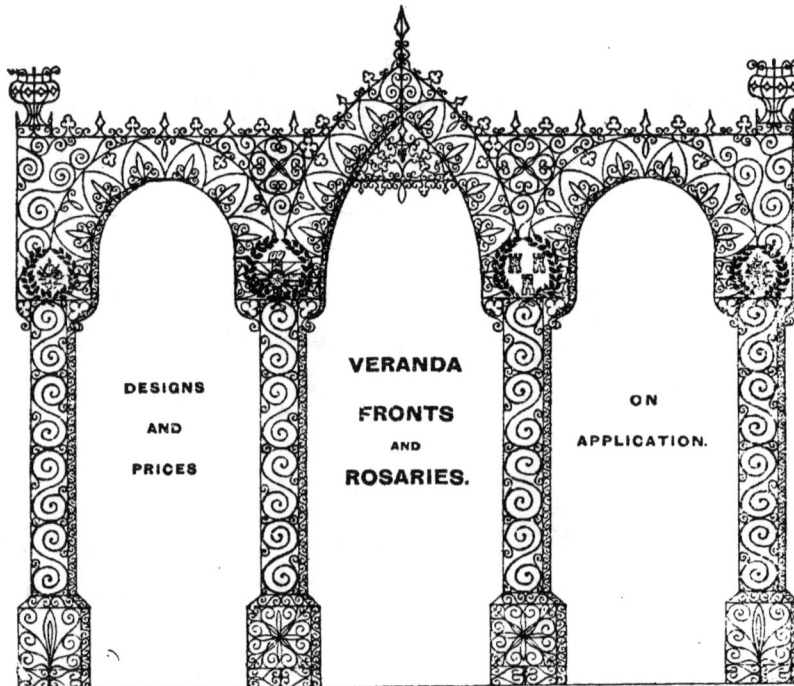

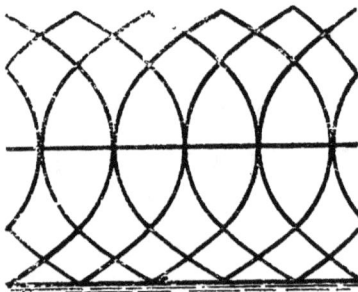

☞ From a NEEDLE to an ANCHOR. ☜

T. A. Moffitt & Co.,

The Hardware Shop in

HIGH STREET, GATESHEAD

(A Few Doors above GREY HORSE INN.)

―――――――

We hold one of the Most Extensive and
――― *Up-to-Date Stocks of* ―――

STOVES,

MANTELPIECES in Marble, Slate and Wood,

KITCHEN RANGES, etc.

All kinds of

BUILDING HARDWARE

and

FURNISHING HARDWARE.

―――――――

LARGE STOCKS.   KEEN PRICES.

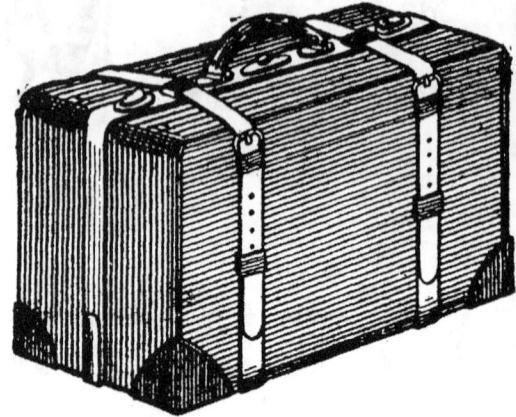

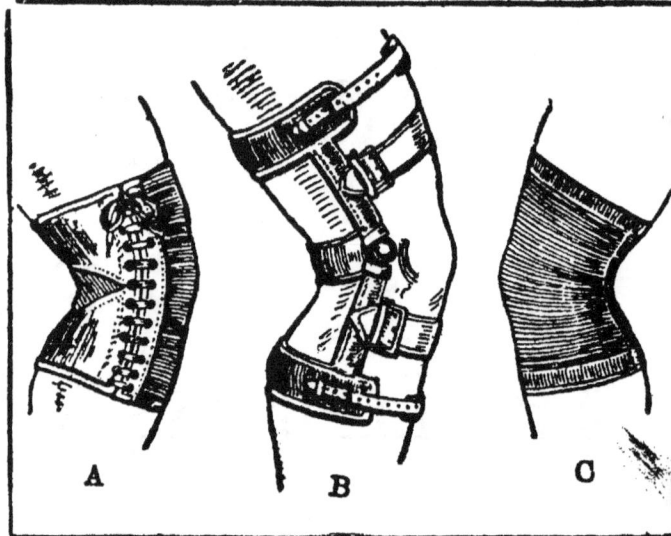

www.ingramcontent.com/pod-product-compliance
Lightning Source LLC
LaVergne TN
LVHW081346060426
835508LV00017B/1447